BALTIMORE: A NOT TOO SERIOUS
HISTORY

MARYLAND PAPERBACK BOOKSHELF

Also of Interest in the Series:

The Amiable Baltimoreans, by Francis F. Beirne
Happy Days: 1880–1892, by H. L. Mencken
Baltimore: When She Was What She Used to Be,
by Marion E. Warren and Mame Warren

BALTIMORE

A NOT TOO SERIOUS HISTORY

by

LETITIA STOCKETT

With a New Foreword by

HAROLD A. WILLIAMS

THE JOHNS HOPKINS UNIVERSITY PRESS
BALTIMORE AND LONDON

To

William W. Norman

I dedicate this book
In memory of
The Fun he had in its planning
The Confidence he felt in its substance
The Pride he took in its craftsmanship

Foreword to the 1997 Edition © 1997 by The Johns Hopkins University Press
All rights reserved
Printed in the United States of America on acid-free paper

Originally published in 1928 by Grace Gore Norman, Baltimore, and released in a
limited illustrated edition in 1936.
Maryland Paperback Bookshelf edition, 1997
06 05 04 03 02 01 00 99 98 97   5 4 3 2 1

The Johns Hopkins University Press
2715 North Charles Street
Baltimore, Maryland 21218-4319
The Johns Hopkins Press Ltd., London

Library of Congress Cataloging-in-Publication Data

Stockett, Letitia.
    Baltimore : a not too serious history / by Letitia Stockett : with a new foreword by
Harold A. Williams.
        p.   cm. — (Maryland paperback bookshelf)
    Originally published: Baltimore : Grace Gore Norman, Publisher, 1928, 1936.
    Includes Index.
    ISBN 0-8018-5670-1 (pbk. : alk. paper)
    1. Baltimore (Md.)—History—Anecdotes. I. Title. II. Series.
F189.B157S76   1997
975.2′6—dc21   97-6122
                                                                              CIP

A catalog record for this book is available from the British Library.

CONTENTS

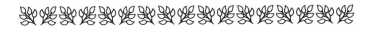

ILLUSTRATIONS

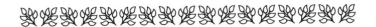

FOREWORD TO THE 1997 EDITION

Letitia Stockett had been teaching at Friends School for ten years when in 1926 a colleague suggested that she write a book about Baltimore. Nothing had been done, she was told, since J. Thomas Scharf's *The Chronicles of Baltimore* in 1874. The challenge appealed to her, and for some time she kept her project a secret. "I simply gave up my friends and spent every minute I could spare on my book," she later said in a newspaper interview. "It was great fun. I didn't tell a single soul that I was writing it. I just said, 'I have some work to do,' and let it go at that!"

Baltimore: A Not Too Serious History appeared in December, 1928, to cheering reviews. In the *Baltimore Sun* Samuel C. Chew referred to the "quaint and picturesque and romantic spots which the discerning eye of Miss Stockett has discovered all over the town." "She has told me," Chew added, "of a quantity of places I never knew before, and has discovered the beauty that lies in the heart of the familiar and the charm of tradition to be found underlying the modern commonplace." Even the *New York Times* praised Stockett's "whimsical humor": "with a light touch that skims over the years, barely touching here and there, she reviews a variety of incidents and scenes that help to make history."

"Would you know Baltimore?" she began her story. "Then put deliberately out of your mind the fact that the town makes more straw hats than any other city in the world. . . . Forget, too, that Baltimore is the centre of the oyster packing industry. Worse, far worse than a straw hat is a packed oyster; Baltimoreans ought to know better. In truth they do; they export the tinned bivalve to unsuspecting, unsophisticated Westerners." Thus she dismissed "commerce." Ignored, too, are government, politics, and crime. In that era of Prohibition, she said nothing about the city's popular speakeasies.

9

She starts at the Washington Monument—"the true axis of the town"—and "rambles" all over. The Baltimore she describes could have been seen from its observatory. She refers to the Fountain Inn or reminisces about the Jones Falls, then she whisks us off to another subject, remarking jauntily, "on another day we shall return" (and chapters later she does). She is not to be hurried. After introducing George Peabody, she assures the reader that "later we will sit down upon the bench in the sun and recount his remarkable career." "Sit here upon the courthouse steps," she directs her readers, "and while you feed the pigeons I will tell you the story of Baltimore's part in the war of 1812."

She calls upon the past to set scenes. At Pratt and Light Streets, she asks us to imagine for ourselves Captain John Smith's pinnace "gliding nearer and nearer." Or Count de Rochambeau's soldiers encamped in Howard's Woods in 1782. Now, "walking on Charles Street at dusk," she attests, "one meets the ghostly figures of these French officers, a breath of the court of old France." (Although she taught English and English history, Stockett displays a far deeper love for France—particularly "old France," dropping such names as Voltaire, Rousseau, Pompadour, and DuBarry.)

She knows how to use colorful detail. On the stepping stones that once enabled pedestrians to cross streets with dry feet: "Ah, what a delight after a storm to stand perilously upon these high stones and look down into the turbulent stream dashing away to the Falls, and gurgling so enchantingly as it dashed." Washington Place, she writes, "runs down hill with a blithe skipping step."

Letitia Stockett was born and educated in Baltimore. She attended Western High School, where one of her teachers was Lizette Woodward Reese, the Waverly poet of whom Mencken thought so highly and who receives much mention in *A Not Too Serious History*. Stockett graduated from Goucher College in 1904 and spent her vacations doing social work and supervising playgrounds. She taught for four years at a girls' boarding school in Stamford, Connecticut, before joining the faculty at Friends School, where she remained for thirty years. Her first book, a collection of poems entitled *The Hoofs of Pegasus* (she called it "plain ordinary poetry"), was published in 1923.

FOREWORD, 1997

The *Sun* review of *Baltimore* called Stockett a "child of that happy decade," the 1890s. She seemed to agree—despite the upheavals the country was undergoing at the time. In Hookstown, beyond Druid Hill Park, she remembers youthful moments hearing like the clattering a herd of steers made on cobbled streets. "It was a lovely exciting sound; above the ringing hoofs came the sharp masterful cries of the man who carried the goad." She recalls, too, the horse cars of the '90s: "The floor of the car was covered with straw to keep the passengers feet warm, and the driver, standing on an open platform, was securely wrapped in a heavy blanket from the waist down. At Eager Street the car generally went off the track, and all of the men promptly arose and aided the half-frozen driver to restore the car to the proper position on the rails." When winter storms struck, housekeepers along the route would sent out hot coffee to the conductors. Stockett once paid her streetcar fare with three cents and postage stamp.

She shares succulent memories of the Lexington Market of those days. Housewives, some with chauffeurs, made leisurely selections from a vast array of stalls. The Italian fruit stands, ablaze with "scarlet and warm yellow fruits," made her think of the same beauty that "enriched the canvases of Titian and Correggio." Outside the market, the horseradish and coconut vendor did his grinding with the "rub-a-dub-dub of his flying wooden wheel."

A Not Too Serious History covers all that one would include in any discussion of Baltimore—Fort McHenry, the Enoch Pratt Free Library, the Peabody Institute, the Johns Hopkins Hospital and University, the Baltimore & Ohio Railroad, Federal Hill, the Shot Tower, Betsy Patterson, and bay steamers. Stockett describes the Washington Monument in mist and cloud as a "silver loveliness." She is less kindly about other outdoor memorials. Severn Teackle Wallis's statue she judges to be inadequate. "Wallis was great and his statue is so little. . . . Perhaps the awful clothes has something to do with the effect." The Women's Temperance Christian Union fountain on City Hall Plaza "has a lesbian air." The Armistead monument on Federal Hill she calls "utterly hideous." The Centennial Fountain on Eutaw Place strikes her as "a monstrous ugly thing. . . . Originally fat cupids placed at neat intervals about the bowl blew water through their cast iron conch shells. Mercifully their respiratory tracts became impaired, and they are no more."

She pays special to attention the history of churches like Old St. Paul's, Otterbein, the Methodist Meeting House, the Unitarian Church, the First Presbyterian, the Friends Meeting House, and the first Roman Catholic Cathedral in the United States, the Basilica of the Assumption. She takes us into the Basilica's belfry to admire the bands of tracery adorning the large bell and to copy the long French inscriptions.

She adds depth to her account when she writes of a street's history, tracing it back by examining old prints, maps, or historic records. Before the Emerson Hotel was built, for example, the northwest corner of Calvert and Baltimore streets formed "the edge of a pleasant green field sloping gently down the high cliff which overhung the Falls." Before long three frame houses were built, which included garden plots and were "certainly shaded by sycamores and honey locusts for which the neighborhood was noted." Over the years the houses fell into decay and were replaced by a fine brick house that became the Baltimore Museum and Gallery of Fine Arts, owned by the famous Peale family. Then Barnum bought the building, and it later "sank to Kunkle's Ethiopian Opera House." In the late nineteenth century the corner was the headquarters for the B&O Railroad, a building destroyed in the great fire of 1904.

Streets were one of Stockett's passions. "Each street has its own flavor and savour," she declared, and all street names were rich in history. Among others, she relates how Eden, Conway, Barre, Camden, Montgomery, Hanover, York, Aisquith, and Armistead got their names. She has much to say about Charles Street, which was first called Forest because it reached into the forest where the Washington Monument now stands. The lawyers' offices below Mulberry, she wrote, hung onto the hill "with their eyelashes," each one with a foot scraper at the door. Their gardens were enclosed with thick walls. She described the lawyers of old as the "most genial of men, living half in Dickens and half in Baltimore." About the area north of 25th Street, when it was Huntington Avenue, Stockett writes, "This road, very straggling, ran out into the real country—a region of fields, streams, locust trees and violets." At what would become University Parkway there stood a toll booth and a box of a house for the toll keeper. How many remember the extended name of Charles Street? "For some years," she writes, "the name of Charles Street Avenue Boulevard was common currency. This is slightly redundant, but it has the advantage of being very precise."

Stockett relates anecdotes that otherwise would have fallen from public memory. At one point (it was in 1919), after being "unceremoniously dragged" from his first position across from the Walters Art Gallery, "poor" Severn Teackle Wallis—his statue, that is—"lay prone on his face" elsewhere in the park. William Rinehart's statue of Endymion in Greenmount Cemetery "prompts someone every year to put into the hands of the sleeping boy a flower suited to the season—a small chrysanthemum for All Saints' Day, a sprig of holly at Christmas, and a daffodil at Easter." One of the unique ground rents, once a popular Baltimore investment, was that on land under the lake at Druid Hill Park. Every year the water department paid $200 to the owner of the submerged property.

A product of the 1920s, A *Not Too Serious History* offers an often-embarrassing time capsule of racial attitudes. Stockett refers freely to "coloured people"—always employing the English (we would add, colonial) "ou." On a fashionable street a casting of a "delightful little Negro boy" served as a hitching post. Today, the reader stirs uneasily when Stockett describes "pickaninnies skating madly [at Mount Vernon Place], their chalky eyes on the police." She has nothing good to say of neighborhood change, and today her words badly jar us. "Biddle Street, once the home of gentlefolk, is now given over to the darkeys. A few courageous artists have salvaged a house or two. . . . Otherwise the neighborhood is 'gone' as we say."

What, if anything, can we tell about this work from the space Stockett gives her subjects? She dwells the longest (for eight pages) on what was surely the biggest and most colorful civic event to occur while she was compiling her history, the Fair of the Iron Horse—an event that celebrated the centennial of the Baltimore & Ohio Railroad in 1927. H. L. Mencken's house on Union Square gets a full paragraph, but on Mencken himself Stockett limits herself to the phrase "his berserkian gusto."

13

FOREWORD, 1997

After her foray into history, Stockett continued to teach at Friends School and do a little more writing. In 1936 *A Not Too Serious History* reappeared in a limited, autographed, highly illustrated edition of 975 copies. Stockett may have used some of the income from the book's success to travel. With two friends she drove to Colorado and California in the late 1920s, and then, in *America, First, Fast and Furious* (1930), she published her generally unflattering impressions of the far west.

She lectured frequently, not only on Baltimore but also on Lizette Woodward Reese, Amy Lowell, and the heroes and heroines of the Eastern Shore. In the course of one lecture during World War II, an air-raid drill cut out all lights in the hall, leaving Stockett at the podium in the dark. She decided to stay there and continue to talk, wondering all the while whether her audience remained or had crept out in the darkness. She gave up public speaking when a women's group said it had no interest in what she chose as her subject so long as she was funny for an hour.

For years she spent her summer vacations in South Duxbury, Massachusetts, where she took daily ten-mile strolls, followed by a brisk swim. She died in a Boston Hospital on March 13, 1949, after an operation following two accidents while riding her bicycle.

Stockett's "contribution was a highly individual one," the *Sun* said in its editorial. "She saw our urban life with a detachment few of us are able to achieve. Also, being blessed with a sense of humor containing more than a dash of kindly cynicism, she could tell the stories and legends of the local past with a Barrie-like piquancy, stylized but entertaining."

Although seventy years old, Stockett's story of old Baltimore still sparkles—a history that Baltimoreans and would-be Baltimoreans cannot fail to enjoy.

Harold A. Williams

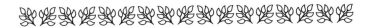

FOREWORD

The writing of this book has been sheer joy. Foreign travel is exciting, but travel in one's home town is even more thrilling, and the life and adventures of Baltimore Town are romantic and rich to a degree. There is the fun of pouring over old charts, of rooting out dusty volumes, of pursuing an elusive fact. But even more rewarding is the actual discovery of the city in a hand to hand, or rather face to face encounter. Much of old Baltimore has vanished never to return, but much is still left—a hint here in the turn of a gable, a trick there in the tilt of a chimney. A street sign leads one straight into the Revolutionary War; Crooked Lane suggests an Indian Trail.

There are no doubt many flaws here; for all corrections the writer will be very grateful and will gladly incorporate them in a "bigger, better" BALTIMORE at some future date. But here I must thank my chief aid and support—J. Thomas Scharf. He, certainly, has written the best and biggest book on Baltimore and to him I am deeply grateful.

My thanks are very gladly rendered to the following for their loan of valuable illustrations: Messrs. Hambleton and Company, through Mr. William E. Bauer, of many interesting maps and pictures of old Baltimore from their unique collection; the City Hall through the City Librarian, Mr. Benjamin S. Applestein, and his department, of a great number of their illustrations of early Baltimore; David Bendann, of the etchings by Miss Clements; the Baltimore Association of Commerce and Mr. M. Paul Roche, of one of the latter's etchings which form part of his great portfolio on Baltimore; Purnell's Art Galleries, of the etching by Mr. D. P. Tyson "A Vista of the Christmas Tower of Emmanuel Church"; Mr. Arthur Stanley Riggs, editor of "Art and Archaeology," of the illustrations of Homewood; and the Reverend Cawley H. Stine of the illustration of Otterbein Church.

IN THE SHADOW OF WASHINGTON'S HAND

CHAPTER I

WOULD you know Baltimore? Then put deliberately out of your mind the fact that the town makes more straw hats than any other city in the world. Aesthetically speaking, that is a fearsome thought. Forget, too, that Baltimore is the centre of the oyster packing industry. Worse, far worse than a straw hat is a packed oyster; Baltimoreans ought to know better. In truth they do; they export the tinned bivalve to the unsuspecting, unsophisticated Westerner. These two enterprises are worthy and profitable, but a knowledge of these facts will not help you to understand this city any more truly than the study of those long lists of products once diligently conned in school gave you an inkling of Tunis, Singapore and Wilkes-Barre.

An entrancing book on the French capital suggests a better method of introduction: "I have spent a great deal of time planning what seems to me the most delightful and alluring way to begin acquaintance with Paris. . . . And I've often debated with myself the comparative loveliness of this spot or that, and which of them I'd choose if I could lead my friend into Paris blindfolded, and at my will tear off the bandages, and cry 'Look!' " The spot finally selected was the Place de la Concorde. This is a good device, and I would choose Mount Vernon Place for such an introduction—the *Monument*, as we call it. This is our Place de la Concorde. I do not make this comparison in any imitative sense, but here, truly, the eye is led on to gracious distances. Here there are dignified facades, an air of repose, of arrival. Strangers looking about them for the first time speak of the French manner, the sauve nobility of design. There is, indeed, a Parisian accent here. But the Monument—and no Baltimorean mistakes your meaning; there are many monuments but only one *Monument*—this gracious Square is the most characteristically Baltimorean thing in the town. The oyster, packed or in his wild state, is not more typical.

So we shall start pilgrimage here, and like all the townspeople we shall pass back and forth through Mount Vernon Place many, many times. All Baltimoreans are born under the shadow of Washington's hand and from a hundred different angles we shall see the marble shaft rising against the sky. It is the true axis of the town. Over Wren's grave in Saint Paul's Cathedral one finds this epitaph:

"Si monumentum requiris circumspice."

You have already found the monument, I take it, but do look about you and orientate yourself. Charles Street, in this town of crooked thoroughfares, runs north and south, and all that lies on your left hand as you ride south with Lafayette is east Baltimore according to the street numbers; and all that lies on your right is west. If you were to walk a few squares south to Baltimore Street you would find there the dividing line for north and south Baltimore. But that must wait for another day; there is much to be seen at the Monument.

When the old court-house was torn down—and the court-house stood on the site of the present Battle Monument which we shall visit later—the citizens begged the Legislature to grant them permission to erect on that spot a monument in honor of George Washington. The privilege was immediately granted, but the War of 1812 prevented any furtherance of the plan. By the time the war was over and the citizens again took up the project, there was a widespread feeling that a column as high as the one proposed would be exceedingly dangerous; it might, nay, it would, topple down on the heads of defenseless Baltimoreans and cause injury and death. This matter was gravely debated, and the idea all but abandoned. Then out spoke that man so generous with his property, John Eager Howard, who practically owned all of the town, and he bestowed upon the city the property needed. This was a knoll thickly forested which lay well out of town. There the lives of citizens could not be endangered, for nobody lived in the neighborhood. It was a peaceful secluded spot. Colonel Howard was warmly thanked for his splendid gift, and thus Mount Vernon Place came into being. But there was no "Place" for many a year. William Wirt in 1822 writes: "After walking about a mile I came to the summit of a hill that overlooked the city, and there I stopped a moment to take breath, and look back on it. The ground had begun to smoke with the warmth of the rising sun, and the city seemed to spread itself out before me to a vast extent. But towering above the fog was the Washington Monument (a single beautiful shaft 160 feet in height, rendered indescribably striking and interesting from the touching solitude of the scene from which it lifts its head) . . . After feasting my eye for some time on the rich, diversified, and boundless landscape that lay before me, meditating on the future grandeur of the city and on the rising glories of the nation, I turned to resume my walk into the country."

Such was the center of town in 1822. The building of this

first monument to George Washington gave Baltimore the title of the Monumental City, and for the project a skilled architect was chosen. He was Robert Mills, a pupil of Benjamin H. Latrobe. Mills was one of those men who in the early nineteenth century had devoted himself to bringing back the old Greek style and manner of building. Latrobe was really the father of the Greek Revival in America, but Mills outdid Latrobe. In the work of the younger man there was no softness, no hint of Attic suavity. His work was severe and plain, Spartan in its austerity. Indeed, in any conflict, Mills would have been brought home on his shield, and a plain and unadorned shield at that. Talmadge speaks thus of his "Draconian restraint" in his design for the monument in Washington: "A man who with that cliff of marble before him refused to scar its face by a single scratch." Such was the architect chosen for the Baltimore work. But I am glad that Washington's monument here is of another type. The Colonne Vendôme was his inspiration, and the Gallic manner is more suited to Baltimore than the bleak severity of Sparta.

At last on July 4, 1815, the procession of dignitaries and simple townfolk moved northward along Forrest Street as Charles Street was then called and mounted the hill where we are now standing. The cornerstone was in readiness and with appropriate ceremonies the great stone was lowered into place. In accordance with the custom of the time a lottery was then opened to raise funds for the completion of the shaft. How early Baltimoreans loved these lotteries! Even stern moralists delighted in them, salving their consciences with the thought of the public good accruing from these games of chance. Churches were built by lotteries, and once in 1753 a wharf was constructed by raising four hundred and fifty pieces of eight. Ah, that must have been a pirates' wharf! Hasn't it the sound and color of the Spanish Main? But here is something even more delectable: one winter when things were evidently dull, a lottery was opened to provide "funds for *any undertaking* early in the spring." Mr. Micawber would have felt a sympathy with such an enterprise. And for the Monument a similar fund was raised; there were thirty-five thousand tickets at ten dollars a ticket. Baltimoreans responded well, not only on the financial side, but in the actual construction of the shaft. Charles Ridgely of Hampton gave the marble, and General William Steuart who was to play such a prominent part in later town annals cut the stone, proud of the fact that he was a good mason. Washington's Monument is in a very real sense the work of the commune.

If you are energetic it will pay you to climb with weary foot the spiral flight of stone steps which leads to the top. The view is fine, and on a misty day, or a snowy one, the ascent is well worth the effort. Of course you may prefer the sharp clarity of an October morning, but there is a silver loveliness in mist and cloud, a romantick quality (romantick with a k.) The monument is surmounted with the figure of Washington resigning his commission, an event which took place not in Baltimore, but in the State House in Annapolis. An old-time negro put another interpretation, however, upon that gesture of the outstretched hand; said he, "Marse George Washington is p'intin' South, sayin', 'Nigger, go South 'cause it's a-gettin' too cold in de No'th.'"

As we come out of the Monument we pass through high iron railings not unlike those that once enclosed the entire square. All travellers abroad, in Edinburgh or London, must have seen many such squares of enclosed greenery shady with trees. Mount Vernon Place was like this within the memory of many people now living, and Hopkinson Smith's story "Kennedy Square" pictures the Place as it was in those distant days. In our own time drastic changes have been made, but beauty can not be driven out. In spite of tasteless balustrades and banal fountains, Mount Vernon Place retains its charm. Let us lean here on the parapet and look at Washington Square as the south square is called. In the center the statue of Lafayette rides proudly before us. It is the work of Andrew O'Connor, a sculptor who could not be hurried. At the end of the Great War Marshal Joffre visited Baltimore, and with due ceremony ground was broken for the Lafayette statue at the eastern end of Mount Vernon Place. But the ways of men and politicians are past finding out. The townspeople suddenly rubbed their eyes, and there lo and behold stood the marble base for the statue firmly entrenched directly below the Monument, under the shelter of Washington's august hand.

Then began the long story of the vacant pedestal, waiting, waiting patiently for Lafayette. One morning the Sunpaper published a cartoon that had the whole town laughing. Two soldiers stood gazing at the empty base, and paraphrasing the words of Pershing exclaimed, "Here we are Lafayette, but where in the hell are you?" Where indeed? At length in 1924 the statue was unveiled, and again criticism poured forth. Lafayette does look somewhat undernourished, but seen from the corner of the Peabody it is a spirited and vigorous work. The Jencks house on the southwest corner makes a fine background. Go over and study the General from this angle. The south square is utterly different from the others. It runs down hill with a blithe skipping step. If the weather is mild, and the taxis not too vociferous we can hear music—the faint rich music of the organ running in and out of the street noises, and in some strange way harmonizing with them. The low grey building on our left is the Peabody Conservatory, and on another day we shall say more about it. But the music comes from there, and that is why I had to explain it. Long ago

WASHINGTON PLACE BEFORE LAFAYETTE CAME TO JOIN HIS LEADER

IN THE SHADOW OF WASHINGTON'S HAND

Washington Square had worn grey stone steps instead of these pebbly treads, and the old pavement was a lovely rose colour, a faint ash-rose very pleasant to the eye. Japonica and forsythia grew thickly and riotously. Where now a characterless basin stands adorned with dolphins, there rose in other years the lily fountain, modelled, so tradition said, from Washington's drinking cup. I can not vouch for that, but it was a thing of beauty, slender in shape like the lotus, with a design of cranes and reeds chased upon its smooth sides. It was deemed old-fahsioned, I suppose, and was moved to Eutaw Place where it still serves as a fountain, but with an alien air. I can see it still in its ancient setting, the water bubbling over the lovely stone lip, falling in streams down the sides, and filling the basin with countless circling ripples. As time went on, the lotus cup wore an exquisite patina of brown and green. The soft voice of the fountain mingled with the Peabody organ, and there arose from the bowl an enchanting smell of fresh clean water. I can smell it now. But beauty is a hardy growth. The lily fountain is no more, and dolphins are a sorry substitute. Nevertheless on April days there are still lilacs, and rhododendrons. In the new fountain a small Sea-urchin, quaint elfish figure, keeps a watchful eye upon the goldfish. Though changes bring loss they also bring some gain, and the stone bench beneath Lafayette's statue is one of them. It is a sunny resting place, and on mild winter days old men a-sunning sit, or rosy children climb up and jump off the seat with boundless energy. Above, thunder the hoofs of the gallant Frenchman whose brave inscription reads

LAFAYETTE IMMORTAL
Because a self-forgetful servant of
Justice and Humanity
Beloved by all Americans
Because he acknowledged no duty more
Sacred than to fight for
The Freedom
Of his fellowmen.   WOODROW WILSON

23

BALTIMORE

The eastern square is the quietest of all. Here with prim dignity is none other than George Peabody, seated for all the world as if upon the lawn of his house. What a homely joy it was to see him sitting in the same informal attitude in Thread-needle Street, as unconcerned as on his Baltimore grass plot. But there is no time now for Peabody's thrilling life; later we shall sit upon the bench in the sun, and recount his remarkable career. Long ago there were trees here, but they languished and finally died. Today the square has a bare look, but the houses are still old-fashioned, and a few pickaninnies skating madly, their chalky eyes on the police, give a little colour, even if it is slightly dusky in tone. At the extreme eastern end of the parterre looking out over the smoky gully of Calvert Street stands one of Baltimore's most famous citizens, Severn Teackle Wallis. Again and again the name of Wallis is interwoven in the fabric of Baltimore's history as a lawyer, reformer, litterateur. The statue by Laurent Marqueste is in my humble judgment inadequate; Wallis was so great, and the statue is so little. Perhaps the awful clothes have something to do with the effect. Men look ridiculous in trousers, and waistcoats, and awkward ugly coats. This site, by the way, was chosen for the Lafayette monument, and it is here that Joffre broke the ground. Then followed the long dispute. For weeks poor Wallis lay prone on his face, for he was unceremoniously dragged from his original position in Washington Square. Even now he wears no assured air. This is disputed ground, and die-hards yet assert that finally La-fayette will be removed, and the line of approach to Wash-ington's Monument will be unbroken. At the western end of the Square on the north corner there once stood a gracious house in the Georgian manner well-beloved by early Balti-moreans. Here a bronze tablet tells us was the house in which Francis Scott Key died. It has of course vanished long ago,

24

and now the Mount Vernon Methodist Church occupies the ground. The church is built in the French Gothic and has nothing noteworthy about it except the charming colour of the stone on a wet day, or when there has been a heavy fall of snow. Then the green serpentine stone has a lovely bloom like ripe almonds or the bright texture of pistachio nuts.

One used to descend into the north square by grey stone steps nicely hollowed by the feet of many generations, and instead of the uniform and dismal concrete there was the warm rose tinge of the old pavements with—oh, shall I mention it? green moss growing in the crevices, moss with rich black dirt under it which one could pick out if the nurse wasn't looking! There were, too, stiff geometric designs in the flagging, circles and stars and quaint pointed borders. Alas, these were removed; we must be modern, and moss is a horrifying spectacle. It will surely grow upon the back if it be allowed to flourish in the pavement, and then—well, even Johns Hopkins Hospital can not save you. There is though one thing that still delights. One fears to mention it—the City Council is so alert—and one dreads Dutch Cleanser: the Barye bronzes have already made delightful green stains on the meaningless balustrades, green from the palest acquamarine to the deepest emerald. But do not praise its beauty too loudly. Remember the bronze lamps at the City Hall! These four groups of sculpture, however, Peace, War, Order, and Force are now well-placed. When one is prowling about the Louvre it is pleasant to find in what is called the "new Louvre" these same groups of statuary—it gives one a homely feeling. Poor Barye! How astonished he must be to find himself in the great French gallery. Barye was a French animal sculptor, who delighted particularly in modelling the tense muscles of wild creatures; this was his special field, and like many another he was unappreciated for years and suffered dire poverty. Late in life

25

when success had come, he exclaimed with bitterness. "They bring me things to eat when I no longer have any teeth." But in spite of his wretched state, he spent long rapturous hours in the Jardin des Plantes studying the living creatures that he so marvellously transmuted into bronze. One day an artist brought him a five hundred franc note to relieve his hunger. In a few days Barye presented himself at the artist's door bearing a huge basket in which were statuettes of lions and rabbits and tigers. As the artist hesitated to accept the generous gift, poor Barye pushed them literally into his arms, saying "They will not sell!" But they did sell—if not these, then other studies of the same sort. William T. Walters was one of the first to appreciate the work of this distinguished sculptor, and in his gallery is probably the finest collection of Baryes in the world. On the Ile Saint Louis, that little backwater in the Parisian capital, there is a monument to Barye—erected, says Georges Cain, at "the very place where this sublime artist, misunderstood and scoffed at, came at the twilight hour from the modest studio on the quai to forget his suffering before the adorable panorama of Paris." One greets him there on the quaint eighteenth century island as a fellow-Baltimorean, for to many of us Barye was the first sculptor we ever knew, and his Lion and Serpent our first objet d'art. I love these links with foreign places. They widen our horizons, and make our town an inheritor of the ages.

Now we return from Paris to consider an American, and a great one—Roger Brooke Taney. He sits in his lawyer's robes as Chief Justice. His lean, ascetic face is skillfully modelled; look at it in the sunlight and see how dexterously Rinehart has managed the subtle planes and contours that make up the human countenance. Sometimes a sparrow lights upon the bent shoulders, and cocks his head impudently, as if he expected Taney to shrug. A twitch of those taut facial muscles would send the bird flying, but, undisturbed, the sparrow perches quietly enough. About this statue there is the suggestion of infinite patience and infinite justice. Taney was appointed Attorney General under President Jackson, and during a long and stormy period he was a power in the councils of the country. But in 1857 affairs began to move toward a climax. Two days after the inauguration of Buchanan the Supreme Court made public its decision in the case of Dred Scott who had sued for freedom. This negro from Missouri had been taken by his master into one of the free states. He therefore claimed freedom on the ground of temporary residence on free soil. The courts, however, decided against him. Taney, as Chief Justice, and the Supreme Court went on to declare that the legislation of 1820 must be considered unconstitutional. Slaves, said Taney, were not citizens but property, and therefore Congress could not legislate against any kind of property belonging to citizens of the states. Slave owners might carry their slaves where they would as they might carry any other property. None but a State could exclude its lawful bondsmen. This decision was known as the Dred Scot decision, and it delighted the South and enraged the North. Out of this discussion grew the Lincoln-Douglas debates, and Lincoln, a new and striking figure, took the field. From Kansas, the immediate centre of slavery agitation at the time, came John Brown notorious for his mad raid at Harper's Ferry. Woodrow Wilson in his American History says, "Brown was a fanatic, but not a common rascal." I wonder what Taney thought.

Francis Scott Key's sister, Anne, became the wife of Roger Brooke Taney, and in Mount Vernon Place these two brothers-in-law are justly celebrated; one by the bronze tablet on the church across the way; the other by the Rinehart sculpture. These two Maryland men were different in temperament

27

and gifts; Key, the fiery poetic nature; Taney, the calm judicial spirit who in debate "spoke like a relentless angel."

North of Taney's statue is the equestrian figure of the Revolutionary soldier, John Eager Howard. Fremiet, the sculptor, has shown him in a noble pose, characteristic of his swift impetuosity. But the story of Howard at the battle of Cowpens reveals more truly than could a dozen sculptors the ardour of the man. Howard particularly relished an encounter with crossed bayonets, and was most skilled in the use of this fearsome weapon. At the battle of Cowpens he rushed at the British in such a ferocious manner that Tarleton's best troops wavered before him. At length, gripping in his fist seven British swords, he stood before the commanding officer, Morgan. Sternly Morgan looked at him and at the sheaf of bloody weapons.

"You have done well" he said. "Had you failed, I would have had you shot, for you charged without orders."

But Morgan was himself an intrepid fighter, and he delighted in Howard's valour. The lines from *Maryland, My Maryland* come back to us now with special meaning—"Remember Howard's warlike thrust." Nor are his glories all military. Indeed I think his zeal with the bayonet was only equalled by his warm generosity. Howard owned practically the whole of Baltimore, his great estate stretching roughly from Biddle Street on the north, to Eutaw on the west, to Pratt on the south, and to Jones's Falls on the east. As the history of Baltimore unrolls you will see how he gives large tracts of land for various purposes. Indeed John Eager Howard gave, as we have seen, this very ground on which we are standing. He was patriotic in the best meaning of the word, and strongly imbued with the sense of his civic responsibilities.

IN THE SHADOW OF WASHINGTON'S HAND

Fremiet is another of those links with foreign countries that enrich our background. Do you remember Jeanne d'Arc riding so gallantly in the Place des Pyramides in Paris? She, too, is Fremiet's work. These children of an artist's brain are blood brothers and sisters; here we have most truly "hands across the sea." Furthermore, the recognition of the tie gives us a sense of the value of our own possessions. Familiarity breeds contempt—or as a quaint old lady said, "too much freedery breeds despisery." Abroad we gape at Fremiet's work; at home we pass it by intent on reaching O'Neill's. Behold the brethren of John Eager Howard—how august a list! The valiant Jeanne at the very gate of old Paris; brave Du Guesclin in the dusty square of Dinan, that little town in Brittany; but most distinguished of all, high in the blue, guarding the sacred Mount, Saint Michael waves his trenchant sword (much in the manner of Howard) over the marvellous pinnacle of Mont Saint Michel. All of these are the work of Fremiet. John Eager Howard, good citizen, brave soldier, finds himself in company with the saints. Think of the windy Mont "and the immense tremour of the sea" when next you pass the Revolutionary patriot. It will enlarge your horizon.

Many critics consider the west square the most beautiful. There, certainly, we get the feeling of repose, the sense of quiet space. To me, the east square is homely and friendly; the north, simply a warm green space, the south, sunny, with a splashing fountain. But the west square is the essence of Mount Vernon Place. It has about it that eighteenth century manner that one finds at old Mount Vernon, the home of General Washington. Here on the balustrades are War and Peace, those fine Barye bronzes. They are well placed and already at home, staining the marble with rich hues of green and copper. Once they stood upon pedestals placed on the lawns, but progress is certainly justified by this move.

BALTIMORE

The Lion stands proudly aloof as ever. Some waggish person has said that Barye's lion has sucessfully treed George Washington; hence the triumphant demeanour. A new statue is Crenier's delightful boy playing in the little circular pool. Of quite another school is Dubois's Military Courage. He is a smug warrior, but he has a handsome profile. How different in effect were those Baltimore boys of the Twenty-ninth Division returning from over seas. On a sweltering September afternoon they marched by, line upon line of grim and impudent bronzed faces under tilted tin hats. Military Courage reviewed them with classic calm. He spoke a different idiom.

Of the houses that surround the Place much might be written. Across Cathedral street, just west of Military Courage is Miss Mary Garrett's Mansion, now the temporary quarters of the Baltimore Museum of Art. The new Museum has been built in Wyman's Park. Sargent has a picture of Miss Garrett, a plain old-fashioned lady of the best Baltimore tradition, but she was by no means stereotyped. All women should remember her with gratitude, for because of her, women were admitted to the Hopkins Medical School on an equal footing with men. When women were in the "wept-with-delight-when-you-gave-them-a-smile" period Miss Garrett believed them capable of intellectual achievement. She had faith. To this house came often her close friend, another Baltimore woman, whose work has been in the neighborhood of Philadelphia—M. Carey Thomas, the former president of Bryn Mawr College. The vast brown stone house on the south side of the Place is the home of Doctor and Mrs. Henry Barton Jacobs. This handsome house was designed by the famous American architect, Stanford White. Next door is the home of the late William T. Walters now in the possession of his son, Henry Walters. Their beautiful art collection will be visited later; you can see the gallery—a fine Renaissance building—just down the hill on Centre Street. No, it is not of the gallery that I shall speak now, but of a story connected with the old house itself. If you are sceptical you may skip this part, and the Maryland Historical Society will probably sustain you. But here is the tale: Passersby in Mount Vernon place will notice just at dusk that a lamp glows in the doorway of the old Walters house. The door is boarded-up and there is no one at home, but the light shines out in fair weather or in storm. Indeed the light burns all day long, year in, year out. Why this should be I do not know, but some say that long ago that lamp was lighted for an erring child, and it has burned perpetually as a signal of forgiveness. Scoff not, gentle readers, such lamps and such stories are all too few in modern towns. Let us cherish them; let us hang haloes on our gate posts while we may.

At the southwest corner of Charles and Mount Vernon Place is the old home of John Hanson Thomas, now owned by the Jencks family. This is a lovely house in the style of the Greek revival so popular in Baltimore in the early nineteenth century. Notice the iron grille work characteristic of that type of architecture, and mark particularly the shell-like ornamentation on the roof. On the day when Military Courage retired before the war-weary courage of the Twenty-ninth Division, all the windows of this beautiful house were set wide open, and rich tapestries and splendid rugs were hung from every casement in honor of the returning troops. It is an old-world custom, and it fitted well with the fine traditions of the Square. But if you love Mount Vernon Place, come out of the Peabody some evening at dusk, a rosy winter dusk. Against the sky you will probably see a flock of homing birds as rhythmically lovely as the flight of notes across a musical score. And always you will see against the west, the fine shell molding of the roof and Lafayette, a gallant figure in this light, riding south.   31

CAPTAIN JOHN SMITH COMES TO TOWN

CHAPTER II

BUT to know Baltimore one must leave Mount Vernon Place, walk south through Washington Square, and ascend the steep slope that climbs up from Centre Street. Baltimore, like imperial Rome, used to have seven hills, but we have no time now for that, nor time either to notice all the old houses and buildings on this most famous of the city streets. On another day we shall return. For the present, we shall walk south steadily until we come to Baltimore Street, and then turn to the left to Light Street. We are on the trail of old Baltimore, and in a few moments we shall find ourselves on the threshold of the town. But we must not be too precise about actual spots; we must get the spirit of the thing, and not rely too exactly upon the compass or whatever instrument is used in verifying historic sites. Now I take it that we have arrived at the corner of Light and Pratt Streets, or perhaps we are wandering down Pratt street easterly toward Calvert. The prospect is neat, modern, and efficient with not a suspicion of an historic site. Sweep all of this view away, and by a strong act of the imagination find yourself walking along a sandy shore where blue water ripples softly, and see approaching you over the waters of the bay an English ship, an Elizabethan vessel, a sturdy boat built by those seafaring men in the days following the Armada. In other words imagine yourself an Indian walking along this very water front, and see for yourself Captain John Smith's pinnace gliding nearer and nearer the site of Baltimore. For the early history of the town goes back to this hardy adventurer. As Macaulay says, "every schoolboy knows" of the Captain's exploits in Virginia, and the incident with the Indian princess Pocahontas. But this man John Smith was not only a figure of romance; he was also a writer of considerable power. In a book of his called *The Sixth Voyage* he describes Maryland and, what is more, the site of Baltimore itself. This was in 1606. He made, too, a remarkably accurate map of the Chesapeake Bay and the rivers of Maryland. To the Patapsco he gave the name Bolus because of the red clay banks which greeted the eyes of those early explorers. Today they are familiar to all of those who travel up and down the Chesapeake or sail around the mouth of the Patapsco River. This red clay resembled "bole armoniack" Smith said; hence the name. According to Lossing "Smith went up the Patapsco and ate maize on the site of Baltimore." Scharf repeats this, and thus it come down to us with authority. But even if there should be an error who would part with such a tradition? It was a fair prospect that greeted the Captain's eyes; the blue waters of the bay, mingling with the tawny river, the land rising in long ranges of gently rolling hills. All the familiar Maryland trees grew untouched to the edge of those red banks, the tulip, the red gum, and the locust. Perhaps a canoe slid stealthily along, bronze savages watching the great ship with unfeigned astonishment. And then the Captain landed, no doubt on the shore at the

head of the Basin, and there he ate his dish of corn meal. I
wonder what it was. Was it a hoe cake, thick and piping hot,
was it a roasted ear, or was it pone, or was it—ah, best of all—
batterbread? At any rate I am sure that he remembered Baltimore most pleasantly. But in case you are literal minded I
must warn you: that last remark is *not* to be taken seriously.
Baltimore was as yet unheard, undreamed of. George Calvert
himself, the Lord Proprietor of later years, was then devoting
his best energies to the service of King James.

At this point it would be well to give an account of the
Cavalier gentleman to whom Baltimore owes her name. It is
possible that in 1628 George Calvert may have visited Maryland while on a journey to Virginia. Again Scharf says that
nothing positive is known on this subject. However that may
be, it is to Calvert that Baltimore owes her finest traditions.
At the court of James the First he was a notable figure, a member of Parliament, and a strong supporter of the king. Went-
worth was his staunch friend, and the two men, different in
temperament, were one in political ideals. As a reward for
his services, Calvert had been made Lord Baltimore, a name
drawn from a little Irish town. It stands today in County Cork
on a bleak promontory, a stepsister of the Maryland town. At
length George Calvert retired from court, and planned to
devote his life to colonization. The attempted settlement at
Avalon in Newfoundland had proved discouraging because
of the "sad fare of winter." His thoughts therefore turned
south, and he asked the king—now Charles I—to grant him
land on either side of the great bay called Chesapeake. Charles
was Calvert's friend, and though there were strong protests
from many influential people, the charter was granted. But in
the meanwhile George Calvert had died, and the actual colonization of Maryland was the work of his son Cecilius. On
the Feast of the Annunciation, March 25, 1634, the Maryland

colonists landed. For the subsequent history of the colony we have no special concern here, but one fact stands out like a bright light in those dark days of bigotry. Maryland was the first colony to grant religious toleration. Calvert was a Roman Catholic, and he secured for his colony an enlightened legislation unknown in any other place in America. This Act of Religious Toleration remained in force until those boasted defenders of liberty, the Puritans, repealed it in 1654. "They did not use their power gently," says one historian. After several years of Puritan goose-stepping the colony was given back to the civilized control of the Calverts.

It may be that you are weary of standing on the corner of Pratt Street and Light, and this paragraph may seem to have no bearing on the history of Baltimore. But it has a most profound bearing. This temper and attitude—this liberal and tolerant point of view—has coloured the whole thought of the city and state. The great Proprietor has left us a priceless inheritance.

Before we begin the story of Baltimore Town of 1729 it might be advisable to walk up Light Street to the Southern Hotel, which stands on the site of the Fountain Inn, a hostelry beloved by Washington. The present modern structure is very different from the low, old-fashioned building shaded by a row of trees which the old prints tell us was the Fountain Inn. A large sign bearing a picture of a fountain—an exceedingly founting fountain—hung outside the door. Redwood Street—formerly German—was named for George Redwood, the first Maryland officer killed in action in the Great War. Light Street itself has sadly changed. I do not say that it is not a fine wide thoroughfare in every way suited to advance the business interests of the city. It is all this, but to one who remembers it as it was in the late nineties or early years of this century there is a heavy change. The cobbles were rough and uncertain, and down by the wharves the houses did lean upon one another for support, but there was colour and there was flavour and there was a goodly smell! In those days when one went "down the bay" in the summer, there were huddled rows of fruit and candy stores, most unsanitary even in the eyes of the nineties, but oh, how tempting! Candy of lurid hue was heaped upon the counters, and in the glass jars swam luscious sour pickles. From fried fish shops there blew whiffs of bay mackerel done to a turn. Old colored men sold devilled crabs, of Lucullan flavour, crying all the while,

"Devil, devil, devil, devil, c-r-a-a-a-b!"

At the doors of the tobacco shops stern faced Indians stood holding out packages of cigars, favoured by Baltimoreans of an earlier day (before the nineties) as a preventive of yellow fever. These carved figures are rarely seen now, but there is still one on guard outside of a shop on Calvert street, just north of the court-house. In those days, too, there were saloons from which came "the robustious laughter of youth," as Walt Whitman would say. With all these colours and smells and sounds was mingled the tang of tar and salt water and, most potent of all, guano—that rich Baltimorean reek that delighted the hardy nostril, and made the returning excursionist know that he was nearing port. Well, we do things differently now, and not so vividly, so vigorously.

But Baltimore is a port—"the most western of eastern ports; the most northern of southern ports; the most southern of northern ports." Three railroads have large terminals in Baltimore, the Baltimore and Ohio, the Pennsylvania, and the Western Maryland. These connect directly with the industrial, agricultural, and mining sections of the country. The largest and best equipped pier for loading coal in the world is owned by the B. and O. A model of this marvellous pier was shown at the Fair of the Iron Horse, the centenary of the Bal-

CAPTAIN JOHN SMITH COMES TO TOWN

timore and Ohio Railroad. The Pennsylvania has an immense plant for handling grain. Those who are interested in the city's commercial development will find little material in this volume; this is not the place for such data. But if you are interested, Bond's "Guide to Baltimore" will help you, and the City Library in the City Hall will gladly furnish information.

William Henry Davies, a Welsh poet who has tramped across the world picking berries, peddling, and working on cattle-ships, has put Baltimore into his poem in a way that means more (to me) than a page of statistics. I can see the boat dropping down past the Fort, past the Seven-Foot Knoll, past the shores of red clay, the "bolus armoniack," through the Capes and out to the open sea. It is not a great poem, but a poem about one's town is always interesting; like having one's portrait painted. Here it is. Skip it, if you don't like verse, but it is good. I wonder whose sheep it was.

A CHILD'S PET

When I sailed out of Baltimore,
　With twice a thousand head of sheep,
They would not eat, they would not drink,
　But bleated o'er the deep.

Inside the pens we crawled each day,
　To sort the living from the dead;
And when we reached the Mersey's mouth,
　Had lost five hundred head.

Yet every night and day one sheep,
　That had no fear of man or sea,
Stuck through the bars its pleading face,
　And it was stroked by me.

And to the sheep-men standing near,
　"You see," I said, "this one tame sheep?
It seems a child has lost her pet,
　And cried herself to sleep."

So every time we passed it by,
　Sailing to England's slaughter-house,
Eight ragged sheep-men—tramps and thieves—
　Would stroke that sheep's black nose.

37

BALTIMORE

When we step out of the Southern we plunge at once into the heart of old Baltimore Town, but before we take this step there is an interesting bit of history that must be told. Few people except the historians know that there was once another Maryland town that bore the name of Baltimore. This town, Old Baltimore, as it is called, was situated on the Bush River about seven miles south of Perrymanville, and two miles northeast of the Philadelphia and Wilmington Railroad bridge. This little town had been the port of entry and the county seat for no one knows how long—probably for some years before 1683. Scharf speaks of six maps which give the location of the town very accurately, and in addition to these proofs there are lines of cedar trees planted carefully as if to mark off fields. All traces of the town had disappeared by the seventies of the last century; only a few log huts occupied the site, and a rude fence enclosed the supposed location of this once thrifty little village. In 1712 the county seat was moved to Joppa—another interesting settlement, now too, fallen to decay. With Joppa our story has no connection, but this transfer of power probably brought about the ruin of the first Baltimore. Speaking, however, of Joppa, you will notice in driving through the suburbs that you will meet several Joppa Roads. These were named thus because Joppa was the center of the tobacco industry, and as many roads led thither as once led to imperial Rome. In this connection, too, one might mention the Rolling Roads. These got their names from the custom of transporting tobacco in the old days. A pin was fastened to each end of the hogshead and shafts attached. Thus the hogshead of tobacco was easily rolled along to the nearest port for shipment. Such a port was Joppa, and such was Elkridge Landing. In 1768 Baltimore was made the county seat, and here our story begins. It has had a long but necessary preamble.

38

CAPTAIN JOHN SMITH COMES TO TOWN

As early as 1661 Peter Carroll surveyed three hundred acres of land for David Jones on the line of a clear but turbulent little stream that flowed down from the rolling hills of Baltimore county. On the banks of this stream where Front Street intersects French Street Jones built himself a house, and gave his name to the stream which has played a considerable part in the history of the town. Of Jones we know scarcely more than this. His house was pleasantly situated and had a fair prospect. To the north and east the land sloped gently in the characteristic Baltimore fashion. To the west across the Falls, as streams were called in those early days, steep cliffs of red tawny clay rose up from the edge of the water, and the sun went down behind a range of hills. To the south lay swamp land, vivid green in the hot summers, and in the autumn full of reed birds—a fine place for a marksman. Such was David Jones's environment. In a few years, in 1668, to be precise, Thomas Cole received three hundred acres of land known as Cole's Harbor. Roughly this tract ran from the mouth of Harford Run on the east to a point on the shore about one mile distant, and then northward for half a mile. In this rhomboid lay the heart of the future Baltimore town. Around Cole's Harbor were many farms whose names have been preserved in the town history, or in the names of streets. Far to the northwest lay Mount Royal, a fine tract which later gave its name to the broad avenue leading to Druid Hill Park. In the west lay Chatsworth; Huntington spread its rich acres on the northern edge of the future city. Those Baltimoreans who have come to mature years will well remember when Twenty-fifth Street was called Huntington Avenue. A wide and generous tract lying approximately in the neighborhood of Union Station was named, oddly enough, Salisbury Plain. Perhaps some Wiltshire man had settled there. But there were other names more picturesque—Carter's Delight, Spicer's Inheri-

39

tance, Parrish's Fear, Hale's Folly, and David's Fancy. Nor
should we forget Haphazard, Roger's Inspection, and Welsh
Adventure. All of these farms were rich and fertile, and the
raising of tobacco was the chief industry. At length the early
settlers petitioned the Legislature to give them a town of their
own, a port of entry for their great crop. It seemed wise to
these petitioners to establish the town on the Middle Branch
of the Patapsco called Spring Gardens, as it is called to this
day. They met, however, with unexpected opposition from
John Moale. On David's Fancy—we shall pass through this
land on the way to Fort McHenry—Moale believed that iron
ore existed. Consequently, he refused to give up his land. The
petitioners, nevertheless, held firmly to their project, and now
cast about them for a new site. Cole's Harbor was the very
place. Here was a good haven for ships; the waters were shallow because of the alluvial sands brought down by the Falls
and several smaller streams, but the slope of the land was
down hill, and tobacco could easily be rolled along the simple
roads—those rolling roads that have been mentioned before.
In August, 1729, the bill for the establishment of the town was
passed, and signed by Benedict Leonard Calvert, Esquire, Governor on behalf of Charles Calvert, fifth Lord Baltimore. It
read: "A bill for erecting a town on the north side of the
Patapsco in Baltimore County, and for laying out into lots
sixty acres of land, in and about the place where John Flemming now lives." This John Flemming had a house near the
present Charles and Lombard streets. The price of the land
was set at forty shillings an acre in current money of Maryland,
or tobacco at a penny a pound. Thus the whole town site was
sold not for quite six hundred dollars! The next step was to
survey the town, and this task was given to Philip Jones who
commenced at the "bounded red oak" at the corner of Light
and Pratt Streets. That, you see, was the beginning of the

town, and that is why I led you thither. John Smith may have eaten that meal of Indian corn on this spot; beyond doubt "the red bounded oak" grew here.

The shape of the town was an Indian arrow head, with the point toward the west. From the red oak the town line ran northwesterly along Uhler Run—now Uhler's Alley—toward what was then the Great Eastern Road and a "great gully" or drain near the present intersection of Sharpe and Redwood Streets. Then the boundary turned north across Baltimore street, and ran parallel with the Great Eastern Road as it turned north through what is now McClellan's Alley. This road was later known as Church Road because it led to Saint Paul's Church, but that belongs later in our story. A bronze tablet on the rear wall of O'Neill's store at Charles and Lexington Streets makes clear the route of this old road, and Baltimore's boundaries in this part of the town were almost identical with the line of the road. The northernmost point of the town was at Charles and Pleasant Streets. Here was a precipice behind which David Jones often saw the sunset. The line now dropped to the bank of Jones's Falls which in those days flowed merrily in the bed of Saint Paul and Calvert. It followed the bank of the Falls to land which lay ten perches west of Gay street and then turned sharply south running in a straight line to the harbor. These were the confines of Baltimore Town as it was laid out in 1729. There were three streets: Long, now Baltimore; Forrest, now Charles; and the third, the chief street, evidently, for it led directly to the water —Calvert, but oddly enough not named at first. Baltimore street was at one time called Market Street, but Calvert has always borne the name of the Proprietors. Charles Street, now one of the chief thoroughfares of the town, was a modest straggling little road meandering casually uphill, and called Forrest, possibly from the fact that north of Pleasant Street there was only the silence of the woods on the Howard estate. The name of Charles Street may be derived from the Calvert family or from Charles Carroll of Carrollton, a signer of the Declaration. In addition to the three streets there were nine lanes: Second, South, Light, Hanover, East, Lovely, Belvedere, Saint Paul's and German. The water in those days came up farther into the town than at present—indeed as far as Lombard Street. And Jones's Falls, that belligerent stream only subjugated within recent years, flowed in a deep bend around the foot of a cliff where the Battle Monument was afterwards built. Calvert Street was then a short road leading up from the Basin to the brow of the precipice. Always this street has been thwarted in its development. First, the Falls stopped its northward march; then Belvedere, the home of John Eager Howard stood in the path; next the Falls—ubiquitous stream —had to be crossed; last barrier of all, the old Blind Asylum blocked the way. The march northward however lay at this time in the bosom of the future.

On January 14, 1730, the first lots were taken up. Titles were secured by beginning and finishing on the lot a house that covered at least four hundred square feet of ground. The work of building had to be complete within eighteen months, but so in earnest were the citizens of the little settlement, that no time was lost, and the sound of the hammer rang out cheerily. Speaking of titles and such brings to mind some of the queer ground rents for which Baltimore was at one time famous. One of the oddest is the ground rent on land under the lake in Druid Hill Park. It is one of the kind known as irredeemable, and every year the Water Department pays two hundred dollars to the owner of the submerged property. Another curious arrangement dating back to an early period in the life of the town is an irredeemable ground rent on a row of houses on Pratt Street. For this property a kernel of corn must be paid yearly. It is said that the reason for these strange terms is obvious. A man who buys a title to land in fee simple owns real estate, and his wife's signature is necessary if he wishes to sell the land. On the other hand, a perpetual lease at the small rate of one cent if it is demanded makes the land personal property, and a wife's signature is not needed for its disposition. All this, however, is off the subject, but it is certainly of interest.

Baltimore Town was by this time—1730—firmly established, but it had a lusty competitor. In 1726 Edward Fell had settled east of Jones's Falls, and in 1730 his brother William bought the tract of land known as Corpus Harbor, and called the land Fells Point. Later we shall wander around on the Point. At present we shall merely mention it. Thus in 1726 there were three dwellings, a mill, a tobacco house and an orchard on the east side of the Falls. This was the nucleus of another settlement to be incorporated as Jones Town. In point of settlement and building operations it preceded Baltimore, and hence it was called Old Town. Old Town it still remains, and the neighborhood is very proud of the distinction. Its special history will be discussed later. Now let us confine ourselves to Baltimore Town.

If you are a good walker, and feel inclined, it is quite possible to trace out the arrow head boundaries of the early city. It will lead you from the wharves up through the edge of the wholesale mercantile business, to the retail section, and thence to the first church built in the town. From that point it will take in the steep hills sloping down to Calvert Street, embracing the municipal buildings, and ending with the Custom House. If you wish to work this out on a map, do so; or even the mind's eye will give you a good outline of the old town. An old map made by John Moale, son of that first John who owned the iron mines, gives a fair picture of the town in

1757. From a neat square of blue water the land rises in gently rolling hills until it reaches the crowning eminence on which stands Old Saint Paul's. North of that there is nothing but a steep ravine, and then in long lazy rises the land slopes upward toward what is now Charles and Chase Streets. Then of course all this hilly land was covered with primeval forest. But let us come to the harbor. There two ships are anchored. On the right hand, Jones's Falls, a pure and limpid stream, flows softly into the Basin. On the left where now the excursion boats lie at the wharves two or three men are artlessly hauling a seine. And I bet it is full of crabs. A wharf juts out into the harbor at the foot of Calvert Street. That is the beginning of our famous docks. In all there are twenty-five houses, two taverns and one church—a well-proportioned town! Several of the houses are substantial and comfortable, but on the whole, the little settlement has a straggling hobbledehoy air. Stand at the corner of Baltimore and Calvert Streets and imagine this simple pastoral scene. In the nearby fields men are cultivating tobacco to the very water's edge. How incredible it would have seemed to those men, the seine-haulers and the field hands, had some one told them that one hundred and seventy years later tall towers of stone would rise against the blue Maryland sky, that this little harbor would be the second port in the country.

But before this picture was painted the town had made itself safe against the attacks of hostile Indians. A strong wooden stockade had been built around the town as a guard against those subtle enemies. There were two gates large enough to admit carriages, one at the west end of Baltimore Street, which then ended at McClellan's Alley, and another at what is now Gay Street, not far from the Fallsway. At the top of the hill near Saint Paul's Church there was a small wicket gate through which foot-passengers might pass. The stockade was well-built and encircled the town as completely as the walls enclosed a mediaeval city. At length, however, a severe winter came, and Baltimoreans fearing the cold more than the redskins, tore down the old wall and use it for fire-wood. Gradually all trace of it disappeared. The fear of the Indians was intensified later, following Braddock's defeat. When that disaster overtook the English arms, the people in the western part of the state flocked along the roads to Baltimore. It was a long and toilsome journey, and the townspeople with their customary hospitality gave a sorely needed welcome. Almost every day reports, true or false, came to the town that the Indians were drawing nearer and nearer. Such was the excitement of the times that ships were prepared in which to dispatch the women and children to safety. Finally the Indians did approach within thirty miles of Baltimore, but they came no nearer, and the tension was lessened.

In this connection it is interesting to recall that Saint Thomas's Church at Garrison, Maryland—commonly called the Garrison Forest Church—was a chapel established by Old Saint Paul's the mother church of the diocese for the care of "the forest inhabitants," at the garrison ten miles beyond the town. This garrison was maintained to keep off the Indians. Thus one sees that the fears of the townspeople were by no means exaggerated.

No doubt this inrush of refugees brought many new settlers who found in the growing community a desirable home. Those twenty-five houses in John Moale's picture are comfortable, peaceful looking homes. The climate was mild, the harbor promising, and best of all the Great Eastern Road ran through the town. This road was the chief artery of travel north and south. It was originally the old Sinequa Trail by which the Senecas travelled to Virginia or the Carolinas. Then after the white men had settled the eastern seaboard what was

45

more natural than that they should use this well-established trail? Bond, whose interesting book on Baltimore devotes much space to this subject, goes so far as to say that this road "welded the straggling colonies into a nation." The Great Eastern Road entered the town from the northeast, and passed along Monument Street cutting the grounds of the Johns Hopkins Hospital, and running to the Harford Road. Then it crossed the Falls at Hillen Street, and climbed the hill to Saint Paul's Church. There it turned sharply south through Crooked Lane back of O'Neill's store. A tablet on the wall here records part of this history, and, too, I have reminded you that this part of the road was once called Church Road because it led past Saint Paul's. Down McClellan's Alley went this old trail, and out Baltimore Street it ran on its long journey south, passing along what is now Columbia Avenue, and on and on until it reached the Potomac. Such a road as this brought the town into touch with other communities, and gave to Baltimore even at this early period contact with national affairs. Later we shall see the great men of the country riding north and south, stopping awhile at Baltimore's famous inns, delighting in her oysters, her toddies, and enjoying to the full the wit and sparkle of Baltimore women. We shall see that rich pageant of the eighteenth century if you will go with me along these modern streets. There as upon a page rewritten we shall decipher the old script plainly visible through the modern text. It shall be our joy to make those antique words speak again in all the measured beauty of that bygone age.

A BATTLE AND A MONUMENT

CHAPTER III

HE year 1755 brought not only Braddock's defeat, but also the arrival of the Acadians. You will remember how the Acadians in the Nova Scotia peninsula persisted stubbornly in being French. To root out this perfectly reasonable desire, the English forcibly exiled six thousand of them to different parts of the British colonial possessions. All of us recall Evangeline, a somewhat discredited heroine with moderns, but I confess that I like her constancy, and her "Norman cap and kirtle of blue." Well, some of these poor Acadians found a refuge in Baltimore. Stand for a moment on the corner of Calvert and Baltimore Streets and watch them as they toil along the little crooked street which then straggled up from the waterside. As usual the town made them welcome, and put a house at their disposal. And such a house—the best in the town! About the year 1750 a Mr. Edward Fottrell, an Irish gentleman, had built the first brick house in Baltimore, on the northwest corner of Fayette

47

and Calvert Streets. Recently he had gone back to Ireland and his house was empty. Here was the solution of the housing problem, and in a short time the Acadians were established in this old mansion.

Among those famous exiles in the story was Rene Le Blanc, the notary. You recall him—

"Bent like a laboring oar that toils in the surf of the ocean,
Bent, but not broken, by age was the form of the notary public.
. . . His forehead was high; and glasses with horn bows
Sat astride on his nose, with a look of wisdom supernal."

This old man—"father of twenty children"—came to Baltimore, it is said, and his descendants called themselves by the name of White. He died, according to Longfellow, in Philadelphia; well, most people do. But let him live in Baltimore! He lived in all likelihood in this neighborhood, and I like to see him building up a new life in this country, old man that he was. No doubt he told Baltimore children those tales of the Loup-garou, and the stories of the oxen who talk on Christmas Eve. René Le Blanc is a noble ancestor, and I would make haste to claim him were I named White.

One of the first needs of the forlorn exiles was the administration of a priest. At this time there was no Roman priest nearer than the chaplain at Doughoregan Manor, but an arrangement was made with Father Ashton, and he agreed to come in for Mass once a month. In the unfurnished house an altar was set up, simple no doubt but sufficient, and here these faithful people gathered to adore their God. Later the little congregation settled on Charles Street near Lombard, and the locality was called French Town.

In the old days before the monument to Washington was erected, Monument Square was the centre of the town. Prints of the period show us a square neatly swept and garnished, devoid of traffic except for an elegant cabriolet. In the centre arises the shaft known as the Battle Monument, and around the neat rectangle are the homes of eminent citizens, solid and prosperous mansions, yet with a sleepy old world air to our more hectic eyes. Even this, however, was a recent devlopment. When Baltimore was young, Jones Falls flowed cheerily down the bed of Calvert Street, and though this is hard to believe, ships lay at anchor at Lexington and Calvert Streets! Ah, what a sight this must have been! Not unlike, perhaps, the wonderful tale told (not by an idiot, but by a staid and sedate citizen) of skating in those good old hardy, ice-bound winters from Towson to Baltimore on the sleet covered pavements, or skating to Annapolis from the foot of Calvert Street. Nor was this the only odd thing to be discovered on the familiar site. Where the Battle Monument stands there was a high cliff of sixty feet or more, and it was on this hill that the citizens determined to build their first court-house. This was not a matter to be decided lightly, but upon mature consideration this was deemed the best possible location, and the work went forward. The building was of brick and two stories high, surmounted by a spire and a gilded weather-cock which fisherman could see at a great distance. It really was a building to be proud of, and the square was called Court House Hill. But the townspeople had reckoned without Jones Falls. Furiously did the waters of that untameable stream beat against the face of the cliff with the result that in 1784 the court-house had to be under-pinned. A public fund was raised for this project, and the work was given to Leonard Harbaugh. It was a difficult piece of work, but Harbaugh succeeded in building an arch beneath the old court-house. Now the town when it went strolling on warm summer evenings could walk under the arch and proceed for a short distance out Calvert Street, which had recently been graded.

BALTIMORE

This old brick building stood until 1809. The new building was of alternate red and white which certainly must have given it a lively aspect. The site, too, was changed, and the new hall of justice was on Lexington and Calvert Streets facing north, an excellent location, but by no means so engaging as Harbaugh's stilts. In the prints of the day ladies, languishing, go by upon the arms of their swains, but nary a glim of the eyes could be caught, protected as they were by huge scoop bonnets. At the hitching post, before the court-house door, one lone horse stands meekly. I wonder if his ghost appears at those yearly Christmas dinners that the Animal Refuge Society holds in the Square.

In those days the Battle Monument was not dreamed of; in truth, the Revolution had not yet occurred. Here, before the court-house, stood the whipping post, the pillory and the stocks. These things sound like Massachusetts. Let no one be deceived. Religious toleration by no means meant a weak-kneed policy towards evil-doers. Blasphemers were branded with a B, and sturdy rogues were publicly whipped to the encouragement of good citizenship. It was not, indeed, until the early days of the nineteenth century that such punishments went out of use. By the way, if you should chance to see an old gentleman wrapped in a scarlet cloak, and wearing a three-cornered hat, do not be astonished; it is none other than Samuel Chase, a member of the Supreme Court, and a Signer. The quaint costume which he wore, long after it had gone out of fashion, will mark him out among the modern hurly-burly, and probably you will find him in Court House Square, his favorite haunt.

Where nowadays the Equitable Trust stands was once the famous Barnum's Hotel. It was a large and florid building decorated in the "most chaste and elegant manner." The façade was adorned with iron balconies of ornate design. Within, all

THE BATTLE MONUMENT
NOTE THE OLD WILLIAMS HOUSE IN THE BACKGROUND

was in keeping. "The door leading from the hall to Fayette Street has been changed to a most imposing and tasty semicircular frontispiece, the novel and bold design of which renders it an ornament." Thus a contemporary account describes the splendours of old Barnum's. You can see that superlatives were popular. Nor should all of the adjectives be used for mere architecture and decoration. The food deserves a separate chapter. That "tasty frontispiece" was as nothing beside the terrapin and wine, the oysters and old ham, canvas backs and devilled crabs. Ah, those were the days! Thackeray came here, and the incomparable Jenny Lind appeared upon the garish balconies and waved her lily hand to the love-lorn swains who had slept all night around the Monument waiting for this moment. Alas, that an office building should rise on this site once devoted to gastronomic and sentimental charms! Such is progress.

The court-house is now on the corner of Fayette and Lexington opposite the site of the old hotel. It is the third structure of its kind in the town. The first was the little court house on stilts, then the second, built on this spot but much smaller, and now the third, completed in 1899. Before the western entrance stands a bronze statue of Cecilius Calvert, second Lord Baltimore. It was designed by Louis Weinert, and presented to the city by the Society of the Colonial Wars. Within, the murals are by men of the highest international reputation, and all except one are by American artists.

On the east wall of the Criminal Court corridor is Charles Yardley Turner's *Barter with the Indians for land in Southern Maryland*. In March, 1634, Governor Leonard Calvert and the first Maryland settlers landed from the Ark and the Dove, at the mouth of the Potomac River. "They were met by friendly Indians, Yaocomicos, under the sovereignty of the Emperor of Piscataway, from whom they bought a tract of land for axes, hoes, and cloth, and laid out the plan for a city which they called Saint Mary's." In the central panel Calvert is in conference with the Indians, Captain Fleete acting as interpreter. On one side the Indians are examining their new treasures, and on the other, a group of settlers are walking along the river bank planning their new home. But the idea that permeates the entire work is the theme of peace. Maryland was obtained by purchase, and the violence and bloodshed of other settlements was mercifully absent from this colony. It was natural that Turner, a member of the Society of Friends, should emphasize this point. On the west wall of the vestibule of the Criminal Court is *The Burning of the Peggy Stewart*. All of the characters here are Annapolitans, but the spirit of the sister towns was one in those stirring days; the mural is well worth careful study. No masked men burned this ship; in truth here the ship owner fired his own bark, as a protest against illegal tax on tea. In the centre, the Peggy Stewart herself is in flames. In the foreground Charles Carroll of Carrollton leads the way; opposite to him is Charles Alexander Warfield, leader of the Whig Club. Here are the impetuous Annapolitans, ladies, lovely, but none the less determined. A small boy has been lifted in his mother's arms that he may see this day's work and remember it. Nor are the coloured people absent.

Another famous mural is Blashfield's painting of Maryland's finest achievements, *The Toleration Act*. In 1649, under the Roman Catholic Lord Baltimore, complete religious freedom was granted to all men. Such a declaration had never been set forth in this country before, and this unique act was fittingly glorified in Blashfield's symbolic painting in the Circuit Court. Lord Baltimore, the central figure, commits his people to the charge of Wisdom, Justice and Mercy. A boy holds the balance true, and points upward to the motto of the

52

A BATTLE AND A MONUMENT

Calvert's—"Thou hast covered us with the shield of thy good-will."

Another fine piece of Blashfield's work is found in the Court of Common Pleas. It represents Washington resigning his commission. There is a special fitness in having a Frenchman add his work to that of the Americans in the decoration of the court-house. Lafayette is remembered with affection even in these late days. Jean Paul Laurens was an old man of seventy-two when he executed this work. The old painter exhibited the mural at the Paris Salon, after which the work was brought to Baltimore by Julian Le Roy White and an artist. In the scene of the surrender of Cornwallis the aged artist has put both fire and vigor as the troops of the English defile with lowered colours before the victorious Americans and French.

This, however, is but guide-book material. Many are the quaint and humorous characters that have haunted these regions. There was for instance Mrs. Kilburn—a tragic figure, though ludicrous enough in appearance. She, poor lady, spent day after day in the court room while her son was on trial for some misdeed. At last the strain was too intense and the wretched woman lost her mind. Those of us who have long memories remember well the strange fantastic figure mincing along beneath a tiny parasol. Of a different kind was Gallegher, supposedly a real estate agent. Mockers said that he bore the real estate about his person, but of that I can not say. He wore a long bushy beard, and carried always a small satchell. In this he supposedly transported his fortune. The bag never left his side, and all men imagined the fat rolls of green backs that old Gallegher had safely stowed away in his bag. When, however, he came to die the bag was opened, and there was nothing there at all—that is, no coin of the realm.

Gallegher, in all likelihood, had a sense of humour and greatly enjoyed his little hoax.

But all this time not one word have we said about the Battle Monument. It looks dingy now, and diminished with the tall buildings that have arisen around it. The tallest so far is the skyscraper which towers above the site of the Williams house. In its day many a distinguished Baltimorean crossed the threshold. The hall was of a gracious width, and a fine spiral staircase led to the upper floors. There were handsome marble mantels where candles gleamed softly, long before electric light was heard of. Below in the wide fireplaces great logs roared on many a New Year's Eve while the wassail bowl went round. The Williams family lived here and in the same neighborhood lived their kith and kin. Then the house passed through several hands until it came into the possession of Thomas Wilson. This Wilson was a member of the Society of Friends. He was born in Harford county just at the time when the French Revolution was stirring all Europe. When only a lad he came to Baltimore and entered the counting house of Thorndike Chase, one of the merchants of the day. But do not imagine that Wilson, the Friend, lived a quiet and uneventful life. He did not. This Quaker followed a career as replete with daring and danger as the life of Saint Paul. When Napoleon and Nelson were contending for the supremacy of the seas, Wilson had many adventures in the deep. He represented his firm on ships sailing to the West Indies. During the War of 1812 he had thrilling escapes. Once he had the yellow fever, but recovered marvellously. He went to and fro upon the earth, amassing an immense fortune for those days. Then he would lose all of his possessions, and with indomitable pluck he would start in all over again. At ninety he went to Colorado, following a life-long passion for travel. Nor was he lacking in a strong social spirit. He incorporated and

54

endowed the Thomas Wilson Sanitarium for The Children of the Sick Poor and thus used his wealth for the benefit of the helpless. At his death the building became the home of the Metropolitan Savings Bank. Famous men had their offices over the bank—James J. Ringgold, Joseph Packard and William Marine. "All, all are gone now, the old familiar faces." A towering skyscraper rises on the spot, but the very contrast of the new and the old has, for me, great charm. In the afternoon the reflection of sunlight from the upper stories of the skyscraper throws a strange orange glow into the Square. The Battle Monument stands out boldly against the modern background. Yes, I think that the new building has made its contribution to the place.

And now, at least, after many divagations, for the Monument itself. Sun and rain and city grime have subdued the marble, once white, to a ripe persimmon brown, a sort of rosy brown with a purplish bloom. It is an improvement, but we must go back a bit and review the passing years.

When the court house was moved in 1784, the space in the centre of the Square was grassed and left vacant. Fine houses arose in the neighborhood, and the Monument as it was then called became the centre of fashion. It was the Mount Vernon Place of early Baltimore. Then came the War of 1812 and the defense of the city against the attack of the British forces. In 1815 the citizens wished to erect a monument to the heroes of North Point. Therefore on September 12, 1815, the corner stone was laid, but it was ten years before it was completed. The townspeople, however, had an opportunity to see what their monument would be like. Maximilian Godefroy, a French emigré, had made the design, and a model of the shaft was borne in the procession. Baltimoreans dearly loved a parade in those artless days. A funeral car for the dead heroes was drawn by six milk-white horses. Nor were distinguished men absent.

55

BALTIMORE

On this anniversary General Samuel Smith was present, as was Colonel George Armistead, and Brigadier-General John Stricker. But for all this, it took ten years to raise the necessary funds. The design was made by Godefroy, and the sculpture by Cappelano, a pupil of Canova's. The monument represents the fasces bound by the fillet on which are cut the names of the defenders of the town in the Battle of North Point. The bas-reliefs depict the battle itself, the death of General Ross, and the bombardment of Fort McHenry. The figure on the top is Baltimore, one hand upon a rudder, as a symbol of maritime power, the other bearing the wreath of victory. To modern eyes this is exceedingly trite, but consider how well these classic ideas fitted into Godefroy's charming background of warm Colonial brick, with porticoes suggesting in every line the spirit of the Greek revival. So characteristic of Baltimore was this bit of the town, that as early as 1827 the Battle Monument was selected as the design for the city seal.

If this were an out-and-out history an account of the Battle of North Point would not be placed here, for truth compels me to state that such an account is out of the strict chronological order. Nothing has yet been said about the Revolution, and here we are plunging into a second war. Most unhistorical! Well, let it be so. The Revolution will not be slighted; all in good time, as the old fairy tale used to say. But for our purpose it would be neither wise nor sensible to leave the Battle Monument without some account of the battle. All well-informed Baltimoreans—if any ever read these pages—may omit this portion of our pilgrimage. Strangers will naturally ask: What battle? Who was General Smith? Where is North Point? Sit here upon the court-house steps, and all these questions shall be answered. Feed the pigeons, if you like. They have grown fat and insolent, but even now they are not above some well-distributed peanuts. And while you feed the birds I will tell you the story of Baltimore's part in the War of 1812. But only a part of it; the attack on Fort McHenry must wait awhile.

From the earliest days of settlement Baltimore had been intimately associated with the sea. Indeed Baltimore owed her very foundation to the desire of the settlers for a port of entry. The three little ships in Moale's picture were a prophecy of great fleets yet to be built, merchant ships and ships of war. We shall find later the home of the Baltimore clipper on Fells Point. And no matter where one walked in that small colonial town he was seldom out of the sight and the smell of salt water. Thus it is not surprising that the War of 1812 should have aroused the keenest interest. Twenty-five years later, in 1839, the "Baltimore Clipper," a journal of the day, comments upon the celebrations at North Point: "A quarter of a century has elapsed since Baltimore was saved from the polluting step of an hireling foe." The very words of Francis Scott Key come back to us—

> "Oh, where are the foes who so vauntingly swore
> Mid the havoc of war and the battle's confusion,
> A home and a country they'd leave us no more?
> Their blood hath washed out their foul footstep's pollution."

These are hot words. Baltimore temper was at fever pitch in those stirring days. We sit calmly here in the sun and tell the story, but the men of Baltimore in 1814 were full of fears for the young republic, and equally full of courageous resolve to repulse the enemy, should he appear on Maryland soil.

On September 11, 1814, the devout and peaceable citizens were on their way to church. Market Street, now Baltimore, was full of gentlemen in their Sunday clothes and tall beaver hats; the young girls walked demurely by their parents, lifting an occasional eye to some ardent swain; the matrons went attended by little pickaninnies who carried their mistresses' prayer books. Saint Paul's bell rang sweetly. No sooner had the last echo of the bells died out than shrill and confused cries arose in the streets: "The enemy is at our doors. To arms! To arms!" Instantly the services were discontinued, and men of all classes hurried to the Court House Square, to this very place where we are sitting. As you know, the old court-house had been taken down in the years following the Revolution, and where now the Monument stands there was a smooth grassy place. This was soon swarming with men, who had hurried thither, bringing with them any weapons that they could find. The drummer boy was stationed in a conspicuous vantage point, and his sharp tattoo called all men to the defense of the town. The report spread that the British forces had determined to annihilate Baltimore, "that nest of privateers." Indeed General Ross had boasted that he would winter in Baltimore though the heavens "rained militia." The towns-people were described as "truculent," and no doubt it was a good adjective, for Baltimoreans are fiery and impetuous—the "Gascons of the South," as someone has well called them.

Meanwhile the wharfs and shores of the town were black with old men and women and children peering under their hands across the long reaches of sparkling water. At last, toward evening, an indistinct cloud drew nearer and nearer. finally resolving itself into the British fleet. There they lay off North Point, fifty ships with the British colours flying, ships manned with Nelson's sailors, and warriors who had fought with Wellington. How was a group of simple colonials to withstand these tried veterans, fresh from the destruction of the Capital? The President himself had fled before them. This was a foe by no means to be despised. The British on their part were secure in the thought of victory. They longed to smoke out this "pirates' nest." So for a short time the two forces confronted each other.

Then all was activity. Faced by certain disaster, citizens of every age set to work upon the fortifications on Hampstead Hill. General Smith was in command of the whole military force of the city. His history we shall note later when we see his monument in Wyman's Park; at present we are in the thick of the most exciting part of his life, so we shall go on rapidly. At Fort McHenry across the harbour, Lieutenant-Colonel George Armistead was in command, and at the Lazaretto, the old pest-house of the town, Commodore Rogers kept vigil.

It was thought wise to send out a party "to feel the enemy," as it were, and General Stricker claimed it as a right that he should lead his brigade in this dangerous work. His men were all Baltimoreans and it was only meet that they should have the honour of dying first for the defense of their homes. Delighted, and proud beyond words at the choice, three thousand men marched along Market Street to the old Philadelphia Road. Flags flying, fifes shrilling, the gallant troops stepped out like soldiers on parade. Near the head of Bear Creek they bivouacked for the night, but the riflemen were posted in the scrubby pine woods, and the cavalrymen advanced to Gorsuch's farm. Under the brilliance of a hunter's moon the little army lay at rest. And a strange army it was, for some wore uniforms, and some plain homespun garments. As the morning of September twelfth dawned, word came that the British were disembarking. Cautiously the enemy advanced over the marshy ground and through the tall reed grass until they came to a piece of woods on a higher level. They were commanded by a skilled soldier, General Ross, and with him went Admiral Cockburn.

BALTIMORE

The whole body of troops marched on to Patapsco Neck, and came at length to Robert Gorsuch's farmhouse. Peremptorily they ordered him to prepare breakfast for them. This Gorsuch did, though most unwillingly. Before the British officers would touch a mouthful they made Gorsuch taste the food. But it was good Maryland food, and the British ate with intense relish. Indeed a pleasant hour was spent at the farm. The bluejackets had been ordered to revictual the ships, and they made merry as they darted here and there pursuing the pigs and skittish young calves who were too patriotic to yield readily to the foe. Ross was in a delightful mood. He seemed confident of eliminating "the pirates," and in the meantime he and the admiral enjoyed the antics of the sailors and the elusive live stock. But all good times must come to an end, and at last Ross made ready to depart. Rather slyly, though of course the General did not see the joke until it was too late, Gorsuch enquired if Ross would return for supper. To this Ross replied, "No, I'll eat in Baltimore or in Hell." At this there was much laughter, and it was a quick retort for a Britisher.* At that moment the sound of firing was heard, and the men dashed out. The British may be slow at a joke, but they are gallant fighters. Ross saw at once that the issue was joined and he called out "I'll bring up a column." As he turned his horse, a ball struck him in the chest. Horror-stricken, his men carried him into the shade of a poplar tree and there the poor fellow died. One of two Baltimore lads, Wells and McComas, hidden in a tree had fired the shot. Scharf denies this, but there is a monument to the boys over on Gay Street, and it is a good story. A moment after the death of Ross the two young sharp shooters were both killed. Little is known of the boys except that they were both young and very tall for their years. They were privates in Captain

*Discovered later that Ross was born in County Cork, Ireland.

Aisquith's command, and were sent in front to annoy the enemy. This they certainly did, for after the death of Ross new plans of battle were put into immediate effect.

It is not necessary to tell the whole of that day's struggle. The sun blazed down with all the vigour of a Maryland September day. Then in the afternoon came drenching showers. The two armies fought doggedly in a long-drawn and confused struggle. The raw militia of a provincial colony withstood stubbornly the troops toughened in the Peninsular campaign. But the losses were heavy on both sides. In the old Methodist Meeting House near Bread and Cheese Creek the British doctors worked over friend and foe. It would take a Bellows to etch that scene—the low ceilinged room, the fitful light of tallow candles, the surgeons' strong merciful hands. In a steady pour-down the two armies fought on. Early Tuesday morning the British came in sight of the ridge where, says Gleig, "stood the grand army of twenty thousand men." There were only twelve thousand of them to be exact, and they probably did not feel at all grand when they sighted the soldiers of Wellington. However that may be, these defenders of the town put the fear of the Lord into the British. They decided to retire to their ships. Now comes the story of the Fort; but that must wait. The "Old Defenders" have long since gone to their reward, but this monument perpetuates their gallant defense of the "pirates' nest."

From this time on the Monument was the centre of the town, and it has witnessed interesting scenes. In the old days Baltimoreans loved parades, and lost no opportunity to give one. In 1826 the shaft was "chastely shrouded" while a procession was held in memory of Adams and Jefferson. Their demise was represented by a funeral car on which were placed two large coffins draped in black. Perhaps this was not a lively occasion, but you may be sure that the citizens enjoyed it.

61

That was the period of lacrymal urns and all the "trappings and the suits of woe." When Lafayette died, again the Battle Monument played a part in the city's memorial. Here came a sarcophagus drawn by four horses panoplied in black, and here was born—oh, most delightful touch!—a shield with an alligator upon it, symbolising the fact that Lafayette first shed his blood in the western hemisphere. Could anything be neater? Let us hope that the reptile did not suggest to the wicked the crocodile tears. Here, in those days of Civil War when Baltimore was torn by faction, came William B. Hayward, a strong Union man and a writer of verse. The General had, too, a good voice, and he gathered about him all the Federal sympathisers, and gave voice to such sentiments as these:

> "Stand by the Union,
> Stand by the Union,
> Stand by the Union
> Whatever may betide."

To the irreverent, this sounds suspiciously like "Wait for the Wagon." But no matter; merrily the good Union men trolled it out, and then went home feeling intensely patriotic, and warm in the cockles of the heart.

If we feed these pigeons any more they will be too fat to waddle, and then Baltimore will have lost a very charming feature. Notice as you go about the city, what provision has been made for the birds. In many parts of the town certain patrons set out a ration of crumbs daily. One man who has a small tobacco store in the neighborhood of Richmond market, sprinkles corn beneath his window ledge, and every day rain or shine his pets patronize his shop. On an old building at the corner of Eutaw and Fayette Streets a sort of shelter has been built for the pigeons in the second story window. There they may perch out of the wet weather or cold winds. At dusk in the winter flocks of starlings whirl around the tall spire of the First Presbyterian Church on Park Avenue and Madison Street. Their wild creaking cries sound like many rusty hinges, but the distance softens the harshness, and there is something beautiful in their strange dissonances.

"Night thickens and the crow makes wing
To the rooky woods."

The court-house pigeons, however, are the general pets of the town.

THE GASCONS OF THE SOUTH

CHAPTER IV

E shall have to leave Monument Square now, though we shall return to the neighborhood later, and follow the history of the town through those mid-eighteenth century days that read like a page from the De Coverley Papers. What a life it was, spirited, gay and irresponsible. It was the life that Addison and Steele described so vividly in their Spectator and Tatler, the life of the English country and town transmuted in the Colonies into an existence more spontaneous, more charming, if less elegant, less urbane. The little town, stretching from Fells Point and Old Town to "Mr. Fite's property" on Baltimore and Sharp Streets, was an epitome of English society of the eighteenth century. It was a country village, and yet there was a distinction and character implicit in its narrow confines. To begin with the citizens were so healthy that the doctors did not flourish in the town. This is certainly not the present situation, but a century and a half brings inevitable change. The children were sound and vigorous, not a blemish upon them, and the girls were renowned for their beauty and wit. That I can readily believe, and so will you if you have a discriminating eye "for female loveliness," as the seventeen hundreds would have it. But here is news: not an old maid was to be discovered in the city limits; the damsels were so beautiful and entertaining that they were all married off at the mature age of twenty years, and comfortably established in solid Georgian houses, devoting their entire time to the rising generation. Well, allowing for the growth of legend, no doubt the Baltimoreans were a fine and hardy stock. They spent most of their time in the open, for town life had not yet completely destroyed those habits of country living. Many of the citizens lived on large estates bordering on the little town, and they reproduced there the life of "a fine old English gentleman." Fox hunting they delighted in. Then there was no easy ride over four or five miles of cultivated country; a thirty-mile gallop through three counties might easily be the order of the day. Scharf says that he has heard of foxes that started at Queenstown near the Chester River and were not killed until the hounds caught them beyond Lewes, Delaware. That was an Eastern Shore fox, you notice; I vouch equally for Baltimore county in such a competition. The hunts often lasted a week, and a hospitable manor house always made the hunters welcome, spreading for them a haunch of meat and bounteous potations. After dinner came cards, generally whist, or the fiddler was brought up from the quarter and the young people and the old danced until midnight. It was such a regime as this that made the Maryland soldiers fit for severe strains of army life. They were the pick of Washington's army and the Maryland regiments were always complete at the end of a long forced march. The horse races also brought together crowds of people, the ladies taking an animated part in the proceedings. Indeed these ladies were very spirited and up and coming.

65

"They rode to church; they rode to hounds; they did anything except consent to stay at home." In the evening they went to balls, their scarlet cloth riding cloaks tied over their satin frocks. Gad, they must have been a charming sight! And then how they danced! What flashing red heels, what deep curtseys, what languishing glances! But the old people said that in *their* day the youth of the land had been far more decorous and modest, not at all like the bold-faced damsels of the present. It was ever thus!

Nor was fox hunting the only sport. There was cock-fighting, and bear-baiting and bull-baiting. Everybody rejoiced in these innocent games, and the idea of cruelty never occurred to them. They were not a squeamish generation. Nor had our ancestors a passion for improving everything, and emasculating existence. Occasionally a stranger among us who did not understand our customs would make a curious blunder. It seems in this connection that a Frenchman was once the guest of Robert Oliver at his estate, Green Mount. Oliver was very fond of the chase, and delighted in turning a bag-fox loose and then enjoying a hunt. He invited his guest to join him. The Frenchman not knowing the point of the game, no sooner saw the fox released than he drew a pistol and shot him, and carried him off in his bag. Immediately the hounds rallied around the unfortunate man, and it was with difficulty that Mr. Oliver rescued his guest from the resentful hounds.

To keep up with these robust sports meals equally robust were needed. And they were forthcoming. "Full table; open door"—that was the Maryland motto in the good old days. Here is a sample of the table; judge for yourself whether it be full or not.

Breakfast: Yesterday's food hashed; coffee, tea, chocolate, venison, pastry, punch, beer, cider.

THE GASCONS OF THE SOUTH

Lunch: Beef, veal, mutton, venison, turkeys (plural), geese wild and tame, fowls, and perhaps somewhat more as pies, pastries, etc.

Dinner: Same as above with a small addition and a good hearty cup before bed. This is not, you see, a meal for an anchorite. As to the cups, rum and cognac stood always on the buffet, and maderia was as usual as vin ordinance. ("Once in the dear dead days beyond recall" and so on to soft music).

Country dances, cotillions, and reels closed the day. Always there were cards after the dance, and goodly sums were lost at whist. Another favorite game was chess. The assembly balls were most exclusive and very high priced, the cost of subscription being about twelve dollars. No more than tea and rusk was served at these dances, but they were very popular, the candle light falling softly on the gay brocaded costumes and the powdered wigs of the dancers.

Of course this was the life only of the well to do, the landed gentry. The ordinary merchants and simple townspeople worked hard at their business all day, and at night played the ubiquitous whist—unless they were Methodist—or went to the theatre where they sat in seats according to their rank in society! What a reversal! Of the theatre I have said nothing, but it played a great part in the entertainment of our ancestors. We shall go to the play house by and by. Nor did the bourgeoisie lack for dancing. Jigs and hipsaws were their delight, and a fiddle set all feet tapping regardless of the quality of the blood. Later when the waltz and polka were introduced here by the beguiling Corponi, a handsome Pole, the girls all fell for him so desperately that their parents feared for their lives. At ten all sensible people (all over thirty) stopped dancing, but the flaming youth insisted on staying up until midnight—the hussies!

Such was the social background of colonial Maryland. But let no mistake be made; there was gaiety, there was boisterous humor, hard riding, deep drinking, but from this group came the finest flower of Maryland. In statesmanship, in warfare or in the home these men and women were second to none. Accustomed to command from their earliest youth they put their hands to the rudder of the state and brought the old ship into harbor; a metaphor a little worn perhaps, but fitted to the commonwealth that gave the first officer to the country—Commodore Nicholson of the Eastern Shore.

When the Boston Port Bill was passed intense excitement prevailed. A crowd gathered at the little court-house to hear the communications forwarded by the people of Philadelphia —communications sent by Samuel Adams of Boston. Immediately a committee relayed the communications they had received from the Massachusetts town to the people of Annapolis, Alexandria, Norfolk and Portsmouth. Oh, the slow method of sending news! Along the Boston Post Road to New York; then south to Philadelphia, down that ancient trail of the Seneca's to the little provincial town of Baltimore, and then on and on to the South. It took a long time, but every town was resolute. The people of Baltimore at once dispatched a ship load of food-stuffs for the relief of their fellow countrymen of Massachusetts. Events followed in swift succession. The Peggy Stewart was burned in the harbor of Annapolis; the deputies of Maryland sent a letter to Virginia proposing a "general congress that such a plan may be struck out as may effectually accomplish the grand object in view," *i. e.* to save America from destruction. A Tory sympathiser writes: "Marylanders are in general mad. They are the most ignorant people that live; a moderate man dare not speak his sentiments— a person for drinking Lord North's health was thrown into the fire and had near been killed. This is the genuine spirit of patriotism that these people breathe." I told you Marylanders were the Gascons of the South; now perhaps you will believe it. News of the battle of Lexington came to town on the 27th of April! Eight days after the event, and it was twenty days before the news had been relayed to Georgia!

Preparations now went forward rapidly. The gunpowder magazine which stood on the edge of the Falls just below the court-house was stocked full, and the manufacture of ammunition of every kind was encouraged. Every one who could possibly find an excuse for doing so spent his time in or near the court-house, and the business there was soon buzzed around the town. On July 18, 1775, Michael Cresap set out from Frederick with his band of riflemen, painted like Indians, and armed with tomahawks and rifles. These young woodsmen had assumed the Indian dress in every particular, even the breech clout, and historians tell how they delighted to march single file through Frederick making the walls echo with their war whoops. A footnote in Scharf adds: "In some instances I have seen them go into places of public worship in this dress. Their appearance, however, did not add much to the devotions of the young ladies." All of this is in itself a footnote to the history of Baltimore, but nobody could resist Michael Cresap. He was, by the way, the first man to bring up troops from the South, marching over five hundred miles in twenty-two days; and when he presented his men to Washington not one of them was missing from the ranks.

In the meantime Baltimore was turning its attention chiefly to the business of ship building. The British watched the mouth of the Chesapeake Bay very closely, but this was only an incitement to Maryland blood. A sloop named the Hornet was purchased and placed under the command of William Stone and Joshua Barney. To Barney was allotted the task of raising a crew. Irish was Barney, and Irish was his luck. There

69

arrived in Baltimore at this time the first Continental flag that had ever been seen in Maryland. Here was Barney's golden opportunity. At sunrise he ran up the flag and ordered the fifes and drums to stir up goodly music. This they did, and out of bed tumbled all the Baltimore lads, and the Hornet had more men than she could use. "Rebels" they were called and a jolly bunch they were, ready to pull King George off his throne. In a few days the Hornet, accompanied by the Wasp, crept through the Capes and once in the open sea they were joined by Commodore Hopkins and won a victory in the Bahamas. Now came the Declaration of Independence, read on the steps of the court-house before a throng of citizens. That night the town was illuminated and an effigy of George III was burned to the satisfaction of all. Baltimore, that "nest of pirates," hummed with activity. Within six years two hundred and forty-eight ships sailed out of the Chesapeake. The British fleet at Hampton Roads was unable to cope with this flotilla of privateers. Fine boats they were with brave names—the *Buckskin Hero, Willing Lass*, the *Hercules*, the *Porpoise, Venus, Matilda, the Viper* and the *Antelope*, the *Dolphin* and the *Fearnaught*. Baltimore sailors, like their ancestors in the days of Drake, preyed upon the British ships as Drake had preyed upon the Spaniards. Every citizen who could build a vessel built one; Purviance and McKim each sent out a privateer a month. Van Bibber, Sterrett, Ridgely, Patterson, Yellott and Worthington—all bore a hand in this work.

But there were dark days ahead. This is no place for the details of Maryland's part in the Revolutionary War, but there are a few points to be made in passing. Baltimore's support of Boston after the passage of the Port Bill has already been commented upon, but the town was foremost in other fields of action. While Congress was considering the draft of a Declaration of Independence, the Convention in Maryland before they had heard from Congress at all adopted on July 3, 1776, a declaration of their own. This "noble document," as Scharf calls it, set forth at length the manful determination of Maryland to maintain freedom at any cost. Furthermore from the first governor of Maryland, Thomas Johnson, came the nomination of Washington as Commander-in-Chief of the Continental Army. Finally in 1786 the Annapolis Convention brought sharply to the minds of statesmen and common people alike the necessity for definite action leading to the adoption of a Constitution. Perhaps the most dramatic incident in the Revolution was the Battle of Long Island where the Maryland Line under General Smallwood stood firm in disaster. You recall the spirited verse of John W. Palmer, Baltimore physician and poet, written for the unveiling of the monument in Brooklyn commemorating their valour:

> "Spruce maccaronies and pretty to see
> Tidy and dapper and gallant were we,
> Blooded fine gentlemen proper and tall,
> Bold in fox-hunt and gay at a ball;
> Prancing soldados so martial and bluff,
> Billets for bullets in scarlet and buff,
> But our cockades were clasped with a mother's low prayer
> And sweethearts that braided our sword-knots were fair."

Not for nothing were these men the sons of Cavaliers. Gist— "with his heart in his throat and his blade in his fist"—brave Gist and Smallwood, Smith and Williams, and John Eager Howard are as proud a heritage as Putnam, Wayne, and Greene. Tench Tilghman ranks with Paul Revere—oh, how I should love to tell of his brave gallop—but alas, there is not room for all of the heroism of this romantic period!

In war, however, as in love, all is not plain sailing. The winter of 1777 was one of discouragement, and the Congress was moved from Philadelphia to Baltimore. We shall visit the spot before long, so now we shall do no more than men-

71

tion it. Mr. Fite's house on west Market street was used as the hall for the meetings, and a tablet marks the site today. As usual in war times the women stayed at home and made bandages as they have done for countless ages; small boys pretended that they were George Washington, and played at soldiers in Howard Woods. Over on Fells Point the sound of hammers rang out valiantly, and while the shaving fell, many a lad dreamed of John Paul Jones. Then in 1778 Count Pulaski came, a gallant and handsome Pole, and even though it was wartime the Baltimore girls rose to the occasion and no doubt had thrills just as modern girls would. Pulaski, dark and foreign-looking with a small moustache and long waving hair, was enough to give one—a young one—a thrill. Even historians admit that he had no difficulty at all in raising a legion here in Baltimore; no doubt the girls urged their brothers to enlist and envied them as they were mustered in. This dashing Captain brought with him a scarlet silk banner embroidered by the Moravian nuns at Bethlehem. He treasured this emblen, and carried it with him through all of his campaigns until he fell at Savannah. This is the banner of which Longfellow wrote:

> " 'Take thy banner! And if e'er
> Thou shouldst press the soldier's bier,
> And the muffled drum should beat
> To the tread of mournful feet,
> Then this crimson flag shall be
> Martial cloak and shroud for thee.
> The warrior took that banner proud,
> It was his martial cloak and shroud."

The scarlet is faded now, but the banner is still to be seen at the Maryland Historical Library.

Shortly afterwards came General Lafayette when the tide of war was low. A ball was given in his honor, but the Marquis was in sad spirits, and the beauty of the dancers seemed only to increase his depression. At length he confessed that the poverty, nay, the destitution of his soldiers, was made more striking in contrast with the brillance of this scene. "My poor fellows need clothes," said the Frenchman sorrowfully. "And they shall have them," was the prompt reply. The next morning the girls and women of Baltimore turned the ballroom into a sewing room, and before long Lafayette's men were properly clad. Again, Lafayette, we were there. Vive la France! Later Washington passed through the town, stopping at the Fountain Inn where we too have stopped or at least on the site thereof. Rochambeau arrived as we shall see in good time. Finally in 1783 appears an extra! The *Olive* announces in advance of every other paper in the country that the preliminary articles of peace have been signed in Paris and to make this announcement peculiarly Baltimorean in flavour, the news was brought in a clipper—those ships that made Baltimore famous on the seas. So ended all these troublous days. With this background in our minds we can resume our walks about the town and take note of her growth.

THE RICH ARRAY OF MARKET STREET

CHAPTER V

E began our walks about town at the Monument because in a very real sense that is the heart of the community. It is, however, scarcely necessary to repeat that Mills's great shaft was not thought of for many a day after the *Olive* had published her glad news of peace. Indeed it was not until 1825 that the Washington memorial was completed. To trace the growth of Baltimore we walked down Charles Street to Pratt and then turned sharply east, arriving at Light Street. It was in this neighborhood as we have seen, that the origin of Baltimore is found, though today we can discover evidences of that earlier town. It is the street names alone that give us a clue.

Baltimore was at first Long Street, running east and west, then Market Street, and now for many years as the principal business thoroughfare it has born the name of the Proprietor. The history of this street is the history of Baltimore in miniature. Poetic persons saw in the shape of old Baltimore not an Indian arrow head but a lyre or harp, and if we use this figurative way of speaking of the town then Baltimore street was one of the principal strings of the lyre. Beyond the present intersection of Liberty and Baltimore Streets there were in the old days only green fields and irregular country roads running vaguely off toward the West, that enchanted land from which the great Conestoga wagons came rolling in. On the east the street stopped abruptly at Harrison's Marsh, low swampy land which lay between Holliday Street and the Falls. Between these two points on the west and east a straggling country main street grew up. When the town was first laid out all the riverside lots were sold quickly, but the Long Street land was by no means popular, except those lots on the north side near the Great Eastern Road which turned off toward the northeast at McClellan's Alley. But it was not long before the chief string in this Irish harp showed plainly that it intended to fulfill its destiny. To be sure the old Sinequa Trail had originally run up hill and down dale, climbing up behind Saint Paul's, and dipping down behind O'Neill's, but practical city fathers soon devised a most acceptable cut-off. Traffic now sought to avoid the neck-breaking hills which make our Pleasant and Saratoga Streets. To accomplish this, a causeway was built across the Marsh from the end of Market Street at Holliday to Gay Street. This made it possible for travellers north and south to pass easily along the level ground of the present Baltimore Street, and to take up the old road north at Gay Street, or, if south bound, to meet the old trail again at Jacob Fite's house. This house or Congress Hall as it was called later was a substantial building which stood at the western end of the town. It would, however, be a mistake to think that the buildings of old Baltimore Town were devoid of dignity. No, they were chiefly the homes of well-to-do citizens, and they were comfortable and ample. Many of them stood in small gardens, and later chroniclers speak of the beauty of the sycamores that shaded the roadway. The stores were generally

75

built flush with the street, and through the small neat panes the very latest goods from England were displayed. There were, moreover, comfortable inns for the entertainment of the frequent travellers. And always there was the sight and smell of the sea. The thought of ships was never far away. Gulls flew over head doubtless as they do today, and if there was not the deep hoot of the steam whistle, there was certainly a thicket of masts rising in the little harbour, that harbour where the good Elizabethan Captain had eaten so heartily of Indian corn.

All of these remarks are general, simply given to sketch in a picture of the town as it was in the days before and immediately after the Revolutionary War. The best way to see the history of the town as it unrolls is to choose some definite point such as Broadway and Baltimore, and walk west, noting as we go the gradual unfolding of the complicated story. There are many reels and many close-ups. Of stately buildings there are none; the street in this neighborhood is mean, but if you have the seeing eye you will glimpse the old town beneath the new; and best of all you will see the people who made the town. In the old geographies the directions ran: face the north and your right hand will be toward the east, etc. But now at Broadway and Baltimore Street stand facing the west; at your right hand will be the steep hill of Broadway rising up and up, with the Church Home and Infirmary at the top. That is the place where Mrs. Clemm, Poe's mother-in-law died, an aged woman; and here it is that Charles Dickens came to visit her, seeking on his sojourn in Baltimore to learn something of that strange genius. You remember Virginia Clemm, frail and lovely child whom Poe married, and with whom he lived happily for eleven years. Upon this hill her mother, whose fingers were pricked with ceaseless stitching, died. Here came that author who, too, had written

76

of a boy and a raven in his *Barnaby Rudge*. How scornful was Lowell—

> "Next Poe with his Raven like Barnaby Rudge,
> Two-fifths of him genius, and three-fifths pure fudge.",

Poe himself died also on this site when there stood on it a building called the Washington Medical College. We shall see that genius and that fudge many a time in our rambles. Through all Poe's happiness with Virginia Clemm there ran the black thread of poverty. Then she died. In September, 1849, he came up to Baltimore on the Richmond boat. He stepped ashore at Light Street. Can't you see that shabbily dressed haughty figure on Light Street! What happened to him next no one knows. The town was in the throes of an election, and political roughs terrorised everyone. On High Street, which we shall pass, there was what was known as a Whig "coop" where one hundred and twenty voters were imprisoned. Near this place, in a tavern, Poe was found unconscious. He was sent to the hospital, and in a short time died. His detractors—and they were numerous—were eager to say that he died in a drunken debauch. The doctors at the Washington Hospital denied this absolutely, however, and now the more charitable, less puritanical, are willing to admit that they do not know how Poe came to his death. But in a building on this hilltop his restless, wild spirit found peace. "He has brought up from his brooding a severe distillation of sound and atmosphere, has created out of his tortured dream-experience something that is suberbly weird."

At the foot of the hill is a stiff and conventional monument to Ferdinand C. Latrobe who was seven times mayor of Baltimore. This beats even Dick Whittington's record, but it is a matter of common knowledge that they both made excellent magistrates. Dick had his famous cat, and Latrobe had his old grey mare. This well-known horse and buggy made the rounds of the city. The equipage was driven by a coloured boy, Robert Wilson, who was a member of Saint Mary's Church, and the mayor and Robert were a familiar sight, beloved by good citizens, but a warning and reproof to the wicked. By this buggy and horse Latrobe was able to keep his eye on affairs and to attend to many details of his office. The name of Latrobe is distinguished in Baltimore. Of Benjamin H., the mayor's grandfather, we have already spoken, for he was the foremost American architect of his day. John H. B. Latrobe, Ferdinand's father, has left most delightful memoirs edited by John Semmes. Of him, too, we shall have occasion to speak. Just now the point that I remember with awe is the fact that Marie Antoinette's dancing master taught John the pas seul. He says most charmingly "not that I became very proficient; but it was something to be instructed by the dancing master of the ill-fated queen." If you want to find out all about the political views and civic achievements of the seven-times mayor, I refer you to a delightful book on the mayors of Baltimore. Now look south on Broadway. There at the end of the street the market house bulks large with appropriate solidity, and beyond that is Fells Point where Edward Fell lies buried in a grubby little yard. But now we are ready for our westward swing to the centre of the town.

For some distance this is a street of small mean shops. Jews and Italians throng the pavements, but proceed patiently, and you will have your reward. Central Avenue has a wide road-bed where once upon a time a sleepy canal flowed quietly along to the harbour. Today leisurely freight trains crawl by, holding up the wayfarer and usurping the bed of the long-forgotten canal.

Now Baltimore Street takes a dip southwest, one of those curious twists that one finds in the city streets, giving them a flavour and colour all their own. No checkerboard town ever has the surprise, the air of casual charm that one finds in old communities that, like Topsy, have "just growed." It may be that you are utterly insensitive to this gentle meandering, and prefer neat blocks and squares. If so, go west, young man; you will not find them here, and you are wasting your time and ours. For my part, I love these curlycues, and at the corner of Baltimore and Aisquith Streets we have a good example of these errant streets. Aisquith, named from the commander of Wells and McComas in the Battle of North Point, slants north. Lately its permanent wave was modified somewhat, and the narow little lane widened. There was talk too of destroying the building which stands at the corner of Baltimore and Aisquith. It was just the place—probably—for a filling station; and you must admit that a filling station is more useful than a Greek temple. So it is. The artists and Quakers, however, had a voice in the discussion, and this lovely little building was preserved. Like a Grecian urn it stands in the midst of our alien civilization—

"Thou still unravished bride of quietness,
Thou foster-child of silence and slow time."

Built in 1822 by John McKim as a free school for poor children it has fulfilled its mission down to the present day. Under the direction of Friends Meeting thirty or forty small children attend Kindergarten here in this Doric temple. It is an exact copy of the Temple of Theseus, and is the purest Greek thing in Baltimore. Even the bootblacks can not touch it for Greekness.

At the corner of Baltimore and Lloyd Streets, near the Mc-Kim Free School, was Baltimore's first theatre of truly metropolitan proportions. Before the Revolution there had been a small affair at King George—now Lombard and Albemarle

79

Streets, but this was a brick theatre and extremely elegant. Maryland was the cradle of the drama in this country, and though Baltimore followed the lead of Annapolis in play-acting, it was no mean second. In May, 1752, Mr. Lewis Hallam and his company embarked in the *Charming Sally* and after six weeks the vessel arrived in Yorktown, Virginia. There was some hitch in the arrangements, and the actors came promptly to Annapolis where a litle theatre had already been erected. On July 13, 1752, the English company presented "The Beaux' Stratagem," and a farce called "The Virgin Unmasked,"—a very twentieth-century-sounding performance, indeed! Such was the beginning of the theatre in America.

Baltimore, devoted to the stage from the time that the town was a mere village, had a more elevated taste. In Christmas week, 1782, the New Theatre opened its doors. It was spick and span with fresh white paint, and the red bricks—brought no doubt from England—though this point is much in dispute—shone warmly in the mild December sun. And our townspeople did not choose farces for their opening night; no indeed. Annapolitans, please take note: our play was "Richard III, containing the distressing death of Henry VI and the inhuman murder of the young princes." The part of the king was taken by Mr. Wall; other parts by "gentlemen for their own amusement." But, alas, we can not lord it over Annapolis. When the "inhuman murder" had been disposed of farces followed briskly enough, as for example, "A Miss in her Teens," the Revolutionary flapper, in the eighteenth century manner, no doubt. In those days, as in these, it was difficult to find new material, worthwhile stuff. Accordingly the programs often bore this notice: "Any gentleman possessed of good farces and willing to lend or dispose of them to the manager will greatly oblige him." What a chance to get on the 'great white way!' But other items of interest were found in the handbills; this for example was discouraging: "No person will on any pretext be admitted behind the scenes." And note this: "Some tunes have been called for by Persons in the Gallery, which have given offense to others. The Managers are resolved that no music will be played but such as they shall order the day before the Representation." What could these songs have been? Monstrous rowdy, no doubt, and all this before the age of jazz. But it does warm the cockles of one's heart to know that the founding fathers enjoyed farces. Maybe some day statues will be erected to us. Perhaps we aren't as hopeless as we think.

Observe, furthermore, the titles of their plays; they have, most certainly, a smack of Hollywood. Here the are: "The Busy Body," "The Ghost," "The Devil on Two Sticks" and "The Wapping Land-Lady." Not so bad for a small provincial town. That "Devil on Two Sticks"—ah, that was probably a wow! But they had their "refined pieces" for the refined: "The Orphan or the Unhappy Marriage" (not so refined as I thought) and "Jane Shore." "Hamlet" was refined (in parts) and "Venice Preserved or a Plot Discovered" was a great favourite.

On the opening night in January Market Street was packed with ladies and their escorts. I would like to say that link boys and the sedan chairs made a traffic jam, but conscience will not permit the link boys, though they have such a charming eighteenth century air. The plays in that period were often given in the afternoon, but I like to imagine the flare of torches and the gleam of candle light on brocade and silk. At any rate all the men were gallant and all the ladies beautiful and distinguished, for was it not a Baltimore theatre? When the curtain at the New Theatre "discovered" the first scene Mr. Wall, in the style of Balieff, stepped forth and spoke thus:

BALTIMORE

"From Shakespeare's golden mines we'll fetch the ore
And land these riches here in Baltimore;
For we theatric merchants never quit
His boundless shores of universal wit.
But we in vain shall richly laden come
Unless deep water brings us safely home;
Unless your favor in full tides will flow,
Ship, crew and cargo to the bottom go."

This was fair warning to the public, but, alas, the hint was not taken, and in four years the ship, crew and cargo evidently sank; the water was not deep enough to keep the venture afloat.

An amusing incident of these early days is told of an actor named Henry. Before 1800 there were not over six four-wheeled carriages in town, but the actor Henry was so badly afflicted with gout that he was compelled to keep a handsome coach. Knowing that he would be the subject of most unfavorable comment for aping the great, he had painted upon his carriage door in heraldic manner, two crutches rampant with the motto "This or These." Thus sarcastic mouths were effectively shut.

Although the New Theatre failed, "the players have come" was a cry that echoed through the town with intense delight. Not even Hamlet heard it more gladly at Elsinore. A royal welcome was prepared at the inn, and crowds flocked hither to see the play-actors. When they appeared upon the streets a throng followed them. Their roles were familiar to all, and men compared the different actors in the classic parts much as the French today recall the old players while acclaiming the new in some well-beloved role. Later on we shall see the "Old Holliday," or rather the site where once the famous theatre stood. Now we must continue our pilgrimage.

Accross the street on the corner of Lloyd and Baltimore was the Second Presbyterian Church built by lottery—those ever popular lotteries—in the year 1804. There were eleven thousand tickets sold at five dollars each, and prizes to the amount of forty-two thousand and five hundred dollars were distributed. The rest of the money was cannily put away into a building fund. Ah, what innocent days those were, when one could even extract excitement in building a church. Behind the church stretching down across Watson Street there were in those early days green fields where the Friends gathered to refresh themselves during their Yearly Meeting.

Between Lloyd Street and the Fallsway there have been many changes since the Fire. First of all there is no rich effluvium from the Falls. Three cement tubes buried deep beneath the roadbed carry the water of the old stream out into the harbour. The broad modern street is excellent for traffic, and an immense civic improvement, but I loved the gloomy ramshackle houses that hung over the dark waters. Unsanitary they were beyond a doubt, odoriferous—yes, I admit it—but for all that there was romance in that turbulent stream; those jutting bay windows and those frail balconies leaning above the water wore an air of secrecy. There was always something mysterious about the Falls. Any stream that flows through a city is unfahomable. It is part of us, and yet, as we watch it, it slips away, swiftly changing before our very eyes. It flows on silently, and yet we must take cognizance of it. There must be bridges, and bridges, too, have in them an element of the unknown. Every stream is in a sense a Rubicon, and no amount of daily passing to and fro deprives them of their heritage of mystery. Be they clear or turbid they reflect the sky; there are eddies in the swift current, and in sinister fashion they slip under the dark piers. These filthy streams, become for a town-bred child his first image of such a river as the Thames or the Seine. How much better the French do these things! The Seine is a joy to every Parisian. The Thames, it is true, is not joyous—nothing British is. But at least it is a living stream. The Fallsway is a hideous object, no matter how beneficient it may be for trade. It will never be like the Falls, a rampaging tawny devil when in flood roaring along under the bridges while fascinated loafers, and a few industrious citizens leaned over the railing wondering—well, wondering whatever people do wonder when they watch swift running water. Sometimes the bridges went down before the flood, and funny little old second-hand Harrison Street would be submerged.

Perhaps some of you are saying, "Oh, I never heard of such foolishness. What was beautiful in old Jones Falls?" And to you I reply in the words of Turner when he rebuked the critics of his pictures: "What, you never saw any sunsets like those? Probably; but don't you wish that you had?" If you don't wish it, I wash my hands of you—and in the Falls, too!

When sleek cable cars went gliding over the bridge at this point, there was a certain Anatomy Musee here that took my youthful eye. The windows were dusty, or had, perhaps, an aquaeous tone as if they were seen under water. In the window behind the sad-coloured glass were large bottles in which floated dimly seen—ah, what? That was the enchantment. I could never tell from the car window, and I was never permitted to investigate on foot. No doubt it was a vague nebulous creature like the embryo cat at the Maryland House in the Park, a cat which has stimulated more scientific inquiry than all the general science courses in existence. Also there was a marble bust of a Cæsarish person with his head neatly divided into segments by red lines and blue. There was an air of disreputable glamous about the whole place. Guilefully my mother diverted my attention—so she thought—but to this day the very word musee has a magic sound. Like the old Falls, this, too, has passed away. So likewise the White Ele-

84

phant has departed, that burlesque house where "The Black Crook", considered a naughty play in its time, delighted the would-be-wicked. All of this neighborhood has suffered a sea change.

Across the Fallsway we come to Market Place, a wide prosaic stretch of asphalt or some admirable material for street paving. Marsh Market Space it used to be called and those were the days when it was full of colour and raciness. There is small doubt that it was also a nest of crime, but virtue is so often the destroyer of romance. The dens and saloons along the water front, and the Space were filled with toughs, seafaring men, thugs, longshoremen, gamblers and rogues of every colour. But at night, or in the dusk of a winter evening, there were lights and shadows, line and tone that would have delighted Whistler or Pennell. It was Alsatia, but there was beauty here, rough beauty of the true authentic stuff. The houses were jumbled one upon another, teetering crazily. The roofs were peaked, and sloped sharply. Gas flared in the shadowy interiors, and through the swinging doors came the wheeze of an accordion, or the gay raucous sparkle of a mechanical piano. Harrison Street is still left—one side of it— and it is, as ever, the abode of the old clothes man. In the short square that runs north of Baltimore the houses are low-browed, as old Baltimore houses are wont to be. Outside of every door hang suits more or less forlorn. Indeed a hasty glance down the street gives one the impression of scarecrows on parade. When a breeze stirs the second-hand garments they swing jauntily. Yellow slickers and blue jeans to say nothing of declasse tuxedos, all keep step to the wind. The windows of the tiny shops are filled with things that delight the heart of man in his wild state, or enchant the boy. Here are second-hand pistols, of ancient make, blackjacks and brass knuckles. In the old days before the Fallsway the people of Harrison

Street were often forced to flee from the raging torrent of Jones Falls. Now all this is changed and doubtless for the better, but I liked Harrison Street best when it presented two lines of scarecrows to the eye of the beholder.

Marsh Market Space itself has had a strange history. Once there was good shooting in Harrison's Marsh, and the reed birds held dominion over all the land between the Falls, then a clean sweet-smelling stream, and Holliday street. Across this stretch ran the causeway, linking up the Great Eastern Road as it ran into Old Town with the Market Street detour. Then, little by little, the Marsh was drained, and filled in until nothing was left but the name of the little crooked second-hand street, and the old Market. The Center Market, as it was called, was built to meet the demands of the growing town. And old prints show it to have been most elegant in design. There was a central covered aisle with sloping roofs over the two side aisles. The wares were displayed upon the ground as they are in European markets to this day, but even then the sophistication of stalls was making itself felt. Here too in the Space was the Central fountain, the water spurting from the mouths of dolphins, and here the townspeople came daily to fill their pitchers. Within a stone's throw lived the cream of Baltimore society, for this location was then by no means given over to mean shops and Jewry. The pitchers that went to the well were carried by servants, their heads proudly wrapped in bright bandanas. The Market Place on a sunny morning was a sight worth seeing. William Wirt says of our markets: "I rose before day, shaved and dressed by candlelight, took my cane, and walked to market. O, what a quantity of superb beef, mutton, lamb, and veal, and all sorts of fowls; hogsheads full of wild duck, geese, pheasants, and partridges." And add to this terrapin, crabs, oysters in season, bay mackerel "and all that move in the waters, bless ye the

86

Lord: praise him and magnify him forever!" Nor must the waters be forgotten. The municipal docks have subdued the water front, but the sea is not far away even in these days. In the early nineteenth century many a lad ran off and shipped before the mast. Read this and note how strong the desire must have been with a Christmas gift in the offing: "Left home on Christmas Day, a bright mulatoo boy named Allick, about fifteen. Fond of the sea. Five dollars for his return to the next door to the Bridge."

Long after the snipe ceased to be plentiful in the Marsh the name remained, and there is a most amusing poem by Doctor Osler in which he celebrates this justly famous spot. In the nineties the town was boss-ridden. The Hopkins men under Howard Kelly made up a reform party to police the polls, and to stop repeaters. This is a poem that in a whimsical spirit Osler complained was circulating in his name. He was of course the author:

MARSH MARKET NOVEMBER 5.
(*With apologies to the late Mr. Keats*)
Much have I travelled in the realms of toughs
And many dirty towns and precincts seen
Round many a ward industrious have I been,
Which bears in fealty to the bosses hold.
Oft of one wide expanse had I been told
That wide-os'd Gorman ruled as his demesne
Yet never did I breathe its pure serene
Till I heard Abel speak out loud and bold.
Then felt I like some watcher at the polls
When a repeater swims into his ken
Or like Steve Kelly when with eagle eyes
He stared at the Marsh Market and his men
Looked at each other with a wild surmise
And said, "Let us, too, vote again."

This entire section was laid low by the Fire of 1904, and there remains here but one remnant of the past—the Mechanical School of the Maryland Institute, which still hold its sessions in the upper stories of the Market Hall. Interest in the development of an Art School had been aroused for some time, when in 1847 a massmeeting was held in Washington Hall of the corner of Baltimore Street and the Bridge. Then and there the citizens decided to hold an exhibition and fair of the national arts and industries. This fair was held as had been planned, and proved to be a tremendous success. Lecture courses were announced, and the first one was opened by the distinguished Mr. Horace Greely. In 1850 the land on the Space was purchased, and the cornerstone of the new building was laid by Severn Teackle Wallis in the same year. This building was the centre of the intellectual life of the community, and was but the beginning of the great contribution that the Maryland Institute has made to the life of the town. When Louis Kossuth, the Hungarian patriot, came to Baltimore, a reception was held here in his honor. Here doubtless Kossuth cakes, that rich confection of chocolate and whipped cream, were first served, for it is to a Baltimore baker that the Kossuth cake is attributed. All of this the fire wiped out, together with the records of the Institute, and Professor Otto Fuchs was in despair. Bu he soon realized the new life which awaited the famous old Art School. The city rebuilt the Market House, and gave two floors for the use of the Mechanical School. Up town on Mount Royal Avenue a new and beautiful building was to house the old Institute. But that is another story.

On the northwest corner of Gay and Market Streets the citizens erected the first town market house long before Centre Market was thought of. Over the market there was a spacious hall where travelling shows were wont to exhibit. There in 1764 Mr. William Johnson, "for the entertainment of the curious," gave a lecture on "that instructive and entertaining branch of natural philosophy called electricity." Over the

BALTIMORE STREET BEFORE THE FIRE
(NOTE THE TELEGRAPH POLES)

THE RICH ARRAY OF MARKET STREET

Bridge that connected Old Town with Baltimore the "curious" came crowding in to patronize the sciences. Then the lecture having improved the interiors of their minds, they gave themselves to renovating the exterior. On Baltimore Street "two doors east" of High an early ancestor of the beauty parlour flourished. This, observe, was the startling advertisement in those days when beauty parlours were not supposed to exist:

"Oh, my Hair! My Hair!
What's the matter? Why, my Hair is turning grey!
It is a great misfortune, for a beautiful brunette
Or blond Head is the greatest Ornament of the Human Frame.
Use Jones' Hair Dye."

Then having adorned the human frame with a head of blonde (remember Anita Loos) hair, it was a simple matter to step around the corner of High Street where lived Madame McLaughlin, "a Christian Jewess" and an astrologer. Evidently this amiable lady, "who can tell your inmost thoughts," was the original of Abie's Irish Rose. Note her name and religio-racial classification. Later in the fifties when we were more sophisticated the "Grand Original Paintings of Adam and Eve in Paradise' were exhibited in the Market Hall. The series of paintings had been made for his Majesty Charles Tenth, and society flocked to see the Temptation and Expulsion. Nearby, in Frederick Street, a man advertised "Five thousand negroes wanted; I will pay highest prices for negroes with good titles. I will also purchase negroes restricted to remain in the state. Families never separated." But, oh, how he would warm the cockles of our hearts, not to mention our other interiors, with a "palatable bowl of Mrs. Hugh Kennedy's green turtle soup highly recommended by the medical faculty." Wise faculty! But 19 Center Space no longer serves "epicures and the public in general" for fifteen cents a bowl.   89

BALTIMORE

Between Market Space and Calvert Street there were many small shops, in the mid-century, as there are at present, but those of a past age were more elegant. In John Murphy's window the *Keepsake* was displayed and here in rich blue was *The Garland* or the *Ladies' Gift*. Bright eyes from beneath the brim of a bonnet were met by the bright eyes of some languishing beauty on the pages of *The Token*. Just beyond, Seth Hance's shop "proclaimed it to the world" (Oh Seth, thee nearly told the world. Fie on thee!) that "Hance's Syrup of Hoarhound is without exaggeration or exception the most safe and speedy cure for all diseases arising from coughs and colds." Again Seth states that "Veritas Vos Liberabit et Prevalebit," but who today would understand him? Therefore, dear reader, when you pass by the gents furnishings of today, do not despise them; they are the literary material of seventy years hence. Before we turn to more weighty matters, I must, however, call your attention to this: "Moderation in eating and drinking is the only rational way of securing a Happy New Year." Thus said I. P. Cook, 76 Baltimore Street. With this ethical comment I go forward.

Holliday Street which runs parallel with Gay at Baltimore Street marks the eastern bound of the original city grant. The next street is South, and on the corner of Baltimore—the southwest corner—stood the old office of the Sunpaper. Newspapers are all very well for other towns, but for Baltimoreans there is just one paper of supreme quality, the Sunpaper. The long and thrilling history of this Baltimore journal will be told when we reach Sun Square; for the present we shall point out the site of the old Sun Iron building. Designed by Bogardus and Hoppin, this structure was most remarkable in its day. In 1839 it was the first cast iron building in the world and it was the admiration of all who beheld it. Meredith Janvier, whose delightful recollection "Before the Fire" have appeared in the *Evening Sun,* speaks affectionately of the old days, recalling with joy the "delightful smell of printer's ink and steam which arose through the iron grille in the pavement." Ah, those goodly smells—who can fail to recall them with bliss? There is even an ecstasy in so-called bad smells— a certain poignant quality. A nose is a joyous thing! Happy the nostril that has inhaled the guano of the old harbour and the piscatory ripeness of the fish market. Once in Cross Street Market I counted ten distinct smells, full, round, robust. Nothing like it!

Across the street from the Sun Iron Building, on the northeast corner of Baltimore and South were the offices of a plucky little paper known as *The Daily Exchange.* In the forties Baltimore was controlled by ingenious bums who called themselves by the picturesque names of Rip Raps, Blood Tubs and Plug Uglies. They dominated the city by the simple expedient of permitting only those citizens to vote for whom they had a liking. The liking, I pause to say, was based on such a sentiment as "You let me do as I please, and I let you vote." This state of affairs continued for years, and the decent citizens either feared to molest the ruffians or were indifferent to them. Finally, in a city like Baltimore, the Know Nothings as the lawless were called outnumbered the Democrats five to one. At this point Teackle Wallis arose. Fearlessly, brilliantly, Wallis assailed the gang of bullies. He poured out vitriol upon them, and it stung even their rough hides. Rumbles of distant thunder were heard. A storm threatened. At length on a sultry August day, the roughs swarmed around the newspaper office. Baltimore Street was packed with their cohorts. At a signal they broke into the editorial rooms, held up the clerks in the style of modern bandits, tore up the fixtures, and pitched the furniture out into the street. But Wallis, with all the spirit of Cato who reiterated the need for the destruction of Carthage, doggedly renewed his campaign for civic decency. In 1860 the reform bills were passed. The Plug Uglies were no more.

This corner, however, was doomed to be a storm center, a sort of political Medicine Hat. When the Civil War broke out the *Exchange,* published on this site boldly championed State's Rights. Butler, the Yankee General, arrested the editors, seized the type and sent the owners of the paper to the Fort. But nothing could quell that fierce little sheet. Under the name of the *Maryland Times* it appeared on the streets of the town. Again, States' Rights! The citizens, delighted, read it with zest. It had wit; it made people laugh. There is nothing so dangerous as a laugh. Therefore Washington took a hand and ordered the complete demolition of the plant. While a mob milled around in the streets, the soldiers smashed the press and destroyed all of the type. So ended the gallant editorial venture.

A third paper appeared upon the scene after the war. Indeed this part of Baltimore was a regular Fleet Street. The *American,* although a newcomer on Baltimore Street, was very old indeed. Its former home was on Fells Point where it was known as the *Baltimore American* and *Daily Advertiser.* This old paper dates back to 1773 and traces its ancestry to the *Maryland Journal.* When the new building was completed in 1876 the following verses appeared:

"Our go-ahead American no obstacle will shun,
But boldly runs its columns up above the daily Sun;
And now the mighty question is, though both spread wholesome leaven,
Which of the two aspiring sheets will make its way to heaven?"

Within a stone's throw of the editorial offices was Bool's auction room at 60 Baltimore street. Here the wags of the day were accustomed to meet for the fun of matching wits with Bool. This worthy man once created a sensation when he threatened to offer for sale a "widow woman" of Old Town. At another time he displayed for sale the "identical piano practised on by Martha Custis before she married George Washington." But ere we leave this neighborhood stop with me at Boyd's cellar in South Street, between Lovely Lane and Baltimore Street. Boyd was a Scotchman famous for the succulence of his oysters. In his cellar gathered the brilliant actors of the day, for rememger that Holliday Street Theater was just across the way. Booth, handsome, dark and fiery came here; Jefferson the elder; Forrest. Here over their porter and oysters they laughed and made merry. To further this end a club was formed called the Quid Nuncs whose object was the collection of all of the jokes and puns made by the frequenters of the Cellar. They were a brisk and lively membership, gathering around the stove whereon the members heated their mugs of flip and toddy. Boyd was a progressive fellow, and it seemed wise to him to purchase a new and elegant stove. One night the new and fashionable model stood in the midst of the cellar, but great was the wrath of the Quid Nuncs. They refused to return until the old stove was reinstated. This was done, and once more the actors, writers and wits assembled about its glowing, paintless sides. Booth, Macready and Jefferson had a table of their own known as the Shakespearean table. Here after the theatre the old cronies met and, warmed by honest toddy, sent forth sonorous speeches rolling along the low beams of Boyd' Cellar.

MORE RICH ARRAY

CHAPTER VI

THE fortunes of the northwest corner of Baltimore and Calvert Streets are both complicated and interesting, and it is to this corner that we come next. Today the Continental Building towers at the southeast; across Calvert Street the low humble structure has a history belying its simple and prosaic exterior. But look for one moment at the Emerson. This hotel, named for a well-known citizen—Captain Isaac Emerson—is famous for its seafood which is served in the Chesapeake Room. But the site on which the comfortable hostelry is built has seen many vicissitudes.

When Long, and later Market Street, was first laid out this corner was the edge of a pleasant green field sloping gently down from the high cliff which overhung the Falls. From this coign of vantage there was a fine view of the water, for in those days the Basin extended as far inland as Water Street. The corner lot seemed central and favorably placed; therefore, before long, three frame houses were built here, the plain and snug houses that early Baltimoreans loved, with garden plots, no

94

doubt, and certainly shaded by the sycamores and honey locusts for which the neighborhood was noted. As the years passed on these houses fell into decay, and finally they were torn down. Then in 1829 a fine brick house was erected. Old prints show its beauty. Over the door was a graceful fan-light. The windows were set with small panes, some of them possibly with the famous amethyst glass now fast disappearing in Baltimore houses. The whole air of the house was one of distinction and dignity. Over the door there was a sign bearing the legend: *Baltimore Museum and Gallery of Fine Arts.* This was in its day the cultural centre of the town. The Peales, a most remarkable family of art lovers, owned this Museum and exhibited here until 1933. Later Edmund Peale established a little theatre on the top floor, and here Baltimoreans enjoyed their favorite recreation—the play house. At times serious dramas were given such as "Romeo and Juliet" or "The Babes in the Woods." But to lighten the tragic vein came an "amusing petite comedy of Mesmerism." Such shows caused the theatre to fall into disfavour with the high brows, but it still retained its hold by the liveliness of its programs, a godsend in the 'forties.' On a hot July night for example this rather sprightly advertisement appeared in the Sunpaper:

"The coolest place in the City.
The Virginian Girl
or
De Bite of De Wild Coon."

That sounds promising for a hot night. At length Barnum bought the stately Georgian hall and gave shows to those who are born every minute. Finally, it sank to Kunkle's Ethiopian Opera House, and "a shooting affray gave it a very bad odour." In 1873 the historian says it was "purged by Fire."

Then after a time the site was the home of the Baltimore and Ohio Railway. That too was burned out by the fire of 1904, and now the Emerson, named for the creator of Bromo Seltzer, occupies the corner.

Peale's Museum, however, did not satisfy the Baltimore appetite for marvels. Read this and weep for the departed days: "Colonel Fremont's Nondescript will be exhibited at 71 Baltimore Street. Nature seems to have exerted all her ingenuity in the production of this astonishing animal combining as it does the Elephant, the Deer, the Buffalo, the Camel, and the Sheep. It is the size of a horse and covered with wool of a Camel. Naturalists and the oldest trappers assured Colonel Fremont that it was never known previous to his discovery. Admittance 12½ cents" Ask me another. And close by the shop where Spalding sells prosaic sporting goods was exhibited "A Wonder of the Age—A Living Skeleton who plays the violin with his leg and one hand. He is intelligent and pleasing in manners and will not offend the most refined lady." This certainly was a recommendation in the mid-Victorian age.

Before leaving the neighborhood, however, you will notice a low marble building stained with the weather, so that now the stone has taken on a warm apricot hue. This is the bank of Alexander Brown and Sons, the oldest private banking house in America. Since the early nineteenth century the establishment of this firm has stood on or near this very corner. The story of the Browns is so interwoven into the fabric of the town that a history of the family will shed an interesting light on Baltimore's own story.

The firm, established in 1800, has for five generations born an untarnished reputation, and maintained the highest integrity. The vaults of this little building—so small and low that the flames of the Great Fire leaped over it—these vaults, I say, are filled with letters and documents written in the precise and beautiful handwriting of the first Alexander Brown. In the Bank itself there is a picture of the old man and his four sons. Thomas Corner is the artist. Alexander, the founder of the firm, looks down, from a painting, upon his four sons. Two are seated, one is standing in the foreground, while the fourth is bending over his brothers. In a corner of the room is a globe, the symbol not only of their world-wide activities but also of their fleets of merchant ships which were Alexander Brown's chief pride. The story of his settlement in the town is worth while. Seven years before Brown's arrival John Jacob Astor of Waldorf, Germany, had landed here a poor immigrant with a pile of musical instruments which he intended to offer for sale. He was induced to exchange his violins and zithers for a bundle of furs, and went north to sell them. Thus Baltimore lost one good merchant, but it was to gain another in Alexander Brown.

In the year 1800 Ireland became part of the United Kingdom, and many Irishmen thronged overseas to seek their fortunes in a new country. Among these was Alexander Brown who took ship for Baltimore, a town with an Irish name, but with a post-Colonial air.

If we were to go back to the Baltimore Street of that period what a different world we should find! Where now tall buildings rise there were then low sloping-roofed houses painted yellow and blue and white. Occasionally a brick house of substantial appearance stood among its more rustic neighbors. The red brick, of course, was faced with white in true Baltimore fashion—a good Georgian style. As yet, however, no Greek portico had arisen. The roadway was wide enough for lumbering Conestoga wagons that had driven in from the West. Nor were sprightly gigs lacking. There were no newsboys hawking the Sunpaper, but no doubt the *Baltimore Amer-*

97

ican and Daily Advertiser sold its sheet like hot cakes, for John Adams was President and French spoliation an exciting issue. The Mayor of Baltimore, Mr. Calhoun, gathered his confreres together at the home of Mr. James Long, in Front Street, where the early meetings of the City Council were held. Large indeed was the town which these men were called upon to govern. Market Street had long since travelled on past Mr. Fite's house where the Continental Congress had met. Now, it reached the far western border of Union Street, or as we should call it, Green. Charles Street, once named Forrest, now climbed the hill to Mulberry, but beyond that there were the fields and woods where Rochambeau had encamped, and where Charles now crosses Franklin there was the entrance to John Eager Howard's vast estate of Belvedere. The town was small but it was full of colour and life. Along Baltimore Street there were inns with gay sign boards swinging over the heads of the passerby. The Indian Queen and the Fountain Inn gave a hearty welcome to the constant stream of travellers passing north and south. The crack of the long whip and the merry tirulieu of the postman's horn gave warning that the mail coach was setting out for Richmond or Philadelphia. Behind low brick walls or neat paling fences flower gardens bloomed in scarlet, blue and yellow. Ladies with "sharp rosy spirited faces" rustled by in taffeta, or, if the day were wet, tripped along in patterns, skirts lifted high above the muddy road. And the gallants—well, it is said that their bows took in the whole sidewalk, and simply blocked the traffic. To and fro among this gay throng went the very popular little chimney sweep, for all the world like those described in Lamb's Essays—sweeps with an "innocent nigritude."

It was into such a scene as this that Brown came. Shortly after his arrival a paper bore the following announcement:

12 North Gay Street.

"The subscriber lately arrived from Ireland has brought with him a complete assortment of 4-4 and 7-8 wide Irish linen which upon examination will be found lower than any inspected for three years past, and which will be sold by the box or by the piece for cash or good acceptance in the city on the usual credit. . . . Alexander Brown.

N. B. He has also imported and for sale three dozen very nice mahogany hair bottom chairs made in the very best construction, and four eight-day clocks which will be sold very low.

December 1800"

Who came to buy this excellent linen and very low clocks I do not know, but in spite of Napoleon's Berlin Decrees and the English Orders in Council, Brown's business prospered. In 1802 the three younger boys came over from an English boarding school. They arrived one piping hot July morning wearing the heavy woolens so suitable to the Yorkshire climate. Their mother was overjoyed to see them again, and, devout soul that she was, longed to hurry off to church to give thanks for their safe arrival. However, as she looked at her boys clad in those hot uncomfortable garments, she felt a practical spirit warring with her devotion. Hurriedly she borrowed some thin clothes from a neighbor, and the lads, more appropriately and tropically dressed, set forth with their parents for divine service.

Hard on to seventy years the firm of Alexander Brown has stood on the corner of Baltimore and Calvert Streets. The elder Brown perceived that this lot would be the business center of the town, and he chose wisely. On the roof of the early building occupied by the bank there was a captain's walk. Here could be kept a look-out for ships, those world-wide fleets that were Brown's pride and delight. On Federal Hill signal flags were run up denoting the approach of some of the graceful

99

clippers belonging to the firm, the *Leila* or the *Grace* or the *Isabella*.

Here we are back at Light Street again the point of departure. Keep in mind that the Fountain Inn stood where the Southern now is situated. The bright gushing fountain on the sign board was welcome indeed to Washington, who always made this house his headquarters. Here, too, came Lafayette, and here Francis Scott Key on the morning after the bombardment of Fort McHenry. On a breakfast table at the Fountain, Key read again the scribbled copy of the "Star Spangled Banner" and revised it with the loving care of a poet, while the waiter drew his ale and brought him—whatever people ate for breakfast in 1814. And the food at the Fountain was Lucullan. Never were there such oysters, such canvasback duck, such terrapin. Never such venison, such meat pies or such lusty draughts of punch and cider—to say nothing of sherry, port and burgundy. Pure gushing water was all very well upon the sign board, but the table told another story.

Nor did the old Inn lack merriment. It was the popular place for dancing. Subscriptions to these dances were only for gentlemen over twenty-one and ladies over eighteen. Six managers were the social arbiters, distributing the places in the quadrilles by lot. At six promptly the dance began, and the refreshments were tea and rusks. But strangest of all, the invitations were often written upon playing cards because, says the historian, there were no blank cards to be had in the colonies. Thus the reverse of the ace of hearts might read:

"The Juvenile Amicable Society requests the pleasure of Miss Cox's company at a ball to be held at the Old Fountain Inn at six p. m. April 18, 1788."

These dances caused the most intense pain to the devout Methodists who had their meeting houses just across the way. It was no uncommon thing to hear the psalms and spiritual

100

OLD FOUNTAIN INN
THE SOUTHERN HOTEL NOW OCCUPIES THIS SITE

songs mingling with the merry dance tunes on the jigging viol. After the Revolution the dances at the Fountain were less popular and the young people met at the Indian Queen on Baltimore and Hanover Streets. This hotel was destroyed by fire—probably from heaven, sent as a punishment for the sinful junketings.

The history of the Methodists in Baltimore centers here in Light Street, and this is the place to tell their story.

Across Light Street from the Southern Hotel, or the old Fountain Inn was the first Light Street church—built in 1785 on the northwest corner of Light and—ironically enough— Wine Alley. This, however, was not the beginning of Methodism in Baltimore. John King, a friend of Wesley's preached the new doctrine from a blacksmith's block on Front and French Streets, and soon afterwards he stood upon a table at the corner of Calvert and Baltimore and set forth the same teaching. It happened to be the day for the militia drill, and the young soldiers thought he was a capital joke, as young men will. They listened mockingly for a time, and then desirous of action they overturned the table, and poor King sprawled in the dust. At this juncture an officer who was passing by stopped and ordered the soldiers to behave themselves. Then he helped the discomfited apostle to his feet. The sermon was interrupted, but all the spectators felt that the preacher had not had a fair hearing, and therefore were predisposed in his favour. It was, nevertheless, Francis Asbury who organised Methodism in Baltimore, and indeed in America.

Asbury was born in England in 1745. His mother believed that God had revealed to her the great destiny of her son: he would be a religious leader and would spread the gospel among the heathen. "But," says Herbert Asbury, maliciously, "God did not specify the Americans." His mother thought that the boy might become Archbishop of Canterbury. In 1772 the famous circuit rider came to Baltimore, stopping at Fells Point, and later crossing the Falls to dine with William Moore. In 1774 two lots were bought on Lovely Lane, and a church was built there in April of that year. This old church was a square plain building, very prim and decorous as a Methodist Meeting House should be. Today on the side wall of the Merchants Club in Redwood Street there is a bronze tablet which reads: "Upon this site stood from 1774 to 1786 the Lovely Lane Meeting which organized the Methodist Episcopal Church in the United States of America." In this little building in 1784 Asbury was elected bishop much to the distress of John Wesley. Later the congregation bought the land across the street—the Wine Alley site—and built a larger church on that spot. At Light and Baltimore stood the parsonage, a sedate and comfortable mansion in good Georgian style. But the Methodists had their trials. One of them was a British army barber named Brydon who had bought Fountain Inn. This worldly man actually erected a dance hall next to the Light Street Church, and all during the prayer meeting the gay notes of the violins ran in and out of the petitions, and the amens were punctuated by the sharp click of red heels dancing Sir Roger de Coverly. Earnestly the Methodists prayed the Lord to destroy the iniquitous place. He did not. Finally Brydon offered the hall for sale, and with fervent joy the Methodists bought the property. No sooner had they turned it into a college than both college and church burnt to the ground; which proves beyond a shadow of a doubt that heaven favours the dance.

For all this austerity, Asbury was greatly beloved. He was, however, difficult to manage especially in any matter that seemed to take time from his work. Many of his converts desired a picture of the preacher, but no one could persuade him to have his portrait painted. One day he stopped to talk to James McCannon, a devout Methodist and a good tailor. In deep distress, Asbury confessed that he was worried over his "boys"; that they were terribly out at elbows. These "boys" were his young preachers. The wily Mr. McCannon now saw his opportunity. With guile he replied, "I have just received a good piece of velvet, and I will make each boy a coat if you will promise to do what I wish."

"What is that?" said Asbury.

"Go with me to an artist and have your portrait painted."

"No," said the obstinate Asbury, "that I will not."

Later in the day, however, he returned rather shamefacedly and said, "As a Christian man I will agree." The picture was painted, and the velvet suits delivered. After a while the painting was lost, but years later a servant of the McCannons found the portrait doing duty as a fire board. A stove pipe had passed through the canvas, but happily the features of Asbury were not marred.

Baltimore Street between Light and Charles is not remarkable in any way. Where the Hub now stands there was once a building known as the Atheneum, a name popular in Baltimore and given to various buildings. The nature of this Atheneum can be imagined when one hears that in the fifties the Ethiopian Serenaders flourished there.

But no account of Baltimore would be in any sense adequate if it failed to take into account that institution known as the Sunpaper. On the southwest corner of Baltimore and Charles Streets stands the Sun Building, a ponderous ugly structure. Here in early days was the modest home of a butcher named Steiger. This substantial citizen owned the Meadows, a name given to the soft marshy island that lay in mid-stream when the Falls looped the loop at Calvert Street, where the butcher fattened his cattle. And here—on the site of the Sunpaper office at the edge of town—the good man re-

103

tired in the cool of the day. That is all we know of Steiger. Of the *Sun* we have a long, honorable record. When it first appeared in 1837 it was to be a penny paper, a most remarkable thing in that day. From the first its history has been marked by initiative and vitality. One lone man, Jesse Reed, was the sole reportorial staff. In his youth he had been with the Hagerstown *Torchlight,* but to the end of his sixty-one years Reed was devoted to the interests of the *Sun.*

The Presidential message of 1838 gave the paper a chance to show what it could do, and the infant *Sun* rose to the occasion. This is the solemn truth; no pun intended. The other journals of the time had been satisfied to obain their supplements with the Presidential message delivered to their readers on the next day. Not so the Sunpaper. A man mounted on a Canadian pony "nimble as a goat, and fleet as the wind" established the pony express. A printed copy of the message was brought by this man to the little office on Light Street, and in five minutes after its arrival forty-nine compositors were at work, and in two hours the first copy was on the streets of Baltimore. The excitement was intense. What, read the President's speech before the words were scarcely out of his mouth! Oh, the dizzy pace of the thirties! The Pony Express became the *Sun's* usual method of relaying news and was used until the perfecting of the telegraph. Those who saw the Fair of the Iron Horse will not soon forget the dramatic Pony Express rider and the swift beauty of his horse. At one time there was a pony relay from Halifax to Baltimore printing news of a shipwreck off the Banks. This determination to get the news is reflected throughout the whole organization of the *Sun.* Not only must the news reach the *Sun* as swiftly as possible, but papers must be delivered to the subscribers at whatever cost. If a Baltimorean is deprived of his Sunpaper he is a lost, distracted creature. When the great blizzard of 1898 buried the town in snow Denny plowed his way through to Towson, arriving in the late afternoon, but the Sunpapers got through. Now when a big storm threatens, a banner bearing the legend, "Remember Denny" is hung up in the circulation department. Such is the *Sun* tradition.

Two years after the establishment of the paper the famous Sun Iron Building was erected on the corner of Baltimore and South Streets. Here, no matter what the fortunes of the town might be (and in the Civil War period Baltimore knew some rather hectic days) the Sunpaper was printed regularly. When the great fire of 1904 swept across the business district the paper was printed in Washington and brought to the city, so that no Baltimorean might suffer the added misfortune of being bereft not only of his place of business but also of his Sunpaper. Later when the burnt district was rebuilt the *Sun* moved to the present corner.

At Baltimore and Liberty Streets on the side wall of a bank one finds this inscription: "On this site stood the old Congress Hall in which the Continental Congress met December 20, 1776, and on December 27, conferred on General Washington extraordinary powers for the conduct of the Revolutionary War." This was Jacob Fite's house, a square stone structure solidly built with wide chimneys and a sloping roof. The mansion stood on the Great Eastern Road—the last house on the outskirts of the town. Here when the Revolutionary cause was at its lowest ebb Congress met, a small discouraged group of men. Dispirited they were, but by no means daunted; they intended to make this their last stand if necessary, but to stand gloriously. Baltimoreans apparently paid little attention to them as they entered the town following in their journey that ancient Seneca trail. Along Market Street they rode, no doubt, stopping, perhaps, for a fine dinner and inspiriting drinks at the Fountain Inn. Let us hope that they obtained both, for they had had a long fatiguing journey from Philadelphia, and their hearts were heavy.

Evidently Baltimore gave the visitors a taste of her mild climate, but it was not appreciated by the Connecticut member who wrote: "No one can walk about here without boots. The air and paths are in the same condition that they are with us at the latter end of March, or the beginning of April." This, however, was comparatively mild. "If you wish to please your friends," wrote Harrison of Virginia, "come soon to us, but if you desire to keep out of the damnedest hole on earth come not here!" Strong words; but remember that these men were overwrought, and Baltimore mud is red and sticky. At first the Congressmen claimed that the tradespeople were nothing short of profiteers, and they cursed them roundly. But it is impossible to hold out against Baltimore for any length of time. Even her climate is insinuating. As soon as the fires were kindled on the generous hearths of Jacob Fite's house things began to look brighter to the visitors. Within three days William Whipple of New Hampshire writes home: "Congress is now doing business with more spirit than they have for some time past. I hope the air of this place, which is much finer than Philadelphia, will brace up the weak nerves." Good William, good boy! If the air did not, I wager that the eggnog did, for remember that this was Christmas time.

> "God rest ye merry, gentlemen
> Let nothing you dismay."

Gerry of Massachusetts records that it pained him to leave Philadelphia, but he must say that it was more exhilarating here. Much! But Samuel Adams crowned it all by confirming what I have always heard of the City of Brotherly Love: "We have done more important business here in three weeks than we had done, or I believe should have done, in Philadelphia in six months."

But all jokes aside, no wonder that these men were disheartened. The British had pressed Washington and his starving army desperately; the Indians threatened; finances were in a muddle; smallpox was raging in the camps. No wonder that the mud and dirt irritated them. But with the coming of Christmas came the news of Washington's victory at Princeton, and the blue skies and pale warm sunlight put new courage into them. Nor did Maryland hospitality fail. The townspeople made them welcome, and in the genial atmosphere of the Howards and the Carrolls they took fresh heart. A little later than this a gentleman writes thus of the town: "Having taken lodgings at Evans's tavern I was astounded by the number of well-dressed men who sat down to table, amounting to about eighty. The houses here are built of brick and many are elegant. As to the ladies, I saw but little of them, and can only say in the language of the Quakers 'They look well.' "

INNS, PRIESTS, AND MERCHANTS

CHAPTER VII

EYOND Baltimore and Sharp Street there
was in Revolutionary days nothing but
countryside, green fields, and a straggling
road. Here the Great Eastern Road turned
south and went on to Washington. But
it was not long after the war that contact
with the West began, and the town pushed out in that direction. Today there is no trace of the taverns which supplied
the needs of the western travellers along these old turnpikes.
Shortly after the Revolutionary War, however, a sturdy
Georgian inn was built on the northwest corner of Baltimore
and Paca Streets. Built of brick, the house had two substantial
chimneys of generous girth, well fitted to accommodate the
smoke of roaring fires. The roof was high-pitched and peaked,
and beneath the eaves there was a graceful fan-light window
for all the world like the eye of a Cyclops. The walls were
built to last for many a year; they were two feet think. The
floors were laid in broad boards, and the low-ceilinged rooms
were of stately proportions. In every one there was an immense
fire-place, and the light of the flames danced upon the

THE GENERAL WAYNE INN

INNS, PRIESTS, AND MERCHANTS

polished wood-work. This noble house stood near one of the
entrances to the vast Howard estate, and the sign which swung
above its hospitable door bore the name and figure of General Wayne. John Eager Howard gave the tavern its name in
memory of Mad Anthony, his friend and companion in so
many warlike encounters. A gallant soldier was Wayne, fighting like a tiger at Monmouth and the Brandywine, storming
like two tigers that precipitous cliff that overhangs the Hudson; "Anthony's Nose" it is called today. His was a fitting
figure for the dashing sign which told travellers that here was
true Maryland hospitality.

Nor did the inn ever lack guests. Here every day came
Judge Samuel Chase, the old Signer who lived a stone's throw
away, at the corner of Lexington and Eutaw. The old gentleman loved his scarlet cloak and his knee breeches long after
they had gone out of fashion. You recall that we saw his
ghost in Monument Square. Well, here at the General Wayne
he used to sit with his cronies, recounting the days of his
youth, gazing into the fire when the talk fell into silence,
relieving in memory the struggles of the young Republic.

Here, too, came General Otho Williams, General Gist and
General Smallwood on many occasions, reviving like Chase
the adventures of their thickly crowded lives. The lesser folk
hung upon the fringes of their conversation and lively anecdotes of war times passed from mouth to mouth. Once Mad
Anthony himself rode up to the old inn door, where he enjoyed
the generous hospitality of his namesake. As the tavern
was situated on the road which led from the North to the
South distinguished men of both sections put up at the
General Wayne. The great Thomas Jefferson was a guest here
many a time, and a whole string of Pinckneys, Lees and
Lowndes made the inn their headquarters. John Quincy
Adams riding down from the North to Washington knew

the solid comforts of the General Wayne Inn. I wonder if his wife—Madam—accompanied her distinguished husband on the long journey. She, as you know, was the niece of Governor Thomas Johnson, "charming as a Romney portrait, but among her many charms that of being a New England woman was not one. The defect was serious." Thus her grandson Henry Adams describes her. "She was Louis seize like the furniture." Yes, I think she would fit well into the background of this old Georgian house.

An inn under the patronage of General Wayne had naturally a strong Revolutionary flavour. Image then the horror of the management when it beheld the Tory principles of some renegade painter. The sun and rain had faded the bright colours of the original sign, and a painter was called in to touch up the General, to give him a smart, military air. But alas, the painter was innocent of history, and had a decided preference for red. He worked diligently for several days, and at length returned Mad Anthony dressed in a coat of brilliant scarlet. "If this be treason make the most of it!" Apparently the management so considered it, and the painter was immediately summoned and ordered to give the General a more patriotic garb. In a twinkling the historical error was rectified, and in Continental buff and blue Mad Anthony once more welcomed wayfarers.

After the War of Independence this part of the town grew rapidly. This quick growth was due to the development of roads and the increased intercourse with the West. As early indeed as 1736 Mr. Digges' wagon road was built for the purpose of bringing Mr. Digges' produce to Baltimore Town. This John Digges was a wealthy planter who had received a rich grant of land from Lord Baltimore. His road was only a rough track, but later it was surfaced with broken stone, and became an important trade artery. Later the highway was known as the Hookstown Road, and only a year ago the last of the old granite markers was removed. This ancient milestone stood at the corner of Pennsylvania Avenue and Robert Street, in the heart of the city, but when it was first set in place it gave notice to the world that Balimore was one mile away. "Balto. 1 mile," it ran. Pennsylvania Avenue was once the Hookstown Pike. And where, you will ask, was Hookstown? Well, it was a snug little settlement on Brown's Hill just beyond Druid Hill Park. It wore a sedate and respectable air, but at Lewin's Hotel the gay blades of Baltimore used to meet the daring, but very charming ladies. All this of course was in the age of innocence, and only the very old now remember it. The Reisterstown Road was linked to the Hookstown Road and thus we had a clear highway from the distant countryside leading straight—or rather biasly—into town, and ending at Greene and Franklin Streets. Along this highway the Conestoga wagons came rumbling in, the bells jingling and the whips cracking over the heads of the sleek six-horse teams. It was a brave sight. Here, too, droves of sheep and cattle stumbled along, enveloped in a cloud of dust. Those of us who recall Hookstown will remember with delight the dramatic moments in our youth when a herd of steers came clattering over the cobbled streets. It was a lovely exciting sound; above the ringing hoofs came the sharp masterful cries of the man who carried the goad. The air was filled with an acrid smell when the cattle had passed by, and at the end of the street they stumbled along in a disorderly, irregular rhythm.

In 1805 a National Pike was built, and Baltimore because of her nearer approach to the Ohio Valley was favoured above Philadelphia. The Frederick Road brought most of this western trade into town. The growth of trade meant that the teamsters must have stabling for their horses and good beds for themselves; hence we find within a few squares of the

General Wayne other taverns growing up to serve the inrush
of travellers. The Indian Queen at Baltimore and Hanover
streets we have already mentioned. By this time her vogue had
passed. You will, no doubt, recall that the fashionable life of
the town was no longer centered either at the Fountain Inn
or the Indian Queen. By 1790, or thereabouts, the Baltimore
Dancing Assembly had opened new rooms at Holliday and
Fayette Streets. There "in an elegant saloon devoted to the
entertainment of fashionable life" a Silver Supper was served
to General Lafayette. This spectacular affair was the talk of
the town for weeks. But the inns that we shall consider now
were of a more robust nature. What hearty names they had.
They sound for all the world like a chime of vigorous bells:
The Bull's Head, the Rising Sun, The Golden Horse, the
Maypole, the Three Tuns, the White Swan. It would not
surprise me at all to see Chaucer himself riding into one of
the great square inn-yards. For miles around on market days
the blue and red Conestoga wagons came jingling in, and the
yards were thronged with teamsters. Before driving the cattle
off to the shambles the men often herded the beasts here. The
air was thick with grunts and neighs and loud bellowings.
Within, the teamsters refreshed themselves with substantial
meat and drink. Around the corner on Pearl Street were the
hay scales, and hay was there offered for sale; horses must have
stout provender as well as masters. Indeed this part of Baltimore became in itself a great market and place of exchange.
Franklin Street was so thronged with wagons bivouacked for
the night that citizens complained to the city fathers for
relief from the congested traffic. They promised to cut through
Centre street; it is still uncut. Nor were all of the travellers
of the teamster class. By no means. At stated hours the stage
coaches stopped at the inn-yards for passengers, and Mr. Pick-
wick's friends-across-the-sea were whirled away to the merry

sound of the horn, and the postillion's crackling whip. The covered wagons set out for the West after a short stay carrying back to the Cumberlands a supply of groceries and gewgaws for the women folk.

In those days when Baltimore was still young; her very streets carried with them a suggestion of merriment. The ingenious device of designating streets by numerals and letters had not yet dawned upon the efficiency expert, and we find thoroughfares rejoicing in such titles as Petticoat Lane and Flat Iron Alley. Both of these extinct articles are proof of the antiquity of the highways. The antiquarian of the future will find here much to interest him; for witness these! Pothouse Alley—oh fie! And then follows a list of famous wines— Canary, Burgundy, Madeira, and even the humble but potent Cider! Scharf, the great authority on Baltimore, says that sack was the favorite drink of our ancestors. It has a jolly roistering sound, but strive as I would I could find no street devoted to sack. I must admit, though, to discovering a Maudlin Avenue. Elbow Court, and Crooked Lane, Half Moon Court, and Wapping have an English flavour, and so too have Fleet and Thames. In the neighborhood of the General Wayne Inn the street names properly recall the Revolutionary days. At the battle of Eutaw and Maryland Line "Swept the field with their bayonets," and there John Eager Howard was severely wounded. The street which bears the name of the victory of the Southern campaign runs parallel to Paca. Greene which parallels Paca on the western side was named for the distinguished Nathaniel Greene, who in spite of ammunition shortage and every possible deficiency brought success to the American army. William Paca, educated in the Middle Temple in London, practised law in Annapolis and held many important positions in the state, notably that of Governor. Fayette once known as Pitt Street, of course commemorates the great Frenchman whom all Americans recall with affection. Saratoga and Lexington speak again of famous battles, and Franklin brings to mind the man whom some have called the first civilised American.

Before we go on to the Market we must stop awhile in the graveyard at the corner of Fayette and Greene Streets. It is a gloomy place, though brighter now than in the days when a dirty chocolate coloured paint covered the walls of the old Westminster Church. Now the bricks are a warm red, and in the late afternoon there is a cheerful twittering in the square tower. We enter the churchyard through an iron grille, and find ourselves in a small enclosure encircled with a diminutive path. Here rests the body of Edgar Allan Poe. The monument is uninspired to a remarkable degree. Ugliness could not be more apparent. As usual the French have done much to relieve the mid-Victorian dullness. The have placed on the monument a graceful scroll which bears the inscription:

A la Memoire
de
Edgar Allan Poe
Eternellement cher dans les coeurs
de ses Amis Français.

A branch of laurel and of palm accompany the scroll, a faithful reminder of the honor in which Poe was held among the French when his own countrymen meted out derision and scorn. The poet deserves a better monument; perhaps I do wrong to speak of it with disparagement, but it is so un-Poeish! Around the grave there are always floral wreaths, or simple flowers, for many visitors come here from all parts of the world. On the right of the entrance to Poe's grave there is a bronze marker which gives the names of the well-known men who lie buried in this graveyard. Visit this place on a sunny day; even then the half-buried stones, the heavy gloomy vaults, the general air of mortality depress the human spirit. Behind the church there is a wide sunny stretch of ground in which there are a number of scattered graves. Here is an ancient stone to "Patrick Allison, Doctor of Theology, Founder and first pastor of the church of the Presbyterians in the city of Baltimore." David Poe, the grandfather of the poet, lies not far away, and nearby there is a curious granite monument bearing the figure of a raven, and the words "Quoth the Raven." Here, the stone informs us, lay the body of Edgar Allan Poe from 1849-1875. The inscription reads: "Mrs. Maria Clemm, his mother-in-law, lies upon his right hand and Virginia Poe upon his left hand under monument erected to him in this cemetery." At least the sun shines upon these with its eternal light, but unhappy are those heavy ponderous tombs shut out from the pleasant light of the sun. On the gate posts of the old graveyard is carved a design of a winged hour-glass. Man's life is like a bird's as the old Saxon poet reminded us. Strangely enough the birds were the only evidence of life in this melancholy burial ground. A recent rain had washed a stream of dust across a flat tombstone. Here the sparrows bathed in a practical fashion, fluttering and scolding and flittering their wings in the dust of patriots and poets.

We are now in the neighborhood of Lexington market, one of the most famous markets in the world. Walk north on Greene Street for one square, but do not expect to see a spick and span new market house. Instead you will find long rows of rather disreputable sheds extending for two squares. In pre-Revolutionary days this hill-top was the fair grounds. It lay on the outskirts of the town; one had to climb a steep hill to reach the site. And when once there, what an ideal location! To begin with it was remote, or perhaps secluded is a better word. Therefore cock-fighting and horse-racing and boxing bouts could be staged here without undue publicity. Even in those liberal days there were some who grumbled at too much cakes and ale. Furthermore the ground was fairly level, perfectly adapted to foot-races, wrestling, football, to say nothing of the greased pole. Here, too, gypsies camped out; bear-wards made it their haunt. In truth the morals of servants and children were being undermined by this naughty spot. Something must be done. As usual, it was John Eager Howard who came to the rescue. He was as ready in social improvement as in bayonet thrust; a remarkable combination.

The land in this vicinity belonged to the vast Howard estate, and furnished excellent pasturage for the Howard cows, no doubt. In 1782, however, with a generosity characteristic of him, the great patriot gave the steep grassy knoll to the city. Immediately plans for a market house were discussed, but it was not until 1803 that the actual completion and opening of the market took place. At first the square from Eutaw to Paca Street was large enough for the needs of the town, but later the market spread farther and farther west. Of that western section I shall say little, but if you are interested in such things visit it yourself on some Tuesday or Friday morning. In 1855 a meeting was held in Cugle's tavern nearby to "establish a dispensary for dried and fresh fish"; from this meeting grew the present fish market. In every way this is one of the most interesting parts of the market, and a journey there is almost as salty and beneficial as a sea voyage. The Lexington Market is one of the most characteristic Baltimore institutions; on no account omit it from your itinerary.

Every now and then some sanitary and highly efficient person proposes to destroy the old market house and to erect a fine new steel structure similar to one in Cleveland, or Kansas City, or Oshkosh. At length these worthy people will prevail, but thank God, their hour has not yet come. Therefore if you have a progressive, reforming mind, stay away from the market; it will be painful to you. If, on the other hand, you enjoy colour, beauty, distinctive charm, you will find it in plenty. Early in the morning when the rest of the town is comfortably asleep the market begins—that is, begins for the market people. They are busy for hours arranging their wares, polishing apples, setting out neat rows of cabbages and kings. For the townspeople, a bell rung by the market master announces the opening of the mart.

But Lexington market is more than a place for vending goods. Here on Tuesdays, Fridays and Saturdays comes that almost extinct American species—the house wife who does her own buying. From stall to stall she goes, selecting her own oranges and grape-fruit, choosing her own fowls, supervising the cutting of her own meat. Nor is the friendly spirit absent. She knows these men and women well. On every side one hears, "Oh, good morning, John," or "Well, George, where were you on Tuesday?" The purchasing is flavoured with pleasant homely greetings. In this democratic atmosphere all sorts and conditions of housekeepers rub shoulders. The rich accompanied by chauffeurs select lettuce with a critical finger; the moderately well-to-do carry their own purchases or adjure Charlie or Jim to put their things "in the right basket." Jim says "Ya'as, M'm" and in go the packages, piled in a tall basket later to be delivered to the house or apartment of the patron. A ten cents a week tip—with an occasional quarter—satisfies Jim; of course he gets a substantial slice of fruit cake at Christmas as well as this largesse. And on Jim's part we get such service as this: "You let me know, m'm if there's anything you want done and I does it." The market people, too, are worth knowing. There was the old horseradish and cocoanut man who had a stand on Paca Street. I loved to hear the rub-a-dub-dub of his flying wooden wheel. He threw out with a rapid circular motion a fine spray of rich cocoanut, drippings not despised by the ragged darkey children who flit across the background of every Baltimore picture. This old man had a fine ruddy face like an English squire's; I have not seen him for several months now. Perhaps he has passed on; if so, God rest his soul! "Pinks" is still with us. He sells rabbits, strawberries, or cantaloupes according to the season. Personally he selects each box of berries, and vouches for the pedigree of each red juicy morsel! If you express doubt, he flings the berries broacast upon the stall and cries dramatically, "Lady, would I cheat you?" This man is an actor as well as a shrewd merchant. There was not so long ago an old, dried-up little match woman, no bigger than a child, who would sidle up to you with the cunning of a gypsy, saying, "Matches, lady?" Woe betide you if you offended her in any way. Billingsgate is found not only in London.

The Italian fruit stalls are marvels of loveliness in colour and arrangement. The darkest day takes on a rich glow from the high-piled oranges, apples, plums and grapes. Rows of pale lemons alternate with the deep coral of pomegranates. Russet pears enhance the wine-dark grapes. The same spirit of beauty that enriched the canvases of Titian and Correggio shines out in the splendid scarlets and warm yellows of these Italian fruit stalls in the market.

And though I know it is unhygienic to admire the candy stalls exposed so freely to the dust, I must delight in those mounds of sleek taffy, and the wondrous clear red and yellow candy that so charmed my unsanitary youth. Those dogs, those horses, those reindeer—all of my childhood Christmases are preserved in their "lucent syrops." Vegetables, too, are not to be despised; and lost indeed is he who does not love the cheese stalls where plump and rosy women peer out from behind the mounds and wedges of thick heavenly cheeses.

118

Talk about colour! Was there ever anything more full of the colour of sunlight from orange to pale blonde? And as we pass by, ah, what an entrancing melliflous whiff!

But to a well-seasoned Maryland nose there is no smell on earth so delightful as the robust odour of the fish market. How the Creator should be praised for fish, and not for fish alone but for

"things creeping innumerable both small and great"

The small things are the gudgeons and smelts, and the great —oh, well, take your choice from whales down. If it's in the water, it is here. Perhaps inlanders may not like the smell of "the dried and fresh fish dispensary." It is a great loss to him. Here in this cool delicious cavern one has a veritable sense of the sea. (Of course if you have no imagination, I cannot help you.) There is a salty tang in the very air. And the fish beautifully mottled in silver, or striped and dotted in the most decorative fashion, gaze at you with such reproachful eyes. Alas for the child who has never felt the purging effect of terror, as he beheld the soft shelled crabs crawling horribly in the slimy weeds, or watched with delight as the skilled and callous market man lifted them with wooden pinchers. And, by the way, have you ever noticed how those who sell fish tend to look like them? It is very marked. There is the same plaintive expression in the eye; the same droop to the mouth. It is extraordinary.

On Lexington and Eutaw there is a flower market, but whether it is more beautiful at Easter, at Christmas or at All Saints, it is difficult to say. Each season has its own perfection. But at Easter there is a special loveliness. The street is thick with bloom as if suddenly a garden had grown up over night. There are tubs of daffodils, and the hyacinths perfume the air in great waves of lilac, pink, and blue. Bees fly unconcernedly among the traffic, as if the city streets were their lawful pre-

serves. They sally in and out of the hearts of tall lilies, but if
the air has a frosty nip, the careful market woman neatly
wraps each bloom in oiled paper! Then the bees patronise the
hyacinths.

On the southeast corner of Eutaw and Lexington there is
an old herb stand. For years this family has sold rue, fennel
and bergamot to all comers. It is a bit of the country still to
be found in a modern city. Lizette Woodworth Reese writes
of The Lavender Woman—

"Crooked, like bough the March winds bend wallward across the sleet
Stands she at her blackened stall in the loud market street;
All about her in the sun, full-topped, exceeding sweet,
Lie bundles of grey lavender, a-shrivel in the heat."

But even better I love her lines on the "black sellers of herbs";

"Black, comely of abiding cheer,
Three times a week she fares
Townward from gabled Windemere
To sell her dainty wares.
and then:
"My snatch of May I get from her,
In white buds off a tree,
June, in one whiff of lavender.
That breaks my heart for me."

Not far from the market in a great triangle bounded by
Paca, Saint Mary's Street and Pennsylvania Avenue is the old
Seminary conducted by the Society of Saint Sulpice. Try as
we may, we cannot escape the "entangling alliances" that bind
us to Europe, and especially to France. Saint Mary's Seminary
has its roots in the French Revolution. You recall no doubt
the gloomy massive buildings on the Rive Gauche, the high
forbidding wall that shuts out the sights and sounds of Paris.
This was the mother-house. In the parlour of this seminary is
laid the fourth act of Manon; around the corner, lived D'Ar-
tagnan; here Talleyrand nourished his intellect for seven

years, feeding his mind upon "histories of revolts and seditions." No place in Paris had a finer tradition than the Sulpician Seminary. Before the Revolution it covered a vast extent of ground. It possessed a fine library, and the chapel designed by Lebrun was a masterpiece. At the time of the Revolution the Abbe Emery, the Superior, was imprisoned in the Conciergerie, but from his cell this intrepid priest directed the maintenance of the faith. In 1790 John Carroll went to London to be consecrated, and M. Emery sent M. Nagot to confer with Carroll on the subject of establishing a new Sulpician Seminary in America. With enthusiasm Carroll listened to the project, and the result was that four men were chosen for this new venture.

A friend of M. Nagot's gave a round sum of money, and the Society provided everything necessary for the services—the linens, vestments and sacred vessels. In addition, the priests brought with them a small choice collection of books, which formed the nucleus for the library of Saint Mary's Seminary. M. Nagot and his three associates, Garnier, Tessier and Levadoux, accompanied by five young men as model students, set sail from Saint Malo in April 1791. After a long voyage of three months and two days they landed in Baltimore. Strangers and aliens, they were met by Mr. Sewall, or as we would say, Father Sewall, who took them to a house on Market Street. When Guilford Avenue was cut through this house disappeared. It was small, no doubt, and of no dignity, but it must have been very welcome to the sea-wearied Frenchmen.

Father Nagot, however, was a man of energy; he immediately looked about for a suitable location for the Seminary. About a mile from the city he found a house known as the One-Mile Tavern, situated on the Hookstown Road. This was a quiet and retired place practically in the forest, and far enough from the dizzy world of the Fountain Inn or the Court-House

Square. Within a week the little company of priests and students moved into their new quarters, and by October the Seminary held its first Retreat and formally opened its doors.

Later on these same grounds a college for boys was founded known as Saint Mary's College. Boys both Protestant and Catholic were enrolled in this fine school, and some of Maryland's most distinguished men were graduated from it. Among these one would mention Severn Teakle Wallis. Today in a classroom at the Seminary there are two paintings by Rubens the gift of Wallis, an evidence of the affection which he bore toward his old school. Other men famous in our history were educated on this old site of the One-Mile Tavern. The roll-call is distinguished: Benjamin Poultney, Odin Bowie, Robert Spence, Benjamin H. Latrobe, Jerome Bonaparte, Joseph Chatard, James Gibbons, Otho Williams, Christopher Johnston, and Robert McLane.

In 1852 the college closed because by that time Saint Charles College was able to provide genuine preparatory education. From this time on the Sulpicians devoted themselves to their real work—that of preparing men for the priesthood. Saint Charles lies far from our radius of interest, but one would mention here John Bannister Tabb, priest and professor of English Literature at Saint Charles. Tabb was the close friend of Lanier's and though, like him, not born in Maryland, they both have an intimate connection with Baltimore. They lived in another world, but they walked these streets.

Now we must retrace our steps to the old market.

In early days when the high grassy knoll was the fair grounds and in the days of the early market, Samuel Chase's house overlooked this spot. Judge Chase, one of the Signers of the Declaration, had lived in Annapolis until 1786. Then he moved to Baltimore. His friend John Eager Howard had urged this upon him, and had presented Chase with a magnificent piece of property bounded by Paca, Eutaw, Fayette, and Lexington Streets. Here where a bakery now stands was the dignified mansion of the distinguished Maryland jurist. The house was very large, with two substantial wings. The three doors were approached by wide flights of steps, and four sturdy chimneys gave assurance of warmth and hospitality within. Along what is now Lexington Street a picket fence ran, shutting off the rear of the property. Trees shaded the house on all sides, and across the back there were long porches. It was a step from this comfortable house to the General Wayne Inn, and often Chase walked across his garden to the old tavern.

Chase was a man of most determined character. When a riot broke out on Fell's Point he ordered the arrest of two ring-leaders, men very popular with the citizens. By pressing the affair he incurred the hostility of the townspeople to such an extent that they threatened his life and property. To this Chase replied, "With the blessing of God I will do my duty, be the consequences what they may." When the case came up he appointed May fourth as the time for the next session. To this some objected that it would be Sunday. "No better day," said Chase, "to execute the laws of our country. I will meet you here and then repair to the house of my God." With a man like this there was nothing to be done. The matter ended. Later Chase was impeached and appeared before the bar of the Senate in January 1805. The charge was that he combined political disquisitions with his charges to the grand juries on his circuit. The accused had Luther Martin for his counsel. The two men had much in common; they were warm Federalists, brilliant lawyers, marked originals. To this old house Martin no doubt came many a time, for Chase lived here until his death.

Martin was the son of poor parents who provided a liberal education for their son. "A patrimony for which my heart beats towards them with a more grateful remembrance than had they bestowed upon me the gold of Peru or the gems of Golconda," says Martin. But alas, education does not make a man provident! With a merry twinkle in his eys he ruefully admitted, "I am not yet, and I was not then, nor have I ever been an economist in anything but time." This he saved so vigorously that he read as he walked along the street—a safe practice in his day, but if, with his nose stuck in a book, he went calling upon Chase in these days the Lexington Street traffic would surely run him down. Chase, however, liked him. Slovenly and awkward in person, Martin dribbled snuff down the front of his waistcoat, and wiped his nose on his sleeve. He had an eminent nose to wipe, but we more squeamish folk—well, nobody will care *where* we wipe ours or trouble to record it. Martin was also a heavy drinker; indeed it was such a habit with him that he was unable to plead unless he had his liquor. A client once made the fee contingent upon Martin's promise not to drink. Midway in the case, the great lawyer faltered, stammered and broke down. Calling someone to him he sent the messenger for a pint of brandy, and a loaf of bread. The bread he soaked in the liquor and thus ate the stimulent observing the strict letter of the agreement. Needless to say, he won the case with his usual genius. Such was the man who defended Chase, and whose massive logic won the day. It must have been a most notable trial; Aaron Burr presided "with all his accustomed self-possession, dignity and grace." But we must not be led off by Burr! Martin and Chase, however belong legimately to this neighborhood.

All of this vicinity has changed since Chase's days, and in our own time there have been many alterations. On what was once Chase's property there was in the days before prohibition a notable restaurant known as the Fox's Hole. Here the very finest of imported beer was sold, and many men prominent in political and art circles gathered here to drink and exchange the news, and gossip.

The steep hill that leads down from the market is Lexington Street. Beyond Liberty it slants sharply to the east, and authorities think that originally Conowago Street, as this slanting part of Lexington Street was called, was in Colonial times a continuation of the old Wagon Road from Mr. Digges' estate, which here joined the Great Eastern Road at the present intersection of Lexington and Crooked Lane. Be that as it may, Lexington Street today is the shopping street of the town.

At the corner of Howard and Lexington is Hochschild, Kohn and Company. Years ago in 1870 Max Hochschild arrived in the steerage, absolutely innocent of English. He went to work in the little shop of a merchant named Bamberger. Strangely enough this shop was at 202 North Howard Street, the present site of the great department store. There Hochschild says he filled every possible position until he became a buyer. But fortune favoured this man, and he soon set up in business on Gay Street in a tiny store large enough for one counter only, and one shelf on which to bestow the merchandise. Money was scarce with Max Hochschild, but not industry. He slept over the store, washed the windows, swept up the shop, ran his own errands, and was head of every department. In the first year he made thirteen hundred dollars net. In 1897 Hochschild and Kohn formed a partnership, and decided to start their business on the old corner where Hochschild had worked as a boy. Gradually the store has grown, until now it claims rank as "Baltimore's Best Store." If you want good service you will get it there. Not alone has the store taken a prominent position in mercantile life, but it has consistently maintained the highest social ideals for the welfare of its employees. As we go on with the story of Baltimore we shall find other immigrant boys arriving here, alien and friendless, but there is not one of whom Baltimore is more proud than of Max Hochschild.

In the seventies Hutzler Brothers was a tiny little shop with one small door, and two small show windows. Plate glass was unknown; the merinos and bombazines were displayed behind little square panes. The little old store has vanished, but much of the old-time flavour remains. In Baltimore shops the salesmen and women are old friends whom one has known for years, possibly since childhood. There was Mr. Ruth of Hutzler's, whose courtesy did much to make life pleasant. Nor should one forget the gigantic footman, with shiny buttons and sleekest of beaver hats. This enormous African had the manners of a prince of the blood. Today another imposing negro takes his place, but he has not the authentic Chesterfieldian air. Nor could the arrival of an automobile, be it Fiat or Mercedes, ever equal in grandeur the slow approach of a Victoria —Mrs. Bonaparte's perhaps. The chestnut horses shone with an incredible glossiness; the silver harness glittered in the sun. And there sat the old lady herself erect and aristocratic, her tiny parasol bent at a right angle to keep off the rays of the vulgar sun. Ah, as a hair-dresser said to me recently, "It meant something in those days when a fine carriage drove up to the door. Rich people stood for something then, and you could look up to them. Nowadays all these fly-by-nights may be as poor as I am next week. I like rich people to *stand* for something." These are shocking sentiments; retrogressive ideas. Nevertheless these were the people whom the gigantic African escorted in splendour to the shop.

Between Hochschild's and Hutzler's there was in the old days a funny little store of tunnel-like aspect called Simon's.

Hochschild's notion department is the rear of this famous old store. At the door of Simon's stood Mr. Cockey, a gentleman of the old school who knew his patrons by name, and enquired solicitously if one had been properly served.

Visit these shops and you will find excellent merchandise, and more pretty girls in one aisle than you will find in the entire city of Boston in a day's journey. Then if you want an attractive lunch in the midst of a day's strenuous shopping try either Hochschild's or Hutzler's; both are excellent.

BETSY AND MINOR MATTERS

CHAPTER VIII

EXINGTON street was not always the crowded garish business street that it is to-day. Long ago it was, as we have said, the short cut to the famous Great Eastern Road, a rather straggling back-woods road that brought one into the heart of the town eventually, but a thoroughfare of modest proportions, a means to an end.

Where the Fidelity Building now stands on the corner of Charles and Lexington, or as they were then called, Forrest and New Church Streets, there was a comfortable house with a red hip-roof set in a garden full of trees and flowers. This house was the rectory of Saint Paul's Church and when it was built there were no houses between the rectory and Market or Baltimore Street. This, of course, was in Revolutionary times, for in 1789 the present lovely rectory, the very sight of which is a refreshment, was built on Saratoga Street. Along New Church Street beyond Charles was a stone wall dividing the graveyard of Saint Paul's from the roadway. A broad flight

128

of stone steps led from the yard down to the street, and great sycamores made a pleasant shade along the low wall.

No part of the town has changed more than the neighborhood of old Saint Paul's. Gradually the land surrounding the church was sold, and handsome stately residences were built along Lexington Street. Later, as fortune changed, these houses were turned over to the lawyers, and such men as John P. Poe and Bradley T. Johnson had their offices there. But distinguished as these men were there is one figure who far surpasses them in historic and romantic interest. In the very house, indeed, where Poe later had his office there lived for years a litle old lady who *would* hang her red flannel petticoat out of her window to the infinite horror of the neighbors. This old lady was none other than Madame Bonaparte, that Betsy Patterson who had such an adventurous and thrilling story. The house has vanished now, and Preston Gardens covers the site, but the dauntless old lady still can be seen in this vicinity—if one has an observing eye. Her history is so well worth the telling that I can not refrain from relating it at this point. You may, however, see Betsy in other parts of town as well as in this.

In 1766 a fourteen-year old boy from Ireland landed in Philadelphia, friendless and alone, but determined to make his way in the world. America seemed to hold out to him unlimited possibilities, and he resolved to try his fate in this new country. A few years later, when the Revolutionary War broke out, young William Patterson had so far achieved his ambition that he was able to fit out two ships for the service of his country. In these he set sail for France to secure the ammunition sorely needed by the Colonies. In 1776 one ship returned, but Patterson himself went on to Martinique, and it was not until two years later, that he settled in Baltimore. He brought with him a fortune of one hundred thousand dollars in gold and merchandise. This was an astonishing sum of money, but it was only the beginning of his wealth. One half of the sum he invested in real estate, but as he always paid cash for land, and never bought for speculation, his fortune acquired solidity, and in a short time he was the richest man in Maryland with the single exception of Charles Carroll of Carrollton. The other half of the money he put into the shipping business. Baltimore was the best possible field for investments of this sort; Patterson rose rapidly in both fortune and reputation. He married Dorcas Spear, and gave to his household the same oversight and attention that he bestowed upon his business. He sounds somewhat like a martinet, but in those days men held the reins with a firm hand. Says he: "I always consider it my duty to my family to keep them as much as possible under my own eye, so that I seldom leave Baltimore either on business or pleasure. Ever since I have had a house it has been my invariable custom to be the last up at night, and to see that the fires and lights were secured before I retired myself. Thus I have found little risk from fires and managed to have my family keep regular hours."

How well this sounds! Betsy, however, had not yet appeared upon the scene. It is not beside the mark to give this long account of William Patterson. Betsy was her father's own child, and the same force and determination that marked his character early showed themselves in the temper of the daughter.

Betsy or Elizabeth Patterson was born in Baltimore in 1785. Very early she gave promise of unusual beauty, even in a town celebrated for its lovely girls. Nor was she at all lacking in brains. The shrewd, hard-headed father was found in the daughter, and added to these qualities was an exceedingly strong "come-hither" of her own. When only ten she could repeat Young's "Night Thoughts", and as to the maxims of Rochefoucauld—the charming minx had them by heart at an infantile age. William Patterson should have looked to this! Here was a fire that should have been "secured." But—purblind man! He was bewitched by her beauty and wit, and no doubt congratulated himself on having a clever daughter. So like her father!

The house on South Street, now long vanished, was the scene of the most brilliant balls and routs. From her childhood Betsy Patterson had met in her father's house the most distinguished men of her time and country. Jefferson, Washington, General Smith, Joshua Barney—men of eminence—thronged the house of the wealthy Baltimorean, and paid court to the slim, enchanting Betsy. One day news came that Captain Jerome Bonaparte was landing in New York, and nothing would satisfy Barney, who had served with the French, but a visit from his brother officer. Napoleon, Jerome's older brother was at this time First Consul, and naturally the French Captain was quite a lion. In September, 1803, Jerome Bonaparte arrived, just in time for the races. The town was in a furore of delight—horse races and a French officer at one and the same time! Life was too good to be true. Balls and parties filled every evening hour, and at one of these entertainments the impeccable Samuel Chase, the Signer, the friend of John Eager Howard, introduced Jerome to Elizabeth Patterson. Little did poor Chase know what mischief he had set on foot. The impetuous Frenchman fell deperately in love with Betsy, and she fell just as tumultuously in love with him. They were engaged. Now William Patterson got wind of the affair, and, like the stern parent in the romance, he sent Betsy off to the Springs to cool her passion. But not so. She protested that she would rather be the wife of Jerome Bonaparte for one hour than the wife of another man for an eternity. She did not know how near this was to the truth. In the meantime William Patterson expostulated, stormed—for he was Irish—but Betsy was married to Jerome on Christmas Eve. A gentleman who witnessed the ceremony gives the following account of the young bride:

"All the clothes she wore might have been put in my pocket. Her dress was muslin richly embroidered, but of extremely fine texture. Beneath her dress she wore but a single garment."

These are astounding details for 1803, and give conclusive proof that Betsy was modern in spirit and deed.

Now more merry makings followed, but the young people danced over a volcano. The august Napoleon was in a proper rage. An ominous silence, however, was more disquieting than threats. At length Napoleon spoke. Jerome received orders to return immediately to France, but "what the First Consul has prescribed in the most positive manner is that all captains of French vessels be prohibited from receiving on board the young person to whom the Citizen Jerome has connected himself, it being his intention that she shall by no means come into France, and it is his order that should she arrive, she shall not be suffered to land, but be sent back to the United States."

What a pity that Napoleon had not himself married Betsy. There would have been a wife for him, and the whole history of Europe might have been different. How much better than that puling Josephine, who dared not smile for fear of showing her bad teeth! Now Betsy could have smiled in the most prophylactic manner. Indeed had she showed her teeth in another way, it would not have been a bad thing for the Emperor. He needed a Baltimore woman to keep him in order. By some strange fatality these ideal matches are seldom made. This, however, is mere aside. Ignore it.

The poor young romantics decided to disobey Bonaparte, to crash the gates as it were (this is only a manner of speaking).

BETSY AND MINOR MATTERS

Consequently they sailed from Philadelphia with an aunt as a chaperon. But of all tragi-comedies! The ship was wrecked near Lewes, Delaware, and they were forced to take refuge in the town. Here the bedraggled Betsy and her husband and Aunt Spear had dinner with a most hospitable man who set before them a delicious roast goose and apple-sauce. To Aunt Spear's horror Betsy cheerily devoured the goose with healthy gusto. The elderly lady suggested that her niece had been better employed offering up prayers of thanksgiving for her rescue. Betsy continued to eat the goose, disagreeing with her aunt at every mouthful. Really Betsy was a trifle hard-boiled even in her youth; no wonder she hung out her petticoat when she was old.

Now things moved rapidly. In 1804 Napoleon was made Emperor, and letters to Jerome became stonier and stonier. Finally the couple arrived in Lisbon where a French guard prevented their landing. Jerome, vowing love until death, fled to Paris hoping to win his brother. Napoleon was a rock. "As to your little love affair with your little girl, I pay no regard to it." And he did not.

Betsy, refused all entrance, went to Dover and with what pride we record that Mr. Pitt had to send troops to the town to keep the populace from overwhelming the plucky girl with their attentions. This in some measure mitigates the sting of subsequent American behavior at Vanderbilt and such-like weddings. At Camberwell, near London, Elizabeth Patterson Bonaparte's boy was born. He bore the name Jerome Napoleon Bonaparte. Bitter and humiliating months passed in which she heard seldom from the caddish Jerome. But Betsy had not learned the maxims of Rochefoucauld in vain. Alone in a foreign country she displayed an admriable fortitude and poise. And well she knew Baltimore, for she wrote thus to her father: "One advantage in my spending the winter in this country is that I escape observation more than in Baltimore where you know people are always on the watch." Shortly after this, Napoleon tried to force the Pope to annul the marriage, but to his lasting credit, his Holiness refused. Then in his Gordian-knot-manner the Emperor ordered the French courts to declare the marriage null and void. This they did. Weak, fickle Jerome, for all his ardent vows, crumpled like paper, and the next alliance was based strictly on fraternal plans. I hope the Wurtemberger made him miserable! The long and short of all this was that Betsy and Bo—the little son—returned to Baltimore. Later we shall see her on South Street. But it was in this neighborhood that she spent her old age, an old age not to be understood without some account of her gallant youth. Here she took her daily walk, wearing one of the twelve bonnets which she had brought with her from Europe. They will last the rest of my life," said she, "for of course there are no civilised bonnets in Baltimore." But evidently the black velvet creation with the orange feather was a Baltimore concoction for it was not listed among the original importation. Cut off in her father's will with a tiny patrimony she still managed to look smart. When she appeared at the theatre she wore plain black velvet, low-cut, and a diamond necklace. The other women in the frills and furbelows of the crinoline age were mere Dolly Vardens. Betsy, like the Dark Lady of the sonnets, moved among them a figure of mystery and romance. Sharp of tongue she was to the end of her life. When some one impertinently asked her how old she was she gave him a keen glance and snapped out, "Nine hundred and ninety-nine years, nine months and nine minutes." The questioner collapsed. Far neater, however, was her reply to Dundas, a figure in the social and political life of England. It chanced that a book on America was under discussion when Dundas turned to Madame Bonaparte, and said,

BETSY AND MINOR MATTERS

"Well, Madame, I see that So and So—the author—says that all Americans are vulgarians."

"Yes," retorted Betsy, "and it does not surprise me at all that such should be the case. Were they derived from the Indians and Esquimaux it would be astonishing, but as they are all descended from Englishmen it does not amaze me in the least."

In an elegant mansion within a short distance of Betsy's last home lived Roger Brooke Taney. He was a spare, ungainly man but the possessor of a marvellous low, clear voice. His opponents said that they might have been able to equal his arguments but that no one could match that infernal apostolic manner. The tiny green oblong called Preston Gardens has eliminated the old houses that once lined Lexington Street. Now the last of them has gone, and on the northwest corner of Calvert and Lexington a bank building now stands. Calvert Street was opened about 1810, and in 1819 Robert Mills, who designed the Washington Monument, planned a row of houses on the new thoroughfare, north of Center. Wags at the time designated them Waterloo Row, and predicted that the architect would come to grief on this venture. Nor were they wrong. The new houses were so far on the edge of the city that few purchasers appeared, and the poor fellow lost all of his money. Today Waterloo Row is a sorry, dingy sight, but thirty years ago Calvert Street was a charming old-fashioned place. On the hill that slopes down from Preston Gardens is the Mercy Hospital. Here in the old days the City Spring was situated. There were five of these fountains, but this one was called the North Fountain, and was the first to be improved by the city. The water sprang from several springs that "anciently flowed from beneath the brow of the precipice that overhung Jones Falls." The spring itself was in a sort of pavilion or belvedere with a dome-shaped roof supported by eight columns. An iron grill enclosed the water to protect it from the dirt. Trees grew about this green and pleasant place. Children played here, and gossip flourished as the townspeople in true oriental fashion drew the water from the well.

In the nineties the dirt and grime of an industrial age had not yet ruined the neighborhood. The houses were the usual cheerful Baltimore brick. Before the homes in the seven hundred block there were small grass plots shut off by iron railings, and neat black and white tiled walks led up to the front steps. Children in stiffly starched frocks swung joyously on the gates of these diminutive gardens. At times life was enlivened by the passage of Miss Kilburn, a poor demented lady who would carry a parasol, rain or shine. Once on a never-to-be-forgotten day a man with a dancing bear came by. That was excitement! In those days, too, Center Street crossing like many others were equipped with stepping stones so that in rain one might cross with dry feet. Ah, what delight after a storm to stand perilously upon these high stones and look down into the turbulent stream dashing away to the Falls, and gurgling so enchantingly as it dashed. Alas, the little girl, the stepping-stones, the dancing bear have all vanished. Only Saint Ignatius Church remains the same with its stern military front, well-suited to a Jesuit Church. But enter it and you will find a beautful and holy place. Loyola College, founded in 1852, was on the south corner occupying the site of a tiny store in the basement of a large old-fashioned house. Here lived an ald woman who dispensed piggies—a most marvelous purple-hued candy of strange composition. Long since she has departed this life and taken her piggies with her.

On the square below Monument Street—in Waterloo Row— stood the most delightful little negro boy who served as a hitching post for horses. This small darkey was of a rich glossy black. He wore a bright yellow shirt which came down modestly to his knees, and his right arm was eternally raised in a gesture denoting safety for horse and buggy. The little pickaninny, just about four feet high, was made of cast iron, but he was companionable, nevertheless. Other hitching posts there were, but they were chiefly unimaginative—simply posts with a horse's head at the top. True, the ring in the horse's mouth gave him a somewhat fiery air, but when all was said and done who could compete with a shiny little darkey in a yellow shirt? This boy had, I believe, a twin brother who stood in front of Enoch Pratt's house, now the Maryland Historical Library, but the Waterloo Row boy was a friend of my youth.

Where Calvert Station now stands there was once a grand Roman Amphitheatre capable of holding five thousand spectators. Many were the thrilling shows exhibited here, bold chariot races and gladiatorial contests of spectacular nature. It had a wide popularity for a short time, but was by no means as famous as the Adelphi located at Saratoga and North Streets. This theatre with the classic name was called in street parlance the *Mud Theatre;* quite a comedown. But the reason is not far to seek. All of this land was once lowlying marsh. The Falls, rough and turbulent ,often spread over the adjacent fields, and the general term, the Meadows, was familiar enough. The Mud Theatre, however, was devoted to the drama and in no sense was a competitor of the Amphitheatre. Here John W. Albaugh took part in amateur performances and perfected his stage presence before his first regular engagement. That came later at the Holliday at eight dollars a week.

On Calvert Street below the station is one of the old wooden Indians once such a familiar sight on Baltimore streets. They

137

are rarely seen now. This one has suffered considerable amputation, but is still here like the star-spangled banner.

Here we are back again at the corner of Lexington and Calvert where the old Williams house used to stand, the site of the Court Square Building. We are now ready for a fresh foray.

Long ago on the corner of Gay and Fayette the Presbyterians built their first church in Baltimore. It was a crude building of logs, unsuited to their needs, so it was not long before they built a new church of "plain brick" at Guilford and Fayette. This was a handsome structure was set back from the street on a grassy terrace and surrounded by a neat wall. In 1785 Noah Webster the great lexicographer visited Baltimore planning to open a school for "young gentlemen and ladies, instructing them in reading, speaking and writing the English language with propriety and correctness." Whether this venture was a success I do not know, but at Doctor Allison's church—the Presbyterian church of "plain brick" Webster gave lectures on the English language.

All this neighborhood has changed. The old Rennert Hotel was on Fayette where now the Post Office stands, and around the corner was Guy's, a hostelry mentioned in Kennedy's journal: "Thackeray lectured on George Fourth—gossipy anecdotal. All went to Guy's and got an oyster, and had a pleasant session until midnight." No wonder! Imagine eating "an oyster" in such company. Across the Square where the courthouse now stands was the Gilmor house afterwards known as the Saint Clair. The Post Office changed all this section, and now there is talk of a new Post Office; surely not before it is needed.

The City Hall on Holliday Street between Fayette and Lexington is typical, architecturally, of the period that produced it, but it might easily be worse. Indeed there is a sort of dig-

138

nity in the east facade where in summer the flowers are handsome and decorative. The old City Hall, however, is a different matter. It is a low-browed building on the east side of Holliday Street. You can not miss it. Your eye is caught by something in the lines, some subtle distinction that marks an old structure, no matter how debased. On the wall near the entrance is a bronze marker which reads:

"Peale's Baltimore Museum, a pioneer art, historical and scientific museum erected 1813, by Rembrandt Peale. Gas lighting demonstrated June 13, 1816. Occupied as a city hall from 1830-1875. Rembrandt Peale, 1778-1860, distinguished Maryland artist, naturalist and technologist, founded first gas company in America, June 17, 1816. This tablet commemorates the American Gas Centenary, 1916."

The marker was placed on the building by the Consolidated Gas and Electric Light and Power Company of Baltimore, but the museum did more than demonstrate the use of gas lighting, valuable as that was. Peale's chief distinction is his work as an artist. The whole Peale family is interesting, and their single-hearted devotion to art marked them out as different from most of their fellow-countrymen of the colonial period. The elder Peale, Charles Wilson, was born in Chestertown on the Eastern Shore. So great was his love of painting that as his wife presented him with three sons he promptly named them Raphael, Rembrandt and Rubens. What Mistress Peale thought privately of this would make good hearing. At any rate there they were—three sturdy boys bearing the names of the old masters. In 1762 Charles Peale moved to Annapolis following there various trades; first he was a saddler, then a harness-maker and then a silversmith. But these, however, were asides. His real interest lay in portrait painting, practically an unknown art in the America of his day. In Annapolis he found men ready to lend him aid in the com-

139

pletion of his work. Charles Carroll of Carrollton and Governor Sharpe raised a large sum of money, and sent Peale to London. There he applied himself with great diligence that he might justify the confidence of his patrons. In the studio of Benjamin West he found a warm welcome. In fact West was in the middle of painting his famous canvas *The Departure of Regulus,* a subject suggested to him by no less a person than his Majesty George III. The well-set-up young colonial seemed to the painter an ideal Regulus, and without much argument Peale was persuaded to sit for the artist. This picture established West's fame as we all know, and before long Peale, no doubt through West's good offices, had so renowned a sitter as Pitt. This portrait of the Earl of Chatham was presented to the Province of Maryland, and is now in the possession of the State.

Nor was Peale content with mastery of a single medium of art. He could make a clock, stuff a bird, paint a portrait, reconstruct a mastodon or make a miniature. In the last art it was said that he sawed the ivory, moulded the glasses, and made the shagreen cases. As a soldier, too, he served his country well. He commanded a corps in the Revolution, and took part in the battles of Trenton and Germantown. But always his first thought was his painting. Continually he was making sketches, studying the faces of the famous men who came and went in that great struggle. These hurried portraits became the basis for many subsequent studies. Indeed the names of Peale's pictures sound like the roll call of honor. There is scarcely a man of prominence whom he did not paint. It is an intense pride that Maryland produced the artist who first made a portrait of George Washington. Indeed he made several; the first shows the General in his youth, in the uniform of a Virginia Colonel. Here is the young Washington, buoyant, energetic, the young Virginian gentleman. Then there is another portrait begun at Valley Forge. Washington himself suggested the background—a view from a farm-house window where he was staying at the time. Gilbert Stuart gives us Washington with the marks of responsibility graven upon his face; Peale shows us the man in those middle years, ruddy, vigorous, before the strains of life had manifested themselves.

After the war, Peale opened a museum in Philadelphia whither he had gone. In Baltimore Rembrandt Peale, that son whose "first recollection was a paintbrush" opened a museum on the southwest corner of Frederick and Water Streets. Sixty four portraits were here exhibited to say nothing of "two hundred preserved birds and beasts and amphibious animals" at last in 1813 Rembrandt Peale bought a lot on Holliday Street just north of Lexington, and built a permanent museum and gallery. This collection was long the chief sight of the town, but it was not profitable to poor Peale. He writes plaintively: "It is not to the credit of Baltimore that the liberal views and purposes of science should be sacrificed to a sordid calculation of short-sighted commercial avarice." Alas, poor Rembrandt! He had much to learn! But though the venture cost him his fortune, he had the untold joy of the artist who knows that he, at least, prefers liberal views to sordid calculation. Briefly, if I were not writing so seriously I would say that he got an immense kick out of the enterprise. A year after Napoleon's defeat at Waterloo (I wonder what Betsy thought) Peale gave a display of carburetted hydrogen gas. This was the first time that such a marvel had ever been exhibited in this country. It created the wildest excitement, and shortly after everyone was asking.

"Have you seen the chaste chandelier of fifty burners executed by Mr. Bouis? I do protest that Mr. Peale is a clever fellow."

BALTIMORE

Peale's Museum was both instructive and diverting. On one occasion the following announcement brought out crowds of the curious.

"Will administer Nitrous Oxide for four evenings. When enhaled it produces the highest excitement of which the animal frame is capable. A practical Chymist will administer it. Admission twenty-five cents. Children half-price" *The Baltimore Clipper,* a paper of the day, announces, "A Family ticket—ten dollars." Surely that was cheap for the highest excitement of which the human frame is capable.

To look at this grimy building now occupied by a printing establishment, it seems difficult to conjure back the past. Yet if you will cross the threshold you will see traces of former beauty in the proportions of the rooms and the lines of the old staircase. Later the Museum was moved to the corner of Calvert and Baltimore where now stands the Emerson Hotel, and its history we have recorded in another chapter.

As you turn back toward the present City Hall you pass the graveyard of Old Zion Church. It is a pleasant spot for a rest, and the gate is always on the latch. One day in spring I found here along the south wall the first hyacinths of the season. The wide stone benches offer a comfortable seat, and perhaps the friendly German police dog will extend to you his hospitality. In the cloisters there are some interesting old tiles setting forth in quaint fashion the stories of the Bible. In the brick wall surrounding the churchyard there are many memorial plaques in bronze well worth your study. There is a report that a fine modern church is to be erected on this site, but God forbid! The present building is venerable and dignified with a life and character of its own, and the little garden has not its counterpart in Baltimore. Here in this pleasant place Pastor Hoffman, greatly beloved by his people, is

142

By Courtesy of Hambleton & Co.

BALTIMORE AND CALVERT STREETS LONG, LONG AGO

buried. Two former ministers lie close at hand with a beautiful cross of antique workmanship erected to their memory.

When you close the gate of Zion Church, you come out upon the Plaza. At first it impresses you as a dreary uninspired expanse of concrete and gravel. But wait. Give the place time to mellow, and the trees time to grow. No, there is decided beauty in the Plaza. It is very French in treatment—all geometric, stiff and gravelly—not even a "jardin anglais" anywhere in sight, but I like it. And apparently the people are learning to like it, for at lunch hour on a mild day the benches are full of office workers. At the western end is a fountain symbolically given by the Woman's Christian Temperance Union. It is a chaste fountain as a W. C. T. U. gift ought to be, but when the pigeons condescend to bathe there or to drink delicately, it has a Lesbian air. Across the Plaza is the War Memorial designed by Laurence Fowler. This is one of the most beautiful public buildings in the country. The exterior is cold and regular, and like Tennyson's immortal heroine: "Faultily faultless, icily regular, splendidly null," but the interior is a perfecet thing. The long rectangular hall is beautifully proportioned, and the warmth of color impresses one at first glance. The stone is a faint rose, while the marble around the walls rising to a height of about twelve feet is palest yellow. Around the entire hall is a raised walk separated from the central floor-space by a parapet of black marble. The ceiling is a clear blue. Twenty-three great silver shields bear the insignia of the various divisions of the American Expeditionary Force. In the frieze are the names of battles, names full of history, "rich with the spoils of time," names remote from the American tradition and now bound up forever with the history of Maryland. Here they are—Chateau Thierry, Malbrouck, Grande Montaigne, Chalons.

"Malbrouck s'en va t-en guerre."

Truly he has. At the west end of the hall is Magill Mac-
kall's mural—a fine allegorical work. This is a hall of which
a Marylander may be proud. It is perfect and correct in
every detail, and yet it has no machine-made precision. It is
warm and beautiful, a worthy memorial to the men who died
in the Great War.

Facing the Plaza on either side of the steps are the figures
of huge seahorses. These symbolize the marine forces of the
state. Some have objected to them as incongruous or meaningless. How absurd. They are fine spirited beasts! As to their
being un-Greek, that does not concern us. They give that
original turn to the whole conception which makes for in-
dividuality and vigour.

The Plaza now covers the site of many old buildings, but
none of them was as famous as the Holliday Street Theatre.
John P. Kennedy says: "I never thought of it as a piece of
architecture. It was a huge mystical Aladdin's lamp that had a
magic to repel criticism." Latrobe in his delightful Memoirs
writes: "So tempting were the alluring posters that I had to
go several squares about to avoid temptation." Then he adds
that money was not particularly plentiful in those days. Of
the other Baltimore theatres we have written in another chapter, but one can hardly over-estimate the importance of the
Holliday Street house. The first theatre on this site was called
the New Theatre, which presented as its opening bill "Love
in a Village" and "Who Is the Dupe?" This was the
announced program, but as there were delays in construction
the actual presentments were, "Every One Has His Faults"
and "The Caledonian Frolics." How refreshing it is to read
that our reverend ancestors had their own mild version of the
Ziegfeld Follies. In 1813, the same year that saw the opening
of Peale's Museum, a fine new brick theatre was built called
the New Holliday. It was on Holliday Street between Fay-

ette and Lexington, and represented the very latest ideas in theatre construction. "When the play came to Baltimore boxes were engaged for every night. Families went together. Smiles were on every face. The town was happy. The elders did not frown on the drama, the clergy levelled no cannon against it, the critics were amiable." Thus a chronicler of those halcyon days records his impressions. The elder Booth played there, while the house hung upon his marvelous interpretation of Shakespearean roles. The best seats were a dollar, and ladies of fashion and the bucks filled the theater with a gay and brilliant crowd. In the balconies the seats were both hard and cheap. The benches were bare, and without backs, but they were by no means empty. "Sit closer" was the cry often heard among the gallery gods, and good naturedly the patrons made room for another spectator.

One of the most thrilling nights at the Holliday was the occasion of the singing of "The Star-Spangled Banner." Key, after his release, went, as we have seen, to the Fountain Inn for breakfast. The brief notes of the poem were in his pocket in a rough draft. His friends advised him to have the poem printed without delay. An apprentice boy named Sands set it in type at the office of the American in Harrison Street, and before many hours it was on the streets of Baltimore in handbill form. Citizens bought it like hot cakes, and every corner had its group reading Mr. Key's patriotic sentiments. It was a timely piece of work. Creditable too. Zounds! Key did not spare the British! Hear this:

> "No refuge could save the hireling and slave
> From the terrors of death and the gloom of the grave!"

At the Holliday Street that night Durang sang the song for the first time, and the enthusiasm of the audience knew no bounds. Every night after this "The Star-Spangled Banner"

145

was called for, and every night it evoked the same wild fervour.

A near neighbor of the old Holliday was the Baltimore Dancing Assembly which was on the northeast corner of Fayette and Holliday Streets. This was by far the finest dance hall in the country, if you could believe the local admirers. This, however, must be taken with the proverbial grain. The hall was opened in 1798, and for many years it was the centre of the social life of the town. Here met the beaux and belles of Baltimore. Here Betsy Patterson outshone in beauty all the women of her day. Here, too, was held the Silver Supper and ball for General Lafayette. How one would have loved to see the intrepid Frenchman riding along the streets of Baltimore. He has of course left his imprint in the names of two of our streets, and in O'Connor's statue at the foot of the Monument. But these are outward shows. One would have rejoiced to see him in the flesh, old in 1823, but still brisk and alert and upright, embodying to the last the spirit of the eighteenth century, a republican, but always an aristocrat. These spiritual links with the past are more vital than the radio, the telegraph, and all of the material paraphernalia that now bind men together. When Lafayette came he brought with him the pale proud ghost of Marie Antoinette, the impetuous ardour of Danton, the lyrical fire of Desmoulins. The beauties who made him deep curtseys at the Silver Supper thought of none of these things as their hearts fluttered with the pride of life. It is, however, pleasing to remember that in our hurly-burly city there was once a guest, fiercely democratic and at the same time inalienably of the old regime.

Later on, Latrobe collaborating with Lucas writes: "The Baltimore Assembly, the resort of fashion in Baltimore occupies the corner of Holliday and Fayette. . . . A large ballhoom and supper room ocupy the second floor, while on the floor below there was a card room which later became a supper room for gentlemen. Here the men may at their ease indulge the gothic practice of cramming themselves with comestibles without fair eyes to gaze at them." Couldn't you tell from the style that the splendours of Versailles had in some measure formed his character? You recall his dancing master, Mr. Dupont. Or does it smack of the Crystal Palace?

OLD TOWN

CHAPTER IX

A T this point it is difficult to decide whether to retreat or to advance. But before we go over into Old Town there is a certain place tucked away behind the Equitable Building that will yield much history. Small trace of history will be found there at present, but shortly after the War of 1812 one of the first literary clubs in the country was founded in this commercial spot. In those days, however, Fayette Street was not commercial. There were great elm trees along the street, and there were grassy traces and small lawns on which the citizens sat in the cool of the day and kept their eyes upon other citizens, as Betsy wrote to her father. The literary club had its headquarters in a yellow house, three-storied, wide, and bearing the name of Tusculum. As classical education is not as common now as then I add for those whose high school Latin is a little hazy— Tusculum was Cicero's favorite residence. In its Baltimore namesake the Delphian Club was organised, and here gathered the most interesting men of the day. To Tusculum came John Neal. Indeed he was the founder, and a man apparently

148

of remarkable force of character. In his novel "Randolph" he lampooned the great lawyer William Pinkney to the exceeding wrath of young Edward Pinkney, who challenged Neal to a duel. Neal was a Quaker, and declined to fight. A fiery statement was accordingly posted which read thus:

"The undersigned, having entered into some correspondence with the reputed author of "Randolph" who is, or is not sufficiently described as John Neal, a gentleman by indulgent courtesy, informs honorable men that he has found him unpossessed of courage to make satisfaction in the insolence of his folly. Stating this much, the undersigned commits the craven to his infamy,

EDWARD C. PINKNEY,
Baltimore, October 11, 1823."

"The craven" had some years before this founded the Delphians and had associated with him in this literary work some of the choicest spirits of the day. Jared Sparks was one of them. Another was Francis Scott Key whom we think of chiefly in connection with the attack on Fort McHenry, but who was in addition to this an author and a lawyer. One of his poems "Lord, with glowing heart I'd praise Thee" is a well-known hymn. Often he was welcomed at Tusculum where wit and good conversation always found an eager circle of listeners. Other poets visited the Club from time to time, such as Samuel Woodworth who wrote "The Old Oaken Bucket." Here too came John Howard Payne taking refuge in this square yellow house from the mob that threatened his life. Poor fellow! His career was a restless one. You remember that lovely square, a pale green emerald set in old silver, the Palais Royal in Paris? Here Payne lived when he wrote his famous song of "pleasures and palaces." I like to think that he found a homely welcome at Tusculum, for the occasion of

149

the mob was not the only time at which he was a visitor. Rembrandt Peale, the portrait painter, was a well-known frequenter of the Club, and so was John P. Kennedy, the friend of Peabody and of Washington Irving, to say nothing of Thackeray. Of the entire group, however, John Pendleton Kennedy is the figure most intimately connected with the life of Baltimore. In an old three story house, "very respectable," on Baltimore Street between Charles and Saint Paul, Kennedy was born in 1795. The "very respectable" house has long since vanished, but the whole neighborhood is still warm with recollections of this most brilliant Baltimorean. The house stood midway in the square, and here says the writer, "I was duly washed, petticoated and kissed." Finally at the mature age of six he was sent to a dame's school in Fayette Street. We shall see him later at Fort McHenry in the War of 1812; we shall meet him arm and arm with George Peabody; we shall see him also with a threadbare gentleman named Poe. But all in good time.

The Delphians were teeming with ideas, and they brought out a publication in 1818-1819 known as The Red Book. Turning over its pages at the Maryland Historical Library one finds himself in the world of the eighteenth century, the world of Steele and Addison, of the wits and the beaux. One envies the leisure of a day when lawyers and men of business had time— and taste—to write for such a Tatler. Hear this modest foreword:

"This little book comes before the public eye, the careless offspring of chance unsupported by patronage, and unadorned by the tinsel of name and fashion." And this is true, for the book itself is small with a thin paper cover, no longer red but rather ashes of roses. The type, however, is strong and admirable and is the work of J. Robinson, the printer who had his establishment at the corner of Market and Belvidere Streets.

Then the Red Book continues:

"The Red Book is old in the British chronicles, and even there exhibits the pageant of folly. It is still destined to be a satire upon human vanity. It possesses this advantage, that let the world slight it as it may, it will still be red—a greater favour surely an author could not wish." From this it will be seen that these brilliant minds were not above a pun; but such was the fashion of the day.

This passage gives a picture of Tusculum written by a Delphian himself, and when next you pass the Equitable think of these things.

"It (Tusculum) stands in a part of the town where it would require an Ariadne to find it. My principal front is upon an alley, and a gate intervenes between the door and the narrow pavement. I have no lordly pillars which sustain my outspreading roof. On either side of the large majestick door are two small rooms, one my study, the other my hall of audience. In the first are a confusion of plans, commentaries, pamphlets, scraps of the Red Book, strictures upon women, Montaigne, Cervantes, Sterne. In the second are the comforts of a neat parlour, with a shining mahogany table that has often trembled with the outflashes of champagne merriment and madeira meditation."

Such was Tusculum. Baltimore was a charming provincial town in those days, and the Red Book, like the De Coverley Papers, commented on the gay kaleidoscopic life of the community. Here is a bit, a description of a Baltimore house. Whether it calls up Sir Roger or Geoffrey Crayon, I leave it to you to decide.

"In one of the retired streets of this bustling city there stands a two-storied edifice of middling size which appears from an inscription on the rainspout to have been erected about the year 'seventy-nine. The chimney is of those ample dimensions which distinguished the days of hospitality and simplicity. In this sober edifice which seems, like a decayed gentleman, to frown darkly from every brick upon the spruce upstarts with which building companies have of late invaded its solitude, there lived a gentleman of retired habits."

Then follows a picture of this "sarcastick gentleman," a bachelor, "to be found more often over his books than over his bottle."

And here is a diary, not a literal one, perhaps, but what light it throws upon the days of the Red Book: "Met Mrs. Blank, and bowed myself into the shape of a Z. Called at the post office to mail a letter. Having my pocket full, I slipped in the wrong one—good joke—told it six times on the way home. Read Chesterfield until ten, and then to bed."

Constantly one finds references to the ladies. What attention they received in the days of their servitude; far more than at present. Perhaps it was bad psychology to display the knee. In those early days—if one may judge by the Red Book —men went into ecstasies over a mere petticoat ruffle. At least I concluded that the article referred to was a petticoat. It was all done so delicately that it was difficult to tell just which garment of the "fair" was intended. There are continual references to the ringlets, the roseate cheeks, the pearly teeth, to say nothing of this delightful picture: "the pert young tenant of a huge merino secure from impertinent glances under her bower-bearing bonnet." Another point of interest is the fact that these girls never walked. They tripped, they floated, they glided. In all ages women have had an immense news value. The bucks stood on the corner of Charles and Market to observe the passing of the "elegant females." "They stand" says the Red Book, "in bundles as if conscious of individual weakness." This, however, is not astonishing, for the paper adds tartly "Baltimore, like ancient Phæacia, is remarkable for its empty heads." Zounds, that is not one hundred per cent.! Indeed the Red Book had a sharp wit, for one finds sentiments of this kind "It is said abroad that Baltimore is famous for three things: its music, its churches, its military. Music is patronized by those who have the least ear; the best churches are built by the worst Christians, and in the military department it is observed that all logic is set at defiance in the making of majors out of minors."

This no doubt sounds puerile and trivial, but not more so than the comments of our own time will appear a hundred years from now. The men who wrote the Red Book were by no means negligible. Kennedy was the close friend of Washington Irving. Indeed Irving was so captivated by Kennedy's book, "Horseshoe Robinson," that he wrote: "I am so tickled with some parts that I could not forbear reading it to my cronies in Wall Street." What a picture that presents! Belles Lettres in Wall Street! Thackeray was so interested in Kennedy's work that several chapter in "The Virginians," it is said, were written by the Baltimorean. This, however, I am not able to verify with chapter and verse; I give you the tradition. Document it if you can.

All this neighborhood has changed now, but around the corner from the Delphians was the Reverdy Johnson house on the northwest corner of Fayette and Calvert Streets. It was a fine house with a marble portico, set back from the street and bounded by a wall as were many Baltimore mansions in those days. But when the bank riots occurred, mobs stoned the windows, and shattered the Greek portico. Not content with this, the crowds poured into the house itself, and carrying out books and furniture burned the entire contents of the old mansion in Monument Square. Later on, the house was restored and occupied by the Chesapeake Club. On Fayette Street, just east of the Monument, was the Maryland Club. It had its home in the house of Doctor Alexander. This mansion, too, was surrounded by a small lawn re-enforced by a wall. Here there were shady trees—sycamores, no doubt, and in their tranquil shadows the members used to sit smoking very choice havanas. So the old order changes; one does not easily associate havanas and shade trees with Monument Square.

We must retrace our steps in Fayette Street now, and turn our faces toward Old Town. But before we go, there is a church here with a unique history. If you look about you, only one church will be found—Zion, on the north side of the Plaza, with the charming churchyard and the interesting cloisters. Today the south side of the Plaza shows no sign of a church, but in the past where the Rivoli Moving Picture house now is located was the old Church of the Messiah. In 1835 the cornerstone was laid, and the new building was a source of just pride. It was a long, low church built in classic style with a row of six noble columns across the front. It soon became the center of a vigorous spiritual life; and, faith, it was needed! It is said that one could "stand on the steps and throw an apple into nine saloons." This is a problem in ballistics which I shall not attempt to solve. Be that as it may, the church played a large part in the life of the town. In 1876 a young priest named Peregrine Wroth was called to be rector, and for fifty-one years he served in that office. During that time there were countless ups and downs. The great fire of 1904 stood out as a land mark in the parish history. When the flames drew nearer and nearer the rector and a few parishioners said the Creed and the Litany and then awaited the destruction of the church that they loved so well. In 1920 a new Messiah was built in Hamilton, and in 1927 the old rector died. Today he lies buried in the chancel of the church. Rest eternal grant him, O Lord. There are still those who see him as they go about the familiar streets around the City Hall, and there are many who remember him with love and veneration.

While we are in this part of town, we must recall that here, where the Plaza lies open to the sun, was born one of Baltimore's most famous citizens—James Gibbons. In a little sloping-roofed house on the west side of Gay street a short distance north of Fayette the future Cardinal was born on July 23, 1834. His father and mother, Thomas and Bridget Gibbons, had but recently come from Ireland, and here they had settled in a small, comfortable house in the heart of the town. It was a very different Baltimore from that town which the Cardinal knew so well in later years. That Baltimore was the home of the clipper ships, and Thomas Gibbons, noted for his honesty, soon became a clerk in an important house. It was the elder Gibbons' place to see that the captains were provided with adequate funds for their out-going voyages. It seems curious to think of a man as modern as Cardinal Gibbons being a link with the eighteenth century, as his recent biographer suggests, but so it is. Let us gather up the threads. It will make the Baltimore of that day more vivid.

The town was then the refuge for San Domingans fleeing from the political disorders of their native land. The dark swarthy faces mingled with those of the young bloods, for the First Gentleman in Europe was still to be reckoned with, although the virtuous Victoria had been on the throne for three years. Many were the Beau Brummels even in the streets of this provincial town. The ladies still languished over "The Beauties of Moore" and "The Keepsake." Not that these delicate females appeared in the rude marts of trade. I mention them solely that you may see that the Byronic lingers with us. It was the day particularly of solid merchants, men of weight in the community. For them, no Byronic curls, no poetic collars. The men who passed Thomas Gibbons' house wore sober grey or black, with stocks and heavy seals dangling at their fobs. To and fro about their business went such men as Johns Hopkins who had a good, prosperous grocery business on Lombard Street near Light. On German Street George Peabody thriftily sold drygoods. Punctually at eight o'clock Enoch Pratt began his business for the day. He dealt an iron. Roger Brooke Taney, Chief Justice of the United States, lived in an elegant house as we have seen. And in the very year in which James Gibbons was born, Betsy Patterson, armed with twelve new bonnets to relieve her tedium, returned to her father's house on South Street. At the theatre Booth the elder was drawing great crowds; Poe was trying desperately to make a living. Into this rich and varied world James Gibbons was born. The first time that he ever entered the Cathedral was for his baptism, and little did his parents dream that this humble child would one day be Prince of the Church.

After his father's death, the family returned to Ireland, and it was not until many years had passed that he found himself a student at Saint Charles College. In the old country he had often heard his mother talk about Gay Street and the Cathedral. He felt that they were familiar ground even though he had been but three years old when the family left America.

It was the foresight of Bridget Gibbons that led them again to the new world; she was keen enough to see the advantages of life in a young country, and thither she returned. But not to Baltimore. The Gibbonses settled in New Orleans; but after many hardships and struggles young Gibbons decided to study for the priesthood. Then Baltimore became his natural objective, and after a long and arduous journey he reached the town. Just beyond the city, in rolling hill country was Saint Charles College under the direction of the Sulpician Fathers.

CATHEDRAL OF ARCHDIOCESE OF BALTIMORE

Here James Gibbons enrolled as a student, and because of this connection throughout his life he was bound to this Order by the ties of warmest friendship. In Paris, the Church of Saint Sulpice was the Cardinal's favorite Church. There are few things more fascinating than unravelling the threads that bind together remote places. That grey severe church on the Left Bank was the Cardinal's spiritual home. Other famous men have loved Saint Sulpice. Victor Hugo, Anatole France (if he loved any) and Huysman. But none surely was nobler or more devoted than James Gibbons. Long after this, in 1858 he received the tonsure in the Cathedral, but that is another story, and we shall come to it in time.

Long ago when the Falls ran through the town one came to the Gay Street Bridge which made a sharp turn at this point. Here Jones had his house; and in early days this street facing the stream was called Jones Street. At present the neighborhood presents a down-at-the heels air, but there was a time when Front Street was the most fashionable part of the town. The houses even yet in many cases have preserved their fine doorways. Here and there one sees a delicate fanlight, but the old days of elegance and fashion have long since departed. Near Fayette Street was the famous Front Street theatre. In appearance it was more like a Greek temple in bad taste than anything else imaginable. But in spite of its looks, its serious demeanour, it had a place of importance in Baltimore life. It was built in 1829, a hundred years after the birth of the town itself, and to the end it held its position in the community. It was here that the Swedish Nightingale appeared.

In December of 1850 the town went wild in anticipation of Jenny Lind, the Swedish Nightingale, as the fashion of the day dubbed her. The newspapers announced her coming thus:

BALTIMORE

"In another column will be found the advertisement containing the program of the first concert of the celebrated songstress. She will sing five compositions in the course of the evening, the Bird Song and the Echo Song being in the number."

Every one turned expectantly to the other column, and there they read: "Miss Jenny Lind will give her Thirty-ninth Grand Concert in America, and her first in Baltimore at the Front Street Theatre Monday evening, December the 9, 1850.

Then followed the program and the stern warning:

"Doors open at Six. Concert will commence at eight. No checks will be issued. The choice seats will be disposed of at an auction at the theatre on December seventh."

Thrills of excitement ran through the town. Philadelphia, the old and staid, already had experienced a mild hysteria over the "Fair Swede." What would you expect of Gascons like the Baltimoreans? The Nightingale stayed at Barnum's Hotel, and half the young men in town—a most reasonable estimate—spent their time lolling in Monument Square, vainly trying to get a glimpse of the prima donna. On Sunday the polite townspeople sent a carriage to ask if Miss Lind would like to attend church. She declined, but P. T. Barnum, her manager, and a lady who was in the party decided that they would go. Loud shouts of joy hailed the unknown lady's appearance, and the crowds happy in the thought that they had at last seen their idol went off to their houses of worship with satisfaction and thanksgiving.

But oh, the great night itself! Front Street is a narrow thoroughfare, and that night there was a terrific traffic jam. As the press stated: "The éclat surpassed the most sanguine expectations. The house presented a brilliant appearance. Every seat was taken, and as the audience was largely of ladies their fashionable attire added much to the splendour of the

158

scene. On Miss Lind's first appearance she was received as she advanced rapidly and gracefully down the stage with a perfect storm of applause." The whole house rose, and her modest air increased the general admiration. (It might have been Lindbergh.) Rapturous tokens of appreciation compelled her to repeat two of her numbers."

And how was she dressed? Well, at the first concert, she "wore a white satin dress with three flounces extending the whole length of the skirt." I see a man's hand in this description. She was a lovely creature, and the flowers fell in "such profusion that her mirth was excited." The American says "the musical furor was intense." The young men who sat out in the Square all night smoked long "segars" to keep themselves warm. The Independent Greys serenaded her at the City Hotel. But at her second concert, "habited in pink satin," she bowled them over completely by singing "Home Sweet Home." Even in this hard-boiled age there is something appealing in John Howard Payne's song. Perhaps some of the sad and lovely spirit of the Palais Royal is in that song. However that may be, when Jenny Lind sang, the Baltimoreans of the fifties wept unashamedly. The third concert, too, was a triumph, for Jenny wore her yellow satin, and the seats sold for six dollars.

It was in Front Street Theatre that Abraham Lincoln was nominated for his second term of office. Baltimore was rent into two camps, the Federalists and the "Seceshes." Friend refused to speak to friend; brother to brother. "Iron clad oaths" were exacted of all who claimed the rights of citizenship. Children appearing on the street in red and white checked ginghams were liable to arrest. Indeed it was dangerous to wear even red and white buttons on a pinafore. Some of these disloyal dressmakers' findings are in the Maryland Historical Library at present. Such was propaganda in the sixties. The Maryland Club which had moved from Fayette Street to the corner of Franklin and Cathedral where now the Y. M. C. A. stands was considered the "focus of treason" in the city. The exact range of the building had been ascertained, and boasts were commonly made that the first shell from Fort Federal Hill would be dropped into the "Latin Quarter" as the Club was called.

But to return to our muttons in Front Street. Baltimore was near Washington, and it seemed wise to hold the convention as near the Capital as possible; Front Street, quiet, dignified, had an air of Georgian retirement and seclusion. But this, alas, was destined to be rudely shattered. All of Federal Baltimore poured into the Theatre, and Washingtonians found their way thither. The decorations on this occasion were most extraordinary. There was "a drugget of green," and pink and blue muslin was purchased at a shop in Baltimore Street. This sounds more like a Delsarte tableau than a war Convention. Delightful music was "discoursed" by the band from Fort McHenry. Then came speeches and more speeches. The wildest excitement was evoked by Lincoln's name. Shout after shout arose; the hall milled with frenzied enthusiasm. At length the Star-Spangled Banner quieted them; I suppose they tried to sing it. However that may be, Mr. Lincoln was unanimously chosen as the Republican candidate. It is strange to think that in that very street had played John Wilkes Booth, the man destined to put an end to the life of the great Civil War President.

Within a short range of Front Street there lived in the middle of the last century two of the greatest artists that this country has produced—Edwin Booth and Edgar Allan Poe. Nor is Edwin Booth the only great actor familiar to these parts. Junius Brutus Booth, the elder Booth as he is often called, walked these streets too, and was a great figure in the theatrical life of Baltimore, and, indeed, of the nation. He came to America with his young wife and a piebald pony in the year 1821. In Richmond he was well received, but he pushed on to Baltimore, and reached the town during one of those epidemics of yellow fever that scourged the city in early days. Consequently he bought a farm nearby, and established himself there. Peacock, the little pony, was the means of transportation between Belair and Baltimore. The summer was spent in the country, but in the winter the family moved into town and settled either in High Street or in Exeter Street.

In 1833 Edwin, the seventh child was born, not in Baltimore, but in Belair. It is said that on the night of his birth showers of stars fell from the sky. This has a true Shakespearean touch, and I believe it implicitly. Booth certainly was the brightest glory of the American stage, and if the stars did not fall they should have done so; it was highly appropriate. The old neighbors on High Street—just beyond Front, and now, a dingy, filthy place—remember Edwin as a dark-eyed fiery boy, riding down High Street on Peacock, and greeted by a throng of his friends who came tumbling out of the prim houses as soon as they heard the clatter of the piebald's little hoofs.

But we must not forget that other brother named for the English agitator, John Wilkes. He, too, like all the Booth boys, was a handsome lad, but wild and intractable. Once he bet some neighbors that he would go sleighing in July, and to make his bet good, he hitched a pair of horses in a sleigh and drove them to Belair. But more of John Wilkes later.

In 1829 Old Town was the haunt of another famous artist. In Milk Street, now called East Street, was the home of Mrs. Maria Clemm, Poe's aunt. On his first visit to Baltimore he very naturally lived at her house, and the warmth of her welcome did much to offset the hardships of a struggling poet. It was a tiny two-story dwelling, crowded with various relatives, and offering as we should think scant opportunity for any literary work. Old Mrs. David Poe lived there, and Henry Leonard Poe, Edgar's tubercular brother. Then there were Mrs. Clemm, and Henry Clemm, and most interesting of all little Virginia Clemm, who afterwards became the poet's wife. The child was but seven years old at this time, and probably was the only gay and happy person in the household. Edgar Allan shared the back attic with his tubercular brother, and in this small, shabby room he tinkered away on his stories and poems. It is pitiful to think of him in these miserable surroundings. But who can tell what dreams of strangeness and beauty gave him consolation. Of one thing we may be sure: no one who saw Poe trudging through Old Town in his well-worn clothes and shabby boots ever thought that a great genius was passing down the street.

While he was living at his aunt's house he was trying desperately to get a publisher for *Al Aaraaf*. Nowadays people stand agape before the first edition when it is exhibited at the Peabody; then it seemed unlikely that it would ever see the light of day. Poe took it to William Wirt, and poor Mr. Wirt, puzzled yet kindly, said: "It will, I know, please the modern reader, but I doubt whether it will take hold of old-fashioned readers like myself." But this did not daunt Poe. Day after day he haunted the offices of The Federal Gazette and the Baltimore Daily Advertiser. The dark, shabby gentleman with a bundle of manuscript became a familiar sight. At length, however, Hatch and Dunning agreed to publish it. Poe went back to Milk Street full of renewed hope and enthusiasm. Let us hope that there was a jolly supper party that night. For it would be quite wrong to think that all of Poe's time was spent in melancholy. It was not. In Aisquith Street lived the Herrings, great friends of his, and on Caroline Street there was a family of cousins. In both of these houses he was the center of an admiring group of young ladies—charming young ladies with languishing glances and ringlets, young ladies who "bridled" and flushed delicately. They delighted in their queer picturesque cousin, and Poe like all young men enjoyed admiration. Heaven knows he got little enough of it!

It was a few years later that Poe won a prize for the best short story in a competition held by the *Baltimore Saturday Visitor.* In John H. B. Latrobe's memoirs a most interesting account of Poe is presented. John P. Kennedy, a Doctor Miller and Latrobe were chosen as the committee of awards, and the pile of manuscripts was sent to Latrobe's house on Mulberry Street. Here the three gentlemen met around a table richly set out with old wine and good cigars. Among the varied contributions there was a small quarto book with the manuscript printed in Roman characters. This looked so promising that the three, according to Latrobe, filled their glasses, lit their cigars and started in to read. The story was called "The Ms. Found in a Bottle." Unanimously the prize of fifty dollars was awarded to Poe. A short time after this the writer was asked to come to Mr. Latrobe's office, and he appeared, a "small erect man dressed entirely in black, with 'gentleman' written all over him."

Through this competition John P. Kennedy became interested in the poet, and it was he who urged Poe to contribute to the *Southern Literary Messenger.* Nor did his kindness stop there. On one occasion it is said he invited Poe to dinner, but so extreme was the poet's poverty that he had not the proper clothes. With exquisite tact Mr. Kennedy saw that his guest was outfitted, and later pressed upon him the use of a saddle horse, saying that the beast really needed the exercise. With much delight Poe accepted this graceful offer. I can see him now in my mind's eye riding through Monument Square, and perhaps turning east toward the home of his young cousins. He was perhaps a little vain of his seat. Only a gentleman like Kennedy could do such a gracious deed; only a gentleman like Poe could accept it.

On the Joppa Road near Exeter street stood the first Baltimore post-office. It was nothing but a rude shack, one story, with a small dormer window. It is startling to hear of the Joppa Road so far from base, but it is a fact that this road did run in a diagonal across what is now the eastern section of the town. The post-office was on Front Street, approximately, and was later torn down to make way for the necessary improvements of the Western Maryland Railroad terminal. Tradition says that this building was used as a post-office as early as 1751. Other authorities claim that mail was sent from a government office at Baltimore and South Streets. Before 1713 letters were sent by "private hand." After that date the sheriff of one county was ordered to pass them on to the sheriff of the next county. Let us hope that the sheriffs were not absent-minded men.

Around the corner from East Street is the old Belair Market, and from this center a street branches off called, from Robert Oliver's estate, Greenmount Avenue, later running into the York Road. Coming down to meet Greenmount Avenue is Gay Street, or as it is called beyond the city, the Belair Road. Along the alignment of these busy city streets ran the leisurely country roads of a few years ago. Here came the farmers with heavily loaded conestoga wagons. Even now on Greenmount Avenue not far from the market there is an ancient hay scales still in use. Down the Belair Road trotted Peacock on many a fine summer morning in the thirties, bringing Booth the elder to town. The city of Poe and Booth, however, has vanished. Only a few landmarks here and there link

BALTIMORE'S FIRST POST-OFFICE, FRONT STREET

the modern town with the past. An old print at the Maryland Historical Library makes Baltimore appear strangely romantic, and Mr. Hervey Allen says it suggested "Lalla Rookh." As we ride along with Mr. Booth we can judge for ourselves of the Lalla Rookhish landscape. There is much in the comparison.

The road in the old days was thickly set with locust trees, no doubt, for even in my youth the neighborhood of the Belair road was heavy in the spring with the warm delicious fragrance. Then as one drew near town he saw on the Monument the statue of Washington, stretching out his hand in a gesture of farewell. Only recently—in 1829—had the statue been put in position. Behind the Monument, a little to the south, rose the exotic minarets of the Cathedral, designed so nobly by Latrobe. In the clear smokeless air these two landmarks stood out boldly. Below the hill, where Mr. Howard's great estate Belvedere spread far and wide, lay the town itself, stretching down to the harbour where the clipper ships rode in from the seven seas. Trot, little Peacock! You have shown us a pretty sight this morning. No wonder Booth felt the death of this horse so keenly that he insisted on reading the burial service over him.

At Forrest and Hillen Streets there stands an ancient hostelry which for more than a hundred years has been a tavern. The Farmer's and Carter's Inn looks out upon a huge square courtyard cobbled with rough stone. Long ago conestogas used to rumble in over the stones, and while the horses were rested the drivers refreshed themselves with stout drinks. Motor trucks and Fords still carry on the tradition, but I will not vouch for the stout drinks. On market days, however, the inn rings with hearty voices, and the inn-yard is used not only as a bivouac for motors, but as a market for calves. Here on certain days the calves are put up for sale, and in the feed store they are weighed, protesting no doubt, but managed with a firm hand. The yard is also a mart for chickens as numerous feathers testify. As far as I know this is the last remnant of those old inns for which Trollope praised the town. He said they were like a bit of old London, and so they were. Even this has a faint but distinct Pickwickian flavour.

The market itself will repay you, if you are fond of markets. It is a rougher, ruder Lexington, and all the more picturesque for that.

QUAKER GREY AND CLIPPER SHIPS

CHAPTER X

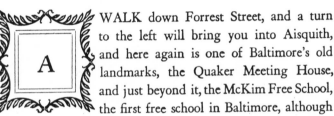 WALK down Forrest Street, and a turn to the left will bring you into Aisquith, and here again is one of Baltimore's old landmarks, the Quaker Meeting House, and just beyond it, the McKim Free School, the first free school in Baltimore, although Saint Patrick's, too, claims this honor. The earliest knowledge that we have of the Society of Friends in Maryland dates from about 1658. After a tedious voyage across the Atlantic by way of Barbadoes and Jamaica, George Fox and his companions reached the Province of Maryland. Already many Friends had settled here because of the religious toleration granted to all Christians. Of late this statement has been so much in dispute that it might be well here to comment somewhat upon the subject. This is the testimony of the son of Cecilius Calvert, explaining why it would be dangerous to scrutinize the religious complexion of the colonists in Maryland:

167

BALTIMORE

"The Reason why such scrutinyes would be thus Dangerous, is that vizt, That at the first planteing of this Provynce, my father, Albeit he had an absolute Liberty given him and his heirs to carry thither any Persons out of any of the Dominions that belonged to the Crowne of England who should be found wylling to goe thither, yett when he came to make use of this Liberty, He found very few who were inclyned to goe and seat themselves in those parts. But such as for some Reason or other could not live with ease in other parts. And of these a great parte, were such as could not conforme in all particulars to the severall Lawes of England relateing to Religion; many they were of this sort of People who declared their Wyllingness to goe and plant themselves in this Provynce, soe as they might have a Generall Toleraccon settled there by a Lawe by which all of all sorts who professed Christianity in Generall, might be at Liberty to worship God in such manner as was most agreeable with their respective Judgement and Consciences, without being subject to any penaltyes whatsoever, for their soe doeing, Provyded the Civill peace were preserved. And that for the securing the civill peace and preventing all heats Feuds, which were generally observed to happen, amongst such as differ in opynions upon Occasion of Reproachful Nicknames and reflecting upon each other's Opynions, it might by the same Lawe be made Penall to give any offense of that kynde. There were the condicions proposed by such as were willing to goe and be the first planters of this Provynce, and without the complying with these conditions, in all probability, This Provynce had never beene planted. To these condicions, my ffather agreed, and accordingly soon after the first planteing of this Provynce, these conditions by the unanimous consent of all who were concerned, were passed into a Lawe and the inhabitants of this Provynce have found such effects from this Lawe and from the strict observance of it as well in relation to their Quiett as in Religion to the farther peopleing of this Provynce That they looke on it, as that whereon alone depends the perservation of their Peace Their Propertyes and their Libertyes. This beinge the true state of the case of this Provynce it is easy to Judge what consequencyes might ensue, upon any scrutinyes which should be made in order to the satisfyeing theis particular Inquiryes."

168

QUAKER GREY AND CLIPPER SHIPS

I hope you have found a clean and comfortable spot where you may sit and ponder over these words of the Third Lord Baltimore so admirably used by De Courcy W. Thom in a paper before the Maryland Historical Society. He then goes on to say:

"Cecilius Calvert, Second Lord Baltimore, and the first Colonists of Maryland thus first founded in what is now the United States, indeed, first founded in the English-speaking world, absolute freedom of religious worship in any Christian form. That is the first and unaccompanied foundational service rendered by Maryland to our American system of government. I make that assertion with full confidence, for, when it fell to me to write the following inscription for the base of the Cecilius Calvert statue which is standing upon the western steps of the Baltimore City Court House I submitted that inscription to such historians as William Hand Browne, Woodrow Wilson and others. They unanimously affirmed it. There, then, is inscribed the proud pronouncement:—

" 'Cecilius Calvert Baron Baltimore of Baltimore in the Kingdom of Ireland Absolute Lord and Proprietary of the Provinces of Maryland and Avalon in America who on November 13, 1663, *with the co-operation and assent of the first Colonists,* proclaimed in England and on March 25th, 1634, established in the Palatinate of Maryland for the first time in the English speaking world Freedom of Religious Worship according to any Christian Form and separation of Church and State.' "

If I were writing a purely polemical article there would be much more to be said on this subject, but the facts remain that "religious toleration was an accomplished fact in early Maryland. . . . —It is equally certain that after the Protestant Revolution and the establishment of the Church religious toleration departed the land for a century."

Now that is nicely settled, and we can return to the Quakers. At first they had no fixed organization, but on the shores of West River they planned to hold a General Meeting. George

BALTIMORE

Fox reached Maryland just in time for the Convocation, and how keen was the delight of his old friends to see this devout and holy man. Fox was the son of a weaver. He had had an exciting life in his witness for theTruth. Like Saint Paul he had known perils by sea and perils among false brethren, but nothing could quench his valiant spirit. Whenever he heard that town officials were furbishing up the stocks in anticipation of his visit, he made haste to go to that town. Such was the calibre of the man who now gathered with his followers at West River, and founded in 1672 the Baltimore Yearly Meeting.

Many Colonial officials who had heard of Fox in the old country mounted their horses and rode down into Anne Arundel County to see what manner of man this was. Lady Baltimore and Lord Baltimore attended some of the meetings of the Friends. Her Ladyship was somewhat sceptical, she said, of the ability of a mechanic to preach. In truth she was right curious to see if it be possible. This was the beginning of Friends meetings in Maryland, but it is not until 1681 that records of meetings in private homes are to be found.

In 1713 a meeting house was built at Friendship, now part of Friends Cemetery on the Harford Road. An obscure little street in North Baltimore still bears the name, and the cemetery itself lies just above North Avenue opposite Clifton Park. In the building of this place of worship the Indians took part. Together with the men of peace they cut the logs and dressed them. At noon they sat under the shady trees and rested from their labours. This was typical of Friendly relations with the Indians. Indeed no sooner had Fox arrived than an "Indian Emperor" invited him to conference in a nearby Indian village. To this opportunity Fox readily agreed, and he gave the Indians a discourse on the Inner Light. What a picture this makes—the sunlight sifting through the leaves, the dark immobile faces of the Indians, and Fox himself aglow with that Inner Light which he so earnestly preached.

As time went on the Friends increased in number, and land was purchased for a meeting house at the corner of Aisquith and Fayette. In short time a square substantial building of grey stone was erected here, set in the midst of a graveyard, and surrounded by fine old trees. A high stone wall kept out intruders. Every First Day from 1781 on through the years sedate Quaker maidens and solid business men entered the doorway and took their place in the old House, testifying as the Spirit gave them utterance. It has been many years now since the Meeting House was used for worship. The neighborhood has changed; the Quaker maidens have grown up and died, and a new generation has succeeded them. Today the grounds have been made into a playground for the children in the neighborhood.

"New occasions teach new duties" and always the Society of Friends has been foremost in social advancement. Always they have been the champions of minorities. In this Meeting house at the close of the Revolution they gave their testimony that slavery was wrong, and the word went forth—"no slave holding by Friends." They were mocked, abused, threatened, but they stood firm, joyfully setting their feet in the stocks like their inspired founder.

All who know the Friends know what a tremendous event Yearly Meeting is. The early records of the town recall the good times that prevailed at Yearly Meeting, even among so austere a people as the Quakers. The crowds of men and women dressed in sober grey were so great that tents were erected on the green meadows south of Baltimore and Lloyd Streets. All hoped fervently for clear warm weather, but rain at this time was proverbial.

"Everybody expects rainy weather because the Quakers are coming to town. Quakers are like the clouds; they bring rain when they collect."

In spite, however, of this tendency, in dry weather or in wet, the shy Quaker maidens and the more worldly Quaker youths cast sheep's eyes at each other, and the elders gravely considered various "concerns." But those were stern days, and woe betide those who married out of Meeting. Even more serious was a hankering for the military. So rigid were they, indeed, that during the Revolution a young Friend was read out of Meeting because he looked at the muster. That is he paused on the green village to watch the soldiers drilling, and looked perhaps with a longing eye at the tactics there displayed. At any rate such conduct was not proper for a child of peace, so out he went.

It may well be that you have not the faintest interest in playgrounds—public playgrounds. If that is the case, skip the first part of this chapter. If on the other hand you do enjoy them, walk a few squares east on Baltimore Street until you come to Spring, and then turn south one block. The neighborhood itself interests me. I love the remnants of old Baltimore, the struggling brick and white stone steps—very struggling—the air of a fine old section gone to seed. After this detour you find yourself in a wide square—City Spring Square. Here long ago was one of the chief water supplies for the townspeople. There were several of these fountains; one on Calvert and Saratoga Streets, and one on Marsh Market Space. This was of the same family. Originally the Square was a shady, pleasant place frequented by the residents, a place of gossip, a place of true refreshment. Then there was a change in the water supply; more advanced methods came into use; the old neighbors moved away. And who came in to take their places? Twenty years ago this community was the ghetto of the town. Old Russian Jews with long beards sat at the doorways conversing in grave tones with their friends. The married women wore the hideous wigs that marked them as Hebrew wives. The children—well, the children in their new-found freedom ran wild. The streets teemed with chubby, dirty babies, rough boys rudely jostled strangers who ventured here; the girls were dirty, lovely, pert.

Into all this came the playground directed and supervised by Mary B. Steuart, one of the pioneer playground workers in this country. She put a young woman in charge. The older people watched with deep suspicion, but the children hailed her with ecstasy. And until you know Jewish ecstasy you have no conception of emotion. When she stepped from the street cars—the funny old-fashioned cars of that day, "summer car" we called them, she was met by an enthusiastic throng who would have carried "teacher" on their shoulders had she permitted it.

The flowers gradually vanished, one must admit, but after all boys and girls are more important. And the comic and tragic things that happened!

After a time a flag pole was erected, so that the flag salute could be given in proper style. To brace the large pole a trench had to be dug for supports. The workmen proceeded with their work, and the director went on quietly with the games and "occupations." All at once she became aware of dark faces watching her over the iron fence that marked the bounds of the ground. They muttered and glanced meaningly at the trench now nearing completion. It was long and deep; two trenches there were, indeed, at right angles to each other. The teacher went on with her games, but at last the children seemed to feel some curious influence. They shrugged their shoulders at their protesting parents, and spoke rapidly in Yiddish. The crowd at the railings grew denser. Now the di-

173

rector knew that something was seriously wrong. In vain she questioned. No use—only sullen shrugs. One or two mothers swooped down upon their children and bore them off willy-nilly. Finally the rabbi appeared. He spoke a few words to the excited groups. Then he came into the enclosure and pointed to the trench.

"They fear it," he said; "it is in the shape of a cross. They fear that you mean to kill their children and bury them in that trench." Then, deprecatingly, "They have seen things like that in Russia."

Together the rabbi and "Miss Teacher" calmed their fears, but not until the iron supports that braced the pole were in position, and the cross-shaped furrows covered were peace and tranquillity restored to City Springs.

In the following years fear was banished. A new attitude made itself felt in the community. The boys and girls learned how to use the new freedom, but at the same time they held fast to the best that their own religion and race had to give them.

On those glorious days when picnics were held at the Park —"Drood Hill," of course—a small boy was offered a sandwich. He was only six, but he inspected it carefully. It was ham. Politely he handed it back to the Teacher, and said, with an air of pride, "If I ate that my mother would give me hell!" Obedient child, mindful of the Law!

It is but a step from here to Broadway. As you turn south you will see a fine church on the northeast corner of Broadway and Bank Street. This is Saint Patrick's, where Cardinal Gibbons when he was simply a priest served his first pastorate. Father Dolan was then in charge. He was called the Apostle of the Point, "a sturdy shepherd with a wild flock," as Wells describes him. The flock consisted of longshoremen, sailors, wastrels from all the ports of the world, men of every sort and condition. If you would like to go into the church for a moment do so, but after a brief prayer plunge into the network of old streets that spreads higgledy-piggledy in all directions west of Broadway.

In Bank Street around the corner from Broadway there was once a famous tavern known as White Hall. Originally it was a small brick building occupied by the Sisters of Saint Patrick's parish. Later it became a public house, and the center of neighborhood jollifications. It was set comfortably in a shady yard bounded by Bank, Gough, Broadway and Bethel Streets. Under the trees in warm weather benches and tables were set out, and here the patrons refreshed themselves with cooling drinks. In the winter there were broad hearths and roaring fires in-doors, for in those days winter was a serious business. When Baltimore was at the height of the Clipper trade it was the custom to meet at White Hall, and drink to the success of the *Fleet Greyhound* or the *Bonny Flora* or whatever the ship might be. What's in a name? A drink's a drink! Often the builders would order a bounteous feast for their men, and then was set forth such fare that it makes me hungry to write—terrapin, turkeys, oysters, old ham and potations of rare order. The favorite drink for which White Hall was renowned was its sangarees. Much mystery surrounded the making of these mighty brews, and no one was permitted to watch the barkeeper at his concoctions.

Not far from this house was another relic of the past. I think that it stood until my own time—it sounds so familiar. It was an old hipped-roofed house built partly of logs, and later a frame was added. This farm house was built when the present Bond Street was a country road, and in 1778 it was sold to a man named Zeigler. Along the Bond Street of that day grew chinquapin bushes, and pleasant fields spread out to the blue water to the south. On clear days there came the sharp ring of the hammers from the ship yards down on the Point. In 1781 Lafayette passed along this road, and stopped at Zeigler's for milk for his soldiers. Yes, but they mixed the milk with wine and sugar, and made what we used to call milk-shakes. Where now the street cars clang and where brick and concrete hide the good red earth, these Frenchmen encamped, and enjoyed no doubt the pleasant Maryland ways. Zeigler planted beside his house a young box tree which later grew to such enormous proportions that it was given to Patterson Park when the old garden was cut up into city lots.

It was in Bond Street that the *Baltimore American and Advertiser* was first published. It came out regularly every day except on the 12th of September when the entire town went out to fight. It is great fun to read these old newspapers, and to meditate on the similarity of human nature in all ages. Note:

"Yesterday the bells of Old Christ Church were removed to the new church. A friend at our elbow says no need to add bells to a church which already posesses so enviable a share of female beauty. He said nothing of the tongues." Same old jokes in 1830! And what about hit-and-run drivers:

"A small colored boy was run over by a doctor in a gig. As the boy received no injury, the doctor passed on without stopping."

All through this section the houses are small, of red brick, with the white doorsteps so familiar in other parts of the town. The streets are dirty and there is a frankly shabby air about the place, but I love its dilapidation—its "nigritude," as Lamb would say. At least there is character here. Each street has its own flavour and savour. The street names are a delight, rich in history. For instance there is Eden Street named for the last proprietory governor of Maryland. Poor gentleman! His lot fell in stony places, but in spite of his loyalty to George III he was greatly beloved by the people of the state. And he had his difficulties. Shortly after the outbreak of hostilities a dinner was held at Barrister Carroll's house, and no sooner were the guests seated than Governor Eden said "It is understood in England that the Congress is about to form an alliance with France." For a moment there was silence. Then Thomas Johnson, who was soon to be Governor of Maryland himself, replied: "Governor, we will answer your question provided that you will answer one for us." To this Eden offered no objection, and Johnson said, "Well, sir, we will candidly admit that overtures have been made to France. But, sir, we understand that the king, your master, is about subsidizing a large body of Hessians to come over and cut our throats." The truth of this Eden was bound to admit. Then exclaimed Johnson:

"The first Hessian soldier that puts his foot on American soil absolves me from all allegiance to Great Britain."

And Chase cried out vehemently:

"By God, I am for declaring ourselves independent!"

The dinner proceeded, but poor Eden dropped his knife and fork and did not eat another mouthful.

The Whig Club in Baltimore "loudly proclaimed the absolute necessity of seizing and securing the person of the Governor as a plan of public safety." After a stormy period the proprietary authority in Maryland ceased in June, 1776, and Eden departed for England "conducted to the barge with every mark of respect due to the elevated station he had so worthily filled." And so dearly did Eden love Annapolis that after the War he returned and died there in 1784.

This is a long story for a humble street, but you may find the thoroughfare enriched by these recollections. Parallel with Eden, most appropriately, is Caroline, named, possibly, for his lady, the youngest daughter of Charles, Fifth Lord Baltimore. Not far away are Albemarle, Exeter, and Plowman, the last named for "Mr. Jonathan Plowman an English merchant newly arrived" who bought ground at Baltimore and High and built himself a fine mansion. On Fells Point a cluster of streets bear these English names, notably Shakespeare, Philpot, and Thames. But Fells Point needs some explanation.

In 1726 a man named Edward Fell had settled east of Jones Falls, then a clear pellucid stream. He had solitude for his companion, for you remember that Baltimore was not laid out until 1729, and even east of the Falls there were few neighbors. However in 1730 William Fell bought a tract of land known as Copus Harbour, and built himself a house on the line of the present Lancaster Street. Shortly after, other members of the family settled nearby, and a tiny community known as Fells Point sprang up. These people were of thrifty Quaker stock, and before long they turned their attention to shipbuilding, and this business for years gave the character and tone to this part of the town. Even today the streets have the charm of the sea. There is the background of water and the harbour. Go out upon the Recreation Pier and look about you. Municipal docks are not beautiful, but there is always the shifting light and shadow upon the water, and the tang of salt air and the wheeling gulls. Or, better still, take the Locust Point Ferry that leaves every few moments from the foot of Broadway. This will give you a fine view of the harbour. But if you take the ferry, do return at once, for I have more to tell you about these streets.

Old Town, as we have seen, was laid out in 1732 on "the land where Edward Fell kept a store," but this was some distance north of Fells Point, and most of the family preferred to be nearer the harbour. Besides, Old Town was very low, situated as it was across Harrison's Marsh, and therefore in

1763 Fells Point became a thriving residential section, built on what had been the old Fell estate. On Shakespeare Street there are rows of old fashioned houses flush with the street, houses of red brick with sloping roofs and quaint chimneys, from which in the old days little sweeps would peer forth like Jack in the Bush. Now Fleet and Lancaster Streets are shabby and out at elbows, but it was not always thus. Stout burghers stepped along with an air of proprietorship; matrons set out for the Market House built on ground given by Edward Fell; and lads in tight jackets and frilled collars for all the world like David Copperfield trundled their hoops along the shady walks.

In a small neglected plot of ground on Shakespeare Street lie the bodies of William Fell and his wife and son, Edward. Nothing marks their resting place but a ring of oyster shells, not indeed an unsuitable marker for a family so intimately connected with the history of the state. The Edward Fell who lies here beside his father married his cousin, and for that heinous act he was put out of meeting. Walk about in these streets and enjoy them. Saturday afternoon is a splendid time for a visit. The entire community is out in full force. The staid Georgian Market House is a sister to those at Cross and Hollins. The flaring lamps throw strange lights and shadows upon the dark foreign faces of Edward Fell's modern neighbors. The fruit, orange and red and tawny-brown, glows like the colours in a Picasso painting. There are ripe and varied smells for the delight of the nostrils. Over all, and penetrating all, is a mist from the Bay, and in the dusk comes the hoot of a tug nuzzling through the twilight. Always there are the thoughts of ships. Men and women are still living who can remember when the harbour was fresh and clean, when ships "that lift tall spires of canvas" came crowding up the river. But this is a story in itself, and it must be told.

BALTIMORE

From the very first Baltimore has had a proud naval record. No sooner indeed had the Fells established themselves at the Point than they began to build ships, and this trade increased year by year. When the Revolutionary War broke out a swarm of privateers was let loose upon the British. Fells Point rang with the blows of hammers, and the foremost citizens of the town were engaged in privateering. "The privateer was the nurse of the infant navy," and it was a lusty child, fostered by such men in the town as Buchannan, Hughes, McKim, Patterson and Ridgely. Within a period of six years two hundred and forty-eight vessels carrying letters of marque and reprisal sailed out of the Chesapeake. And what rip-roaring names they bore; the "Lively," "Baltimore Hero," "Antelope," "Intrepid," and the "Fearnaught." Moreover the men who commanded these boats and scores of others were as gallant in action as their ships were in name. Captain Thomas Boyle in his ship the "Comet" seized twenty-nine vessels.

His exploits make even the movies seem a pallid spiritless thing. The "Chasseur" commanded by the same brave officer made eighty captures, thirty-two of them of equal force, and eighteen of a greater. A model of this ship stands in the rotunda of the City Hall. Nor ought one to omit mention of Joshua Barney. His log reads thus: "July 31, seized brig Nymph. Took and burnt the Princess Royal. August 1, Took and manned ship Kitty. August 2, Took and burnt brig Fame, brig Devonshire, schooner Squid. August 3, Took and sank brig Henry, and schooner Racehorse. Burnt schooner Halifax; manned brig Williams and gave schooner Two Brothers forty prisoners to be sent to Saint John's on parole." These were only a few of his daily dozen.

The ships for which the town is celebrated, however, are the Baltimore Clippers. The model for these famous ships is somewhat of a mystery. There are those who claim that this

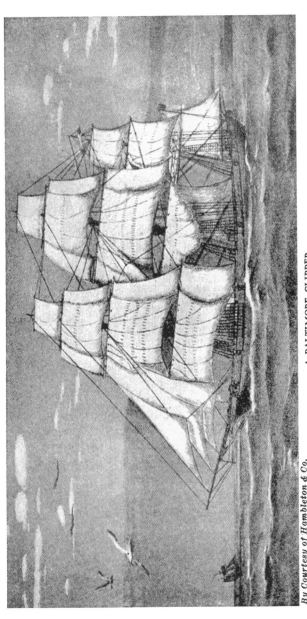

By Courtesy of Hambleton & Co.

A BALTIMORE CLIPPER

"Each with her special memory's special grace,
Riding the sea, making the waves give place
To delicate high beauty; man's best strength
Noble in every line in all their length."

MASEFIELD.

type of vessel originated on the Eastern Shore at Saint Michael's, and was nothing more than a development of Captain John Smith's pinnance with which he explored the Bay. Be that as it may, the clipper was admirably suited for speed, and it is thought that the quality gave rise to the name. There is the well-known colloquial expression "to come at a good clip," and surely these boats clipped over the waves rather than ploughed through them. In the early nineteenth century the eastern trade was largely in pirate-infested waters, and there the clippers had the immense advantage of a swift getaway. The name was used for many types of vessels in the early years of the last century, but Clark in his *Clipper Ship Era* says that no one had ever attempted "to reproduce the lines of a small swift vessel in a large one until in 1832 Isaac McKim commissioned Kennard and Williamson at Fells Point to build a ship embodying as far as possible the lines of famous clipper brigs and schooners." This vessel was named the Ann McKim after the owner's wife. Built of live oak it was sturdy and strong but lithe and swift. This was the boat that suggested the clipper design to other builders.

Romance dwells with these old ships, now long vanished. Their very names entrance. "The Flying Cloud," the "Greyhound," the "Comet," the "Grey Eagle" and the "Shooting Star." Glorious ships they were. The "Sea Witch" was a notable beauty, with ranking masts and a great cloud of canvas. This dusky creature was painted black and a huge scaly dragon writhed along her prow as a figure head. A whole chapter could be written on figure heads alone. The little shops in Fells Point made them at your order. The pots of paint—red and green, blue and yellow—furnished forth an Indian queen, a mermaid or warrior. One does not find them now except in some old New England village, where leaning against the low stone wall of a fisherman's cottage the queen or warrior dreams again those old days on the great waters. "Thrice I suffered shipwreck, a day and a night I have been in the deep, in perils of water, in perils in the sea." Sailors were proud of their figure heads, and took delight in keeping them bright and shining. The "Fighting Cock" was a fine bird with a ruffled crest and a fierce beak. The "Nightingale" bore the figure of Jenny Lind, and the "Romance of the Sea" carried at its prow the figure of a man scanning the deep; such a man as must, many a time, through all the centuries have stood upon the prows of ancient ships and cried "Land! Land!"

If in your imagination you will clear away the railroad terminals, the practical and no doubt excellent docks on Fells Point, you will be able to recreate the old Point as she was in those clipper days. Up the river, gliding as proudly as swans, came ships from China, from Cuba, from Peru. And ever new ships were upon the ways. There was a good reek of tar and paint and oakum. There was the clink of hammer on steel and the smell of shavings. There was a stir of activity, a constant coming and going, the arrival and departure of vessels. To see a ship make ready for a voyage is even today a thrilling sight. But to see a clipper get under way was a picture never to be forgotten. Everywhere on deck and in the rigging there was hurry and excitement, the creak of ropes and the rattle of chains. Voices shouted orders sprinkled liberally with sulphur and brimstone. But over and above the hubbub rose the voice of the chanty man, the leader of the songs, without which no clipper was complete. Often the chanty man was drunk, but that made him troll the merrier.

> "In eighteen hundred and forty-six
> I found myself in a hell of a fix"—

and the "Shooting Star" is off to the Horn!

IN CARROLL'S NEIGHBORHOOD

CHAPTER XI

IF you walk up Central Avenue—once a canal—to Eastern Avenue, and then turn west you will find yourself in the Italian section of Baltimore. Here are to be found the remnant of those street-piano men who in the past generation added much to the pleasure of a summer evening. True, the music was purely nominal, but there was a gayety about "Daisy, Daisy, give me your answer true" or "Down went Maginty" that no "Red Hot Mama" will understand. But I know that Daisy would spurn the Red Hot Mama. In those innocent days the first sign of spring was the sight of the street piano pulled along by the faithful pair, an Italian man and his wife. The instrument was covered with a faded green cloth, and at the turn of a crank the dulcet strains of Il Trovatore or Cavelleria Rusticana came rippling forth. I swear they were pretty tunes! Sometimes they were little wax figures set in a niche in the piano and they went solemnly through their gyrations paying no regard to the "piece" of the moment, for all the world like modern dancers.

These puppets were rarely seen, and their appearance in the neighborhood brought forth all the children and all their pennies. On the corner of Eastern Avenue and President Street there lived a man named Merici whose house was headquarters for the hurdy-gurdy men. He could tell fascinating stories of their lives—Giuseppe was of noble family, but for political reasons had fled from Italy; Angelo had lived in a small town at the foot of Vesuvius, he was working for his family back home; in a brawl Marcio had stabbed a man. Sapristi! Now all this has changed. The hurdy-gurdy men are a vanished race. Occasionally one sees a small hand organ strapped on the back of a wizened old fellow; and very occasionally one sees, too, a monkey wizened as his owner wearing a scarlet cap and a little jacket. Don't you remember the look in Jocko's eyes as he held up his bonnet for your penny? They have all gone now, the old harpers, the fiddlers, and the street piano men, vanished like the bear-wards. Those were thrilling days when bears, somewhat moth-eaten it is true, could be met walking along with their keepers. The city fathers of course required that these bears should be held in leash with a stout chain, but a bear's a bear for all that, and so is a street piano. "O tempora, O mores!"

Once a year Exeter Street, from Stiles to Bank, is in gala attire. When the great fire swept over Baltimore the people around Saint Leo's church were frantic at the thought of losing their homes and all of their possessions. They crowded the church, praying to Saint Anthony of Padua to deliver them, for all know well that he is powerful in his aid against fire or loss of property. Invoking his aid they promised that if their homes were spared they would honor his memory yearly with a great festival. With anxious hearts, and yet with faith, they watched the wall of fire eating steadily eastward. But Saint Anthony heard them. The fire stopped at the Falls;

Exeter Street was safe. Nor have the pious members of Saint Leo's forgotten their promise. Every year sees the neighborhood gay with the flags of America and Italy. There is a band and a carnival and much merrymaking; but there is a religious side as well. The statue of Saint Anthony is carried in procession, and all struggle forward to pin a crisp crinkly bill to his robes. Then there is the Mass and music and hundreds of twinkling tapers. Saint Leo's is a most interesting church. When I visited it I was fortunate enough to witness a wedding, with the church packed with relatives and friends, and the priest saying Mass, and throngs of children outside armed with rice. Looking at the hordes of dark-eyed boys and girls I thought that the rice was not really needed; that little matter would be attended to.

A short walk up Exeter to Pratt, and then one square west brings us to a small old-fashioned house tucked in demurely among its taller neighbors. Here in 1814 lived Mary Pickersgill. The British had burned Washington and were marching north on Baltimore. Nor were the troops insignificant regiments. They were the very best of Wellington's Invincibles who had just succeeded in banishing Napoleon to Elba. One day General McDonald who lived around the corner and Commodore Barney stopped at the little house on Albemarle Street and asked Mrs. Pickersgill to make a flag which should be the signal of no surrender. Now the making of flags was no new art in the family; Rebecca Young, Mrs. Pickersgill's mother, had made Revolutionary flags under the direction of Washington himself. But this visit put her on her mettle.

Aided by her little daughter, Caroline, Mrs. Pickersgill worked night and day on the flag which was to fly over the town. It was a large and cumbersome piece of needlework, far too large for the tiny house, and for that reason permission was gained from a nearby brewery to spread out the ban-

185

ner in their malt room where the work could proceed more rapidly. It requires no imagination to see the bare room lighted with candles and the faithful woman and her daughter working on until midnight.

This was the flag that Key saw from the deck of the Minden when he watched for the coming of the dawn. The house has been bought by the city, and placed under the care of a partiotic group of men and women who will make it a worthy shrine.

On the northeast corner of Front and Lombard Streets stands the old home of Charles Carroll of Carrollton. During the Revolutionary period there were three of these Carrolls of distinguished Irish ancestry. There was Charles Carroll of Carrollton, Charles Carroll, barrister, and the Reverend John Carroll, all descendants of Daniel and Dorothy Carroll of Ely and O'Neill, Ireland. "The Daniel Carroll," it is said, "had twenty sons whom he presented in one troop of horse all accoutred in the habiliments of war, to the Earl of Ormond, together with all his interest for the service of King Charles I. Most of these died in foreign service, having followed the hard fate of King Charles II." Such was the ancestry of the boy born in Annapolis in 1737. When he was ten years old he was sent over to the Eastern Shore to a school conducted by the Jesuits. No longer did liberal and enlightened laws prevail in Maryland, and this school under Jesuit control, though excellent, had to be conducted in the most discreet manner. But this life on the Eastern Shore in "The Tusculum of the Society of Jesus" did not last long. One fine day Charles and his cousin John, destined to be Archbishop of Baltimore, sailed for France, for Saint Omer's where a famous school had long been established.

What a rich and splendid world that was, the world of 1748! Louis the Fifteenth was on the throne of France. Voltaire and

Rousseau were slowly and secretly undermining that throne. In this work they were ably abetted by the caprices of Pompadour and DuBarry. At Aix-la-Chapelle the War of the Austrian Succession had come to tedious end. Clive in India had defeated the wily Dupleix. The little Marie Antoinette had not yet been born in Vienna. Ten years must pass before Robespierre saw the light of day, in a square white bourgeois home in Arras.

Such was the world. But the eleven year old boy thought little of it. He was occupied with his Cicero and Virgil. For six years he remained in the small provincial town. Then at the age of seventeen he went up to Paris, to the College of Louis le Grand. What brave sights he saw! The old grey colleges dreaming under the shadow of Saint Genevieve's hill, the stern front of Notre Dame, the Seine flowing, flowing forever under her bridges. But he saw, too, the writing on the wall. This young colonial saw the king enslaved by harlots; saw Damiens tortured on the Place de Greve, saw the sacred offices of the Church bartered, while the Jesuits tried in vain to arouse the Well-Beloved to a sense of decency. In 1757 Carroll crossed the Channel and going up to London took lodgings in the Inner Temple. There he continued his study of the law until 1764 when he returned to Maryland.

By the time that he was safely married to "an agreeable young lady endowed with every accomplishment necessary to render the connubial state happy"—Miss Darnall by name —political difficulties had arisen with Great Britain. Into these dissensions Charles Carroll threw himself with his entire energy.

This old house, now forlorn and degraded to a vocational school, was once the home of a brilliant and distinguished group of men and women. Here you must allow your imagination full play, and you must see the house set in a garden that ran down to the edge of Jones Falls. There were wide-spreading trees, and bushes of keen, fresh-smelling box. And the ladies, too, were lovely and gracious in their taffetas and laces. The gentlemen wore cocked hats and carried canes under their arms, though of course republican ideas modified the fashions a trifle. The hats were turned up at first on one side and then on the other, but those stiff-necked Quakers wore them straight in protest! Mr. Ward, the wigmaker, had a shop—the Sign of the White Peruke at the end of Market Street, but alas, "the English hair" which he imported became unpatriotic. It became the thing to wear ones own locks lightly powdered. But in truth the beauty of Maryland women needed no artifice. Carroll's own daughter Mary married Richard Caton and became the mother of a famous beauty—Mary, who later was Lady Wellesley. A boorish Englishman once said to her—

"Ah, Lady Wellesley, do you come from that part of America where they 'calculate?"

To which King William gracefully replied,

"Lady Wellesley comes from the part where they fascinate."
Not half-bad for an Englishman!

Great indeed was the veneration and respect which Maryland felt for Carroll, so great that he was called the First Citizen. In 1776 the Declaration was adopted, but it was not signed until sometime afterwards. On the second of August it was presented to the Maryland members then present. It is said that as the signing proceeded, "John Hancock asked Carroll if he would sign it. 'Most willingly,' he replied; and taking up a pen signed his name as was his habit—Charles Carroll. A bystander remarked aloud as Mr. Carroll signed his name, 'There go several millions," alluding to the great wealth endangered by his adherence to the cause of independence. 'Nay', said another, 'there are several Charles Carrolls—he can not be

188

identified!' Mr. Carroll, hearing the conversation, immediately added to his signature 'of Carrollton' remarking as he did so, 'They can not mistake me now.' "

A walk up Front Street today is singularly unrewarding. There is, however, a curious landmark at the corner of Fayette and Front—the old Shot Tower. In the early days of the city's history there was another one of these towers on south Eutaw Street but all trace of that has vanished. This one remains, an odd cylindrical structure of very fine brick work. It was built in 1828 and the corner stone was laid by that indefatigable old gentleman Charles Carroll of Carrollton. How weary he must have been of endless corner stones! The Tower, two hundred and fifty feet high, was built without scaffolding. There were two platforms inside the tower, and from the lower level sizes of shot up to number four were made. From the higher level sizes up to T. T. It is a picturesque old relic, but it must be admitted that a filling station does not enrich its historical significance. Early descriptions of the tower speak of it as the highest shaft in America, but be that as it may be, there is, at sunset, a beauty in the old Tower as one rides west from Broadway. Nor is there a more curious accent for the formal Periclean beauty of the War Memorial than this old shaft of ruddy brick.

No account of this part of the town would be complete without a mention of Saint Vincent's whose gilded domes add another strange note in this architectural medley. Yet indeed the charm of this part of Baltimore is found in precisely that quality. Everything is a jumble. But out of the jumble comes a beauty not orderly and suave, but distinct and definite. Saint Vincent's is an ugly church, but it has dignity. Alone it bears witness to the truth in a neighborhood from which all other churches have fled to more fashionable quarters. Yet it is by no means forlorn or forsaken. Here midnight mass is said for newspaper men, and I have heard that Saint Vincent's was the first parish in the country to establish such a custom.

We have made a wide circuit of old Baltimore, but there is still the Custom House, a fine modern building on Lombard and Gay Streets. The present Custom House, however, concerns us not at all—except when we have to pay our income tax! In Gay Street between Second and Water stood the old Exchange, or as it was affectionately called 'Change.' As early as 1793 there had been an Exchange for the proper transaction of business, but this had not been very successful. In 1816, therefore, was incorporated the Baltimore Exchange with William Patterson as chairman. This company began the building which "in size and magnificence had no rival in America." The architect was Benjamin H. Latrobe. The accounts of the building abound with references to the Ionic columns, the galleries, the colonnades, but after all the dome was the chief source of pride. In this dome was an arrangement by which news could be conveyed by signals from Federal Hill. Thus information that a certain ship was coming up the Bay could be at once communicated to the merchants in the Exchange below. In 1832 this was considered a marvel; and no doubt it was. The contemporary record read: "Thus in a few moments the arrival of a vessel at a distance of thirty miles from Baltimore may be known on 'Change.' "

Opposite the Exchange was the law office of Robert Goodloe Harper, and here in 1821 came the young John H. B. Latrobe to read law. A light is thrown on those days when one considers the methods in vogue. The office itself was as bare and austere as a convent cell, but the personality of Harper was large enough to furnish a dozen rooms. He spoke to young Latrobe about poetry, discussed his literary tastes with him, argued the merits of the great English writers of the day. Further, he advised his pupil to practice the art of poetry. Strange legal preparation! But in those days men were giants. Particularly, Harper suggests *The Faery Queen*. Keats says that *he* romped through it like a young colt in a meadow, but who would expect to find a lawyer recommending such provender. In this office the lad soaked up a marvellous amount of widely diffused knowledge, and received a sound education, not only in law but in life. Latrobe's diary gives us many a fascinating picture of the men of early nineteenth century Baltimore. He describes Robert Gilmour who lived not far away as "a small man stooping yet elegant," a man who had a taste in art and literature, and was noted, furthermore, for the excellence of his cellar.

Nor is prosaic Water Street lacking in melodrama. When excavations were made for the new Custom House many curious underground passages were found in the locality. In several places the thrill of the subterranean caverns was increased by the additional discovery of skeletons long buried in the earth. Conjectures arose concerning these gruesome finds, and a strange story is told in explanation. Once upon a time there lived in Water Street a Frenchman who like most of his countrymen of like profession kept an excellent hotel. Everything that appetite could want found its way upon his tables. Behind the hotel there was a pleasant garden, and there this singular Frenchman lived with his wife and family in a small, secluded house. On no consideration were the good woman or the children allowed to enter the hotel. As time went on it was noted that persons who stopped at this inn were frequently seen no more. One could not say precisely that there was anything untoward in the matter—but the fact remained; guests disappeared. At length one night the wife's curiosity got the better of her discretion and she crept into the hotel, secreting herself in a convenient cupboard. All too soon she discovered the source of her husband's wealth.

In terror the woman and her children fled from the sinister house under cover of night. Immediately the Frenchman bundled up his ill-gotten gains, and fearing that his wife would betray him to the police fled likewise from the accursed spot— but fled in the opposite direction. Years later building activities revealed a number of devious underground tunnels, and in them were discovered the skeletons of human beings. Then the oldest inhabitants recalled that Frenchman who served the so excellent ragouts, and recalled, too, the fact of the uncanny disappearance of his guests. This Ginevra-like tale may help you to see a bit of romance in an exceedingly drab and commercial neighborhood. If you do not feel disposed to credit it, very well; but the French do make admirable ragouts. You must admit that.

And now the tale shifts again to that Baltimore girl who was nourished upon Rochefoucauld. To the Patterson house on South Street Madame Bonaparte returned with her son whom she called Bo. Young, witty and beautiful, she was the leader of the social life of the day. Gilbert Stuart painted her portrait, and she said "It looks like me; the others looked like the portrait of any other woman." But how she hated Baltimore, and laughed as its smug respectability! Later from Europe she wrote to her father in this disrespectful vein: "As to the opinion of old Mr. Gilmour and other very reputable and worthy persons that I ought to be in Baltimore, they only tell you this because they know that their daughters might come here and never be known. Look how they run after the poorest sprigs of the nobility and you will know what they think of my standing in Europe. . . . Let people think that you are proud of me, which indeed you have every reason to be, for I am very prudent and wise."

To this old William replied, "God grant that it may be so."

There was, however, one in the family who adored Baltimore, and that was Bo. "Since I have been in Europe," he writes, "I have not found a dish to my taste as the roast beef and beefsteaks I ate on South Street." Nor did his Baltimore predilections stop there. In 1829 he married Miss Susan May Williams, and Betsy's intense disgust knew no bounds.

"If he can be satisfied with living in Baltimore I have nothing to say against it." This the lady said, but meant the opposite. Soon there was great excitement in the family, for a son was born to Bo and his young wife. Betsy again was disappointed. "I had hoped that there would be no children, but as nothing happens as I desire, I do not flatter myself with the accomplishment of my wish."

Nature proceeded unimpeded. Ah, the danger of rearing a child on Rochefoucauld!

CHARLES STREET LONG AGO

CHAPTER XII

HARLES Street is the axis of the town. From the Middle Branch of the Patapsco it runs north with only a small quirk at Barre Street and a westward turn in Guilford. It is, moreover, the dividing line, marking off the eastern and western sections of the town. Its history, growth and development are in a peculiar sense the history, growth and development of Baltimore. Once it was the fashionable residence street, but now it is given over almost entirely to business. Beyond Twenty-fifth Street, then known as Huntingdon Avenue, there was in the dim nineties only a country road. This road, very straggling, ran out into real country—a region of fields and streams, locust trees and violets. Charles Street from its rural atmosphere became Charles Street Avenue. This has an odd sound to barbarians, but not to real Baltimoreans. Then came modern improvements. The trees were hacked down, the streams piped, and the violets uprooted. But did the townspeople change the name? They did not; they simply added a more elegant word, and for some years the name of Charles Street Avenue Boulevard was common currency. This is slightly redundant, but it had the advantage of being very precise.

But we are covering the ground too rapidly. This street named for the Signer, Charles Carroll of Carrollton, is uphill; we must take things in more leisurely fashion.

South Baltimore has its own story which we shall leave for another day. But take a blue bus at Baltimore and Charles Streets and jog out to University Parkway. You will ride through Baltimore history in a most remarkable manner. Here at this corner we are in the midst of things. South of us in the neighborhood of Lombard Street lay Frenchtown, the part of city where the Acadians settled. That building on the southwest corner of Charles and Baltimore is none other than the Sun Building. Opposite is the Baltimore and Ohio, and thereby hangs a tale and a long one. From this point Anton Schutz, the famous modern artist, made an etching. To his mind it was the most suitable vantage-ground in the city. Of etching I am innocent, but I know many views more characteristic than this. Looking up the hill one sees nothing more violent than the traffic officer controlling the flood of machines and trucks, but in the thirties the spectator would have witnessed a very different scene.

Baltimoreans were exceedingly prone to riot, selecting, indeed, almost any occasion for this diversion. In 1835, however, there was much justification, for claims against the Bank of Maryland had been dishonored, and the directors had announced that the business would shortly be wound up. "Here's a how-de do!" The depositors and many roisterers were in a fine and proper rage, and vowing vengeance on Reverdy Johnson and John Glenn they assembled at the foot of the Battle Monument. Reverdy Johnson was a great and distinguished lawyer, subtle and acute. He could sway any audience, so it is said, be they simple ploughmen or learned savants. Scharf reports him as "delightful as a draught of old south side Madeira." Alas, his subtlety and madeira-like qualities were as nothing to the mob that swirled and raged around his fine home in Monument Square. Bent on destruction, the rioters dragged forth Johnson's furniture and household goods, and piling them high under the shadow of the Battle Monument, applied the torch. The crackle of the flames and the shooting sparks brought together an immense crowd, which marched next to John Glenn's house which stood in Charles Street north of Fayette. The mob entered and likewise tore out all of the furniture and, barricading the streets, dared the soldiers to interfere. Not content with this dramatic way of showing their displeasure, they broke into Glenn's excellent wine cellar. It was not long before great hilarity prevailed among the citizens. Some with loud damns called down the vengeance of heaven upon poor Glenn, but others said he was probably a good fellow, and was certainly stocked with devilish good liquor.

By this time a troop of cavalry made up of gallant young men drew their swords and dashing down Charles Street (head-on toward our bus) threatened the mob with violence. The hill is steep, and when young Willey, who led the charge, reached the barricade his horse leaped over it like an early edition of Billy Barton. The malcontents were so amazed at this that word to retreat quickly spread. It was further reported that soldiers were advancing from Monument Square. A few whiffs of shot chastened their military ardour, but it was not until General Smith, a defender of 1812, seized a flag and called on all good citizens to follow him that peace was finally restored.

In Latrobe's memoirs there is the most delightful letter from William E. Bartlett that I must quote

"Dear Edward,

Thine of 7th inst is before me. We have seen things awfully strange this week, I tell thee. On fifth night a considerable number of folk, good, bad, and indifferent, assembled in Monument Square before the door of Reverdy Johnson, (of Bank of Maryland memory).

* * * * *

I do not know what Glenn's losses were but when I tell thee his wines alone are said to have cost over four thousand Dollars I am very sure thee would not pay all of his losses for a sum under twenty thousand Dollars.

* * * * *

Had they been able to catch the Obnoctious Directors of said institution they would have been altogether satisfied to have given each a coat of tar and feathers.

* * * * *

Jno Livingston has told the monthly meeting that he intends to Marry Ann Scott.

I am thy friend,

WM. E. BARTLETT.

And William E. Bartlett has good powers of description. He relates how the rioters threw Reverdy Johnson's furniture out into the street "as briskly as fifty lively negroes husk corn." Again, the destructive crowds picked at the woodwork of the house "like wood-peckers." Indeed the whole letter is full of interest. Nor could I forego that bit of gossip tacked on so mildly at the end. Evidently there was mischief here. Observe that capital M for the word marry. That shows determination in Jno. Livingston. I am sure that Edward Stabler enjoyed that letter.

O'Neill's store which stands on the corner of Lexington and Charles marks the northernmost point of the Baltimore

Fire. On that Sunday, when, just as church began, the fire-engines went clattering by, nobody realized the extent that the fire would cover. Little by little as the day went on the flames crept eastward, climbing up the hill to Charles Street. It seemed as if the whole downtown section was doomed. Saint Paul's Church would probably be destroyed again as other buildings on that site had been swept by fire. And surely nothing could save O'Neill's. It is said that Mr. O'Neill prayed fervently that the work of his life might not be wiped out, and as by a miracle the flames stopped short of his store. But long before O'Neill had built here, on this southwest corner stood the home of Doctor Pierre Chatard, a name well-known in medicine. In the year 1797 Doctor Chatard went to Haiti, but the outbreak of revolution in the island led him to the States. By some chance the ship put in at Baltimore, and here he decided to stay. For many years the physician had a residence in Harrison Street, but his son Ferdinand in 1829 established himself on this famous old corner, and hung out the knocker dated 1797. This knocker is still used by the present Doctor Chatard on Calvert Street.

This neighborhood, indeed, is closely associated with the early medical history of Baltimore, and there is nothing, not even oysters, for which the town is more celebrated than its medical learning. As early as 1729 Doctor Walker and Doctor Buchanan were appointed commissioners of health. They had many long and difficult struggles with "winter feaver" or smallpox. Some years later Doctor Henry Stevenson settled in Baltimore, no doubt on Market Street and turned his house into a hospital. This was very advanced for 1754, and people laughed at the poor deluded man, calling his venture "Stevenson's Folly." He charged two pistoles for inoculation ("stimulate the phagocytes!") and twenty shillings a week for board and lodging. Soon other doctors came—Wiesenthal,

Craddock, Coale and Ridgely, but when the Revolution broke out poor Doctor Stevenson was compelled to leave because of his Tory principles. The other physicians agreed to take country produce as payment during the times of worthless currency, and they likewise announced that they would treat the poor "with the usual tenderness and charity."

Quacks abounded. There was, for instnace, Mons. Francis Torres "who cures all ills by means of his Chinese stones and bags of powder at the price of twenty-five shillings a stone." But in spite of these humbugs, the science of medicine made rapid strides, and in 1799 the Medical and Chirurgical Faculty of Maryland was organised. These men elected "twelve persons of medical skill to grant licences to such medical and chirurgical gentlemen as they shall judge adequate to commence the practice of medicine." Five years after Jenner's discovery, vaccination for smallpox was looked upon with favour in Baltimore. Doctor James Smith, physician at the Country Almshouse, which was then located near the present site of Mount Calvary Church, was the father of vaccination in Maryland, and one of the first physicians in the country to adopt the new preventive. Doctor Davidge who lived down on Fayette Street near the first Presbyterian Church gave medical lectures in his house, and later he built a hall for the study of anatomy on the site of the present Rennert Hotel at Liberty and Saratoga Streets. But this was too much. The people would not stand for dissection, and in one of the characteristic riots they demolished the house. For this there was no legal redress, but it all ended happily for the advance of science —"even the wrath of man shall praise Thee." In 1808 back of O'Neill's store, on Fayette Street and McClellan's Alley, the College of Medicine was started. The house where the seven students met was a rough wooden structure with neither light nor heat except of the most primitive kind. The students' hands were so cold that they could hardly write, and in the mornings all the anatomical subjects were frozen as hard as bullets. But the school grew. By 1809 there were eighteen students, and better quarters were found for them on Commerce Street.

Now John Eager Howard comes forward once more in his old role, and gives a large tract of land on Lombard Street for a proper and decent building. This is to be known as the University of Maryland. In 1812 it opened its doors and from that time on it has played a noble part in the science of medicine. But now let us turn to Divinity.

In Revolutionary times Saint Paul's Church was set in the midst of a churchyard extending from Saratoga Street to Lexington, and from Charles Street to Saint Paul's Lane. Across Charles, where now the Fidelity stands, was the old rectory, a house we have already described. The Seneca Trail or Great Eastern Road, you will remember, crossed the Falls in the neighborhood of Hillen Street, and climbed the steep grade which we now call Saratoga Street. Then this road turned south, and cutting corners, ran down through Crooked Lane, back to O'Neill's, to Market Street, and then turned west. All this I have said before in some other chapter, but it will bear repeating, if only because it makes clearer the general topography of this neighborhood. To see Charles and Lexington in the old days you must call up a vision of fields and country roads. Beyond Franklin Street there is nothing but the vast undulating acres of John Eager Howard's estate.

A continous tradition is a hard thing to find in an American city. "Westward the course of empire takes its way"; yes, and eastward or northward or southward. But the story of Saint Paul's Parish is associated with Charles and Saratoga Street in a peculiar manner. Fires have wrecked successive buildings, but always the new church arose on the site of the old. Since 1731 this locality has been associated with the mother church of the town.

In 1692, long before Baltimore Town was dreamed of, the freeholders of Saint Paul's Parish were enjoined to meet together, and make a choice of six vestrymen to manage the church affairs. The Parish was almost as large as the one John Wesley claimed. It extended from Patapsco River and Falls on the south to the Pennsylvania line on the north, and from the country line on the west to the Chesapeake on the east. Nothing niggardly in that! Of this meeting of the Patapsco Hundred no record remains, but there is evidence that they did meet from an extract in the records of Baltimore County for 1693. There is the statement that "Pettetes old field was the best place for a church, and that John Gay was to be clerk of the vestry."

In 1702 the Reverend William Tibbs was made a missionary priest for the Parish, but alas, he was not a very worthy representative of the clergy! In the eighteenth century the Church of England was at a low ebb spiritually. Both in England and in the colonies the parsons cared more for foxhunting than for the cure of souls. However, when one considers that in America for a hundred and fifty years there were no bishops to put the fear of the Lord into these lower clergy, their frequent lapses are understandable.

The Reverend Mr. Leakin drew a delightful picture of these so-called jolly parsons. Said he: "In 1711 a priest wrote to the Bishop of London and reported that he had travelled over two hundred miles in a month besides the care of his own parish which he also visited on horseback, and he complained, 'My Lord, I cannot subsist without some aid, for tobacco, our money, is worth nothing, and all I have received for my ministry and perquisites since October last is a poor ten shillings.' If this parson was jolly under those circumstances it must have been that he gloried in tribulation." In truth, one is left to wonder not so much at the jolly parson as at the ruminations of the Lord Bishop. When one considers how little the average Englishman of today knows of America, what must have been the astonishment of the Bishop of London when he heard of this ten shilling stipend. My word!

So poor Parson Tibbs has come down to us as a jolly parson. Well, at least he was jolly, and that is better than being an ague cheek. May he rest in peace!

Where the first church of this parish was built we do not know. It was probably of logs, and built, of course, in the county, for as yet there was no Baltimore. Another church was built near the Sellers Point and North Point Roads, but that met with bad fortune. In 1729, Baltimore Town was laid out, and it was suggested that a site be purchased nearer town. Various plots were considered, but finally in 1730 the vestry bought the lot numbered 19 on the old plan of the town, the very site which now lies at Charles and Saratoga Streets. This was the highest spot in the village, commanding a beautiful view where the land sloped gently to the harbour. North, the great slopes thickly forested rose and fell like the waves of the sea. Here where Saratoga Street dips sharply downward was a steep cliff which dropped abruptly to the Falls. You remember that in those days the Falls made a deep loop like the handle of a pitcher, and this handle curved beneath the red clay banks of Saint Paul's Churchyard. At infinite risk of their necks to say nothing of detriment to their breeches, small Baltimore boys used to slide down these perilous banks. They began on their stout corduroys but they ended the journey in the au naturel, which caused their long-suffering mothers to apply the rod to that already sore spot. But the thrill of a swift descent is worth a few maternal whacks.

202

Now, however, we must build the church. Up to this time there was no church in Baltimore. The town was young— only a year old in fact—but everyone felt that a house of worship was necessary, and also a metropolitan asset. The work of building took nine years. How Baltimoreans dawdle! But when it was finished it was a goodly building. Clear away now all that impedes your view; remove all adjacent shops and offices; eliminate the traffic policeman. Now you can see clearly a fair and spacious plot of ground and a plain dignified Georgian building of warm red brick. The windows were set with small panes of clear glass. The roof, peaked, with a cornice slightly extending over the corners was crowned with a quaint steeple. Many trees cast their shadows on the churchyard lawn, and before long, members of Old Saint Paul's were buried beneath their shade. An old print shows some of these ancient stones set at rather curious angles. Little by little the graveyard acquired the reputation of being haunted, and, says the chronicler, that drew the young people to its quiet domain. That may be, but churchyards are always popular with young people—possibly for other reasons. But we are writing sober history.

When John King, a Wesleyan missionary, preached at Calvert and Baltimore Streets he received scant courtesy. We have read of the militia captain who gallantly came to his rescue. Now another, and quite unexpected, hand was held out to him—he was actually invited to preach at Saint Paul's! It was not often that Anglican pulpits were so liberally offered, and King took ample advantage of it. He preached heartily, so heartily in fact that as he pounded the cushions on the pulpit, the dust flew out and caused several persons to have coughing fits. Indeed his fervour disgusted the more stolid and discreet Anglicans. Wesley was furious when he heard this, and counselled him severely "Scream no more on

203

peril of your soul!" Poor King, somewhat dashed, asked permission to speak again, but the privilege was withdrawn. Then did King have his revenge. On the next Lord's day he stationed himself at the entrance to the churchyard; and there he preached to a large crowd while the worshippers within doors haughtily looked down their noses and sang "The goodly fellowship of the prophets praise Thee."

At the close of the Revolution there was a new church on this site, grander perhaps, but not with the homely charm of the original building. There was in the east wall a huge window of common glass through which the sunlight poured in all its strength. To prevent this, a green baize curtain was drawn across it, and this gentle subdued light together with the deep square pews made slumber in sermon time a very venial sin. The architects neglected to build a sacristy, and the priest was compelled to robe behind a stiff red curtain. For the altar, or, as it was called in 1785, the communion table, there was one green cloth cover and one pewter basin and one silver plate. Outside in the churchyard the ground was terraced down to Lexington Street, and sycamore trees grew along the southern bounds of the yard. The rectory at Charles and Lexington was obviously shabby in 1788, so with the engaging ethics of the time a lottery was held to build a new one. Of course John Eager Howard gave the ground, and in 1789, the year of the storming of the Bastille, the rectory was begun.

Sally Bruce Kinsolving, the Baltimore poet, and wife of the present Rector of Old Saint Paul's writes thus: "The house seems to have been constructed with the one idea predominating—that the sun should begin to play upon its long façade and travel across it in a riot of glory throughout the day, until finally sending long golden shafts to light into warm colours the books and portraits on the walls."

THE RECTORY OF OLD SAINT PAUL'S

Above the doorway there is a beautiful window looking out over the town. In the old days there was a long sweep of green field and meadow stretching down to the Bay, and as one stood at this casement he had sight of a pleasant heritage. Now all this has changed, but there is a strange beauty to be found in the sharp uncompromising lines of modern skyscrapers. A tradition says that in the room over the doorway—the room with the enchanting window—the House of Bishops of the Episcopal Church met in 1808. Whether the meeting was in this room it is difficult to determine, but certainly it is true that the Bishops met in the Rectory. A messenger sent from the House of Deputies brought back word that he found the Bishops—there were but two—in a room on the second floor of the Rectory seated at a table with a bottle of amber liquid between them. I am glad that the colour was amber; it exactly expresses the tone of this old house. The Bishops' cogitations no doubt prospered. For thirty-five years the Rectory was occupied by the Reverend Doctor Hodges and his family. John Sebastian Bach Hodges, the son of an English organist, brought to the Parish the finest traditions in worship and in music. He is widely known as a composer of both hymns and anthems, perhaps the most familiar of which is the melody used for Herber's Eucharistic hymn, "Bread of the World." Devoted priest, he was also an artist, and often he must have sat here at his piano "transfixing some lovely melody, swaying his spirit with as sure and delicate a touch as the wind the lilacs outside."

In 1906 the Reverend Arthur B. Kinsolving came with his wife and children to Baltimore where he assumed the responsibilities of the old Parish. The traditions established by Doctor Hodges have been consistently maintained, but these will not especially interest us at this point. The Rectory has been the focus of a rich and varied life. Bishops, priests, poets,

painters and musicians have shared in the family life. Notable
among these are the brothers of the Rector—the famous Kin-
solvings—Bishops and leaders in the Church. Nor should one
forget Father Hughson of the Order of the Holy Cross who
for so many years was the preacher at the Holy Week services.
As to poets they are thick as crows—Noyes, Masters, Sandburg, Millay and Markham. It was Sandburg who said that
the beautiful winding staircase looked like a staff of musical
notes. This comment is decidedly Sandburg's best poem.

The drawing room looks out upon the garden, a lovely
spot, but the room itself is full of charm. It is old and assured
like a French lady of the ancient régime. It is full of the
sun, for here no silly curtains shut out the warm amber
light. Could anything be more absurd than cutting squares
in a wall to admit light, and then covering up the said holes
with layers of cloth? No layers here! From the wall portraits
look down at us, especially Elvira Cabell Bruce who first
married a son of Patrick Henry's and later James Bruce.
Erect and beautiful, her dark eyes are full of fire, and her
mouth indicates the fine rectitude which marked her character. There is a gentleman, too, but he is not so dominant. In
this room are held from time to time informal gatherings of
poets, a kind of corollary to the Poetry Society. Writers are
thorny folk, but Sally Bruce Kinsolving disarms any fretful
quills. These meetings are small and intimate enough to be
full of salt—especially if Miss Reese be present, and one carries
away a clear sharp impression of the visiting lion. An occasion, however, that stands out vividly in my mind is Mrs.
Lawrence Turnbull's reading of a poem on Lanier, written by
herself. Very old and very frail, she read in a clear, steady voice
her tribute to her poet friend. Lanier indeed is present in that
room, for here each February a group of men and women
gather to honor his birthday. And that reminds me of Mr.

Gottlieb and his memorable flute. I'll save that, however, for another time, but I would not have you miss the melody for the world.

These are the memories that give the old room its charm, its rich associations. I hear the flute, those wistful prison tunes that Lanier loved; I hear the echoes of old Doctor Hodge's psalms and anthems. Someone reads:

> "I am Thy grass, O Lord,
> I grow up sweet and tall
> But for a day; beneath Thy sword
> To lie at evenfall."

The firelight shines rosily upon the wall; the wood-fire crackles merrily. Yes, warm amber is the colour of this old house.

Saint Paul's is the mother church of all the Anglican parishes in Baltimore. Soon after the first church was built, "the forest inhabitants" established at the Garrison about ten miles out of town wished to have a chapel of ease nearer to them than Saint Paul's. Consequently Saint Thomas's Garrison Forest was built to minister to the handful of military men stationed in the wilderness to keep off the Indians. One by one other parishes sprang up, soon becoming independent; but all of them have their origin in Old Saint Paul's. In 1814 a new church was erected but not completed until 1817. This building stood until 1854 when a disastrous fire destroyed it. Across the street where the old Young Men's Christian Association used to be, there was at that time a large private house. Here the young people were enjoying themselves in merry fashion at a dance, when suddenly the rosy reflections on the wall startled them.

"Fire!" they cried, and in spite of the pouring rain, out they ran into the street, the boys regardless of their thin pumps, the girls undismayed by their tulle frocks. Alas, Saint Paul's was burning, and burning so furiously that nothing availed.

Doctor Wyatt, the rector, and others stood by helplessly, after fruitless attempts had been made to save the structure from utter ruin. But no sooner was the blaze put out than new plans were immediately on foot. To see what the newspapers said on this loss to the city I examined the files of the Sun for April, 1854, and found exactly *eleven and a half lines* devoted to the burning of the oldest and one of the most historic churches in Baltimore. Such was the press in the fifties. It was the forties that roared.

The walls of the old building were used in the construction of the new, and the bas-reliefs of Moses and of Christ used on the present façade were also saved from the church of 1817. In January, 1856, the new—at last—structure was consecrated. The newspapers record that Bishop Whittingham's sermon was "chaste and appropriate," and that the choir directed by Professor Barrington "performed with considerable sweetness and correct musical taste." But, alas, someone had forgotten to order the coal! This frightful oversight was not discovered until it was too late, and the congregation shivered. Indeed all Baltimore had a severe winter in '56. At the Eutaw House—that "elegant hostelry" on Eutaw and Baltimore streets—the thermometer registered four degrees below zero. And at Greenmount twelve degrees! But the town was merry with the sound of sleigh bells. Everything was on runners, and the young men vied with each other in their distinguished equipages. At least that's what the Sunpaper says. Yes, it was a bitter cold winter, and even pride in the new church could hardly keep the congregation warm.

Across Saratoga Street from Saint Paul's there stood in early days—in 1756—the German Reformed Church. An old member, long dead, recalls this church of his boyhood in rather pathetic terms. "There were no cushions, no carpet, no organ, no, not even a stove." Here during the long hours of Sunday worship the northwest wind blew with terrific force, and seemed as if it would tear down the simple and homely structure. There was dissatisfaction with the pastor as time went on, and some of the members withdrew, calling the Reverend William Otterbein to shepherd them. In 1775 they built a church on Conway Street which we shall see later when we go to South Baltimore.

The history of the Roman Catholic Church in Baltimore is full of picturesque incident. I have told how a handful of exiles found their old faith ready to minister to them in Mr. Fottrel's house. But it was not for many years that they had a church, not indeed until 1770. In that year the Roman Catholics bought a lot fronting on Charles and Saratoga, and on the northwest side they built a very plain brick church which they called Saint Peter's. There was a cemetery around the church on the eastern side. The name of Northwest Street was formerly used to designate Saratoga Street. It was on a much higher level than the present thoroughfare, and ran slightly north of the present street alignment. It is difficult to say precisely where this church stood; authorities disagree. As far as I can determine it was on the site of Calvert Hall, or at Mulberry and Cathedral Streets. But the church met with ill-fortune before it was finished. The superintendent failed in business, and the principal creditor locked the door, and put the key in his pocket.

Such was the juncture of affairs when the Revolution broke out. Now it chanced that a troop of soldiers passing through the town desired to go to church—for the day was Sunday. They explained that most of them were Roman Catholics, and that naturally they preferred a church of their own belief. The townspeople looked puzzled, scratched their heads, and then recalled the irreligious creditor who still had Saint Peter's key in his pocket. Immediately the soldiers vowed that

209

they would open the church. Their officers were sympathetic, and Baltimoreans, always eager for a row, swore roundly that they would support the papists in their project, for, by Heaven, it was plain to see that they were zealous men. Accordingly the entire regiment accompanied by delighted hordes of Baltimoreans trooped around to Mr. P.'s house and demanded the key.

. Now Mr. P. had Tory leanings. When, therefore, he heard that the soldiers were on the way to his house he fled precipitately, thoughtfully leaving the key behind him. The soldiers peacefully obtained the key, opened the church, and had the service they so richly deserved.

FROM ROCHAMBEAU TO A GREEK

CHAPTER XIII

T HE first episcopal residence for the Roman Catholic bishop was on Charles Street below Pleasant, set, no doubt, in the midst of a garden. All this land now is built upon and has been given over to business for many years. An interesting place, the Dutch Tea Room, has recently disappeared. This was one of the first tea rooms in the city to be managed by a woman, Miss Natalie Cole. She began the business in a small way on Charles Street near Lexington. Then came the Fire, and hungry men had to eat. This venture gave the needed impetus, and tea rooms sprang up in many directions. It was at this time that the Little French Coffee House was to be discovered, tucked in behind the old Robinson house. In the early years of the century there was a tangle of these old mansions on Saratoga Street set back at curious angles from the pavement. Where now the Colonial Trust Company stands there was in old days the Maryland Jockey Club, headquarters for men interested in horses. Marylanders, indeed, have always loved dogs and horses. As to races, they were so popular in

Colonial times that they had to be prohibited on Sunday, Saturday afternoons and at Quaker Meetings. Races between pedigreed horses were first introduced at Annapolis by General Ogle in 1745, who was the first to import thoroughbred English stallions. Nor has the love of horse flesh died out. Pimlico is the scene each spring of the great racing event called the Preakness, named from the horse that first won this famous purse. Of all the timber toppers none is more renowned than the Maryland horse, Billy Barton, who ran in the recent steeple chase in England and won second place.

How far afield one runs when horses are the theme; let us return. On Charles Street below Saint Paul's church, on the site of the present Masonic Temple, there was in the early days in Baltimore a select school for young ladies conducted by Shamah and Ashur Clarke. Across from the Little French Coffee House was the back door of Eichelberger's, now the firm of Norman, Remington. The store was shaped like an ell, crowded and dark, and probably highly old-fashioned, but it was the gate to the Paradise of books. The clerks let you alone as they do at the new Norman, Remington's. There was no one to say brightly, "May I help you?" Of course not. You could easily help yourself to the whole store if help were all that was required. In a proper book store one needs time to browse, to dream, to dally with temptation. If the meditative mood is broken, in all likelihood, the purchase will never be made. I wish booksellers would remember this. In the same neighborhood, indeed across the street from Eichelberger's, was the New Mercantile Library, which we shall see in other quarters. Once it had its habitation in this squat brick building just north of Saratoga Street. It was here that a young man from the North presented himself one summer morning, and, full of confidence, asked where he could find Mr. Mencken.

With a vast sniff the old librarian replied, "Humph! Indeed I don't know; I believe he is a German."

Alas for the prophet!

A hilly city always lends itself to views. At any corner on Charles Street look off—not across country, but distance—and you will find a jumble of roofs and chimneys, strange masses of light and shadow that will satisfy the soul. Saratoga Street is especially rewarding. At Charles the street plunges down hill with all the swiftness of the descent to Avernus. A more casual inspection will repay you, and I advise you to go down to the lawyer's offices that hang on to the hill by their eyelashes, and ask the barristers if you may see their gardens. These lawyers are the most genial men, living half in Dickens and half in Baltimore. Several old footscrapers still remain, and unless the improver has been abroad there are some good doorways left, and chimneys of a ruddy orange colour. The gardens at the rear are enclosed with walls at least a foot thick and secured with formidable locks. An aged paulonia tree of astounding beauty flourishes in these bricky purlieus. Wicked cats prowl like the troops of Midian and eye the intruder. This breakneck street lies in deep shadow while the buildings across town still glow in the early afternoon sun.

Mulberry and Charles gives an even better prospect, for here the hill is higher, and the range more extended. On clear evenings the lines of the distant streets are strung with twinkling chains; on foggy nights it is a grey world cut sharply with silver fans of light as cars shoulder through the mist. But best of all I love this corner in a winter dusk when dizzy with a draught of books at Norman, Remington's you step forth into the night like Nora in "The Doll's House." You have, perhaps, been voyaging over the Aegean, or wandering in the temple of Artemis, or longing for the towers of Notre Dame that frown above the Seine. With all this in your mind you

BALTIMORE

forget the American scene, but as you pass through the enchanted portals of the shop suddenly you are aware that this is no mean city.

Opposite is the Howard's square brick house with its slender spindled "captain's walk" upon the roof. Down the hill Mulberry Street is lined with prim old-fashioned houses like ladies of another age, and far beyond them lies the broad expanse of the city, a strange theatric blue. It is the colour one sees upon the stage through warmly curtained windows. Now look west where a streak of orange still burns on the horizon. The bold corner of the Cathedral, Latrobe's noble building, stands out against the sunset. The ancient elm here at the corner leans across the street carrying in its heart memories of Rochambeau. But we must get on to more practical things.

To go on, one must go back. And by the way, if you want luncheon and delicious food stop in at the Woman's Exchange on the corner of Pleasant and Charles. This enterprise was started in those early and well-nigh prehistoric days when woman's only economic aptitude lay in the direction of cooking and fine sewing. Here both of these resources are fully utilized. The cakes are especially good. See if you can buy some Lady Baltimore. It had an immense vogue shortly after the publication of Owen Wister's novel. Now we shall walk down Pleasant Street, and see for ourselves some of the old houses still remaining. On the southwest corner of Saint Paul and Pleasant is one of the finest old mansions in the town. Built of brick, three stories high, it bears in every line that broad and generous hospitality that marks the typical Baltimore family. The marble steps are chipped, and the edges are broken, but nothing can mar the lines and beautiful curves of the old hand-rail. The doorway is flanked by fluted doric columns, and on the fanlight are two gay dancing figures. Within, the hall is well-proportioned. A slender, dark ban-

214

OLD HOUSE ON SOUTHWEST CORNER OF PLEASANT
AND SAINT PAUL STREETS

ister curves serenely upward. The whole house suggests an aristocratic face marred, perhaps, by time, but still bearing the fine contours, the noble modelling of race and breeding.

If possible do examine the yard, that is if such things interest you. There are people of course to whom the whole place would be a down-at-heels old house and nothing more. But I take for granted that you are not in that category. The best approach is from Saint Paul Street where you will come upon a deep recess set apparently into the wall of the garden. On the occasion of my exploration a very pretty girl was selling soft drinks in this grotto. A few green tables and chairs invited patrons, but at this early hour I was the only customer. The girl and I fell into conversation, nor was it long before a young man joined us—her young man, I take it. They gave me cordial permission to look about, even proposing to admit me into the garden. For this it was necessary to enter a dark celler at the rear of the grotto. There a flight of rickety stairs led up to a long narrow room that gave access to a spacious yard. This garden lies on a level of twelve feet or more above the street. An immense paulonia grew at the south end, and along the wall were boxes gay with petunias. Verandas wide and shady overlooked the yard, and indeed one might have imagined himself in the kitchen precincts of some old Southern house. Another stairway of stone led down to a big green gate secured by an ancient latch at least a foot long. By this means I let myself out into the street, but I could not leave without thanking the pretty girl and her young man. When she heard that I was interested in all old places and things, she said:

"Oh, you'd like to see the subway."

I agreed, and the three of us went again into the cellar, and there a tunnel black and sinister opened up before my astonished eyes. When I entered my nostrils were assailed with

215

a dank, airless smell, which increased as I penetrated the tunnel. After walking a few feet I decided to return to the grotto.

"They say it was for pirates," said the girl in answer to my question, "or maybe Confederates."

And with a wink the boy added "Today it would be swell for bootleggers." It certainly would.

If you walk north on Saint Paul Street the Preston Gardens are on your right hand. Here in this funny little lane was once a clutter of old houses, where at one time many well-known Baltimoreans lived. The Gardens named for a Mayor of the town are clumsy in design, but they give a feeling of space and fresh air. For years the unimaginative have sought to turn the Gardens into a public garage, but so far they have met with no success. The spring finds the space at Saratoga Street aflame with thousands of scarlet and yellow tulips. These alone would justify the Gardens. At the southwest corner of Mulberry and Saint Paul Walter DeCurzon Poultney is still living, the only old resident left in the neighborhood. In the long-vanished nineties Mr. Poultney was the Beau Nash of Baltimore, always faultlessly groomed, always dressed in the most individual manner. His ties and waistcoats had as much authority as those of Wales. He was kind enough to give me an interview one evening, and several of his interesting anecdotes enliven these pages. His house was the center of a brilliant social life, and invitations to his dinners were highly prized. Today, crowded with rare and beautiful things, it stands alone in a part of the town where once it was one of a number of fine old residences.

On the north wall of Mr. Poultney's house you will notice a curious sign known as a fire mark. These marks have a fascinating history which certainly reveals an odd streak in human nature. It would be difficult to imagine a fire company which would dash to a fire, and upon discovering that the blazing house was uninsured or protected by a rival company would calmly withdraw from the scene of action. But that, however, was the method of procedure in the good old days when fire companies and insurance companies were one organization. The first of these companies was formed in England after the Great Fire of London in 1667, and it was called, most suitably, "The Phoenix." Rivals quickly started up, notably "The Amicable Contributionship for Insuring from Loss by Fire." But it was generally known as the "Hand in Hand." These marks were duly affixed to the buildings insured, and the firemen maintained by each company were rushed to save not the property alone, but the company's money. Many wealthy people took out insurance in several companies and their houses were correspondingly adorned with various gilded signs, and brightly painted marks. Indeed the Prince Regent was described thus: "He looked like a house that has been over-insured." Signs bearing clapsed hands, and others adorned with small hand-engines are to be found in many of the old quarters of the town. The Friends Meeting on Aisquith Street bears a mark of the Fireman's Insurance Company—"F. I. Co."

Over in Old Town Number Six engine house still has the tower or belfry so necessary before the days of the still alarm. Then the bells would ring out—you recall Poe's

> "Hear the loud alarum bells,
> Brazen bells!
> What a tale of terror, now, their turbulency tells"—

and the neighbors, counting the strokes would determine the scene of the disaster. Those magnificent horses plunging down the cobble-stoned street, manes flying, sparks struck out from their hoofs—what an unforgettable sight it was! Wonderful, too, the drills, when at the stroke of eight the gong sounded, and like magic the splendid horses leaped into place, and the harness descended upon their proud necks. Nor will one soon forget the firemen sliding nimbly down the poles which vanished mysteriously into the floor above. How thrilling when the children, too, ran along the pavement crying "Fire, Fire," and the engine clattered by, leaving a thin trail of embers glowing in the night.

And here we are at the very corner from which we set out! The Howards sold their old house last year. Before the door stood not so very long ago one of those forest trees beneath which Rochambeau camped. Together with the old elm in the Cardinal's garden it made a green arch across Charles Street, but the tree was sacrificed to progress as they call it. Bare and dismantled the Howard house still has nobility and dignity, but when the family was living there it was furnished with beautiful and lovely things. Among those the most noteworthy was a set of furniture made by Lindley and decorated with miniatures of famous country estates in and near Baltimore. All but two, Homewood and Mount Clare, have vanished, but these quaint medallions show Belvedere, the home of John Eager Howard, Bolton, owned by Grundy, and later by the Spence family, Montebello, the home of General Smith (you remember how he defended Baltimore), Rose Hill, the Gibson's old mansion, Mount Deposit, where Doctor Harris lived, and Beach Hill, the home of Robert Gilmor. One wonders where these chairs and tables so intimately associated with our history will find a home—whether in Brittany or Berlin.

We have seen how a regiment of soldiers led to the opening of Saint Peter's Church. Now we shall have to camp with another regiment on the hilltop where the Roman Catholic Cathedral stands.

In 1782 Count de Rochambeau arrived in Baltimore and made an encampment in Howard's woods, as the land was then called. Here he was soon joined by the Duke de Lauzun, and the French regiments prepared to spend the hot weather

THE GOODLOE HARPER HOUSE DESIGNED BY BENJAMIN H. LATROBE

of July and August in the shade of the great forest trees that covered all the surrounding country. The camp probably spread out as far west as Howard Street, and extended south almost to Lexington. The stream from which the soldiers drew their water supply flowed in the bed of Center Street, that same stream which has given subsequent engineers so much trouble. While the soldiers were encamped here they were the object of immense interest on the part of the townspeople. Their uniforms, their bearing, their language—all was strange and fascinating. Frequently these soldiers had a military Mass, and this, too, was an event both for Protestants and Catholics. Under the trees an impromptu altar was built, and there, accompanied by all possible splendour that their poor means could afford, the Eucharist was celebrated for these strangers in a strange land. Walking on Charles street at dusk one meets the ghostly figures of these French officers, a breath of the court of old France.

Among these wraiths there is none more interesting than the Swedish Count Fersen, the man who loved Marie Antoinette. He met her at a ball at the Tuileries in 1774 and, falling in love with her, devoted the rest of his life to her service. Nor did she reject his love. It was Fersen who planned the escape to Varennes, Fersen who waited patiently in the streets near the Palace while she dawdled, Fersen who took snuff with the cabbies, and pretended that he was merely one of their fraternity. This man came to America as interpreter and long before the downfall of the monarchy spent weary months pottering between Philadelphia and Baltimore. He wrote endlessly to France reporting colonial affairs and the varied fortunes of war. Often he must have traveled along the Great Eastern Road; often he must have stopped at the Fountain Inn. Perhaps he came here on the very ground where now the Cathedral stands and heard Mass, or talked to Rochambeau and Lauzun. At least I like to think that he did.

After the Revolution the Reverend John Carroll was stationed at Saint Peter's and together with Father Sewell carried on a large and growing work. It was not until 1789 that Carroll was made the first bishop of the Roman Catholic Church in America. As the Cardinal so aptly said: "There was a man sent from God, whose name was John." Carroll was particularly fitted for this work. He was a patriot, brother of Charles Carroll of Carrollton, and a man of infinite tact, a quality much needed in a colony whose background was largely Anglican. Saint Peter's served the needs of the community until several years later when in 1806 the cornerstone of the Cathedral was laid. But the work was interrupted by the War of 1812, and it was not until 1815 that the building was recommenced. The architect chosen for this important project was Benjamin H. Latrobe. Born in England and educated in Germany Latrobe came to America to find a better field for his professional career. His distinction as an architect is manifest in the Cathedral and also in the Goodloe Harper house on Cathedral Street and the old Swann house on Franklin Street, long the home of the Maryland Academy of Sciences. These houses will all be destroyed when the new Pratt Library is built. Many authorities consider Latrobe the father of the classic movement in American architecture, and because of his influence old Baltimore is full of Greek porticos and noble classic façades. The Cathedral is one of the first churches in America to be built in this manner. To many it is distasteful, suggestive of a pagan temple rather than a Christian church, but Baltimoreans love its warm, brown façade, its quiet almost Quaker dignity. The golden minarets may seem incongruous to a stranger, but one does not measure his mother's face by strict canons of art.

A BALTIMORE HOUSE IN THE CLASSIC TRADITION AT THE
N. E. CORNER OF CATHEDRAL AND MADISON STREETS

FROM ROCHAMBEAU TO A GREEK

The nave of the Cathedral is somewhat disappointing for all its fine proportions. The light is too glaring, and there is none of that mellowness that comes from light filtered through the rich colour of stained glass. But this is a consistently Greco-Roman building. One feels at once, however, the venerable association of the place, its spiritual significance. Two paintings, the gifts of Louis Eighteenth of France, are among the treasures of the Cathedral—one of Saint Louis burying the plague-stricken soldiers before the town of Tunis, and the other the Descent from the Cross. The altar, too, is a gift from France, presented by the pupils of Archbishop Marechal who succeeded Bishop Carroll, or as he afterwards became Archbishop Carroll.

Cathedral bells are always full of interest. One has only to recall the Bourdon of Notre Dame de Paris whose terrible reverberation deafened the poor hunchback, or the dancitive silver melody of Chartres. The Cathedral, too, has her bells. It takes a long dark climb to reach them, past the clicking clock from Paris that controls the dial on the Mulberry Street side, and then up until you come out into daylight, and see the city small and diminished, lying beneath you. Under the main bell is a heavy clapper used for all low masses. Six bands of tracery adorn the large bell, but the design of the wheat and the grapes is the most beautiful. On one side is a medallion of the crucifix and on the other the Virgin and Child. The inscription—another link with the old world—runs thus: "La Très Sainte Vierge, Ambrosius Marechal Archiepiscopus Baltimorensis Tertius Ponere Curavit Pius VII Leo XIII." Below is carved "Fait à Lyons par Joseph Frerejean MDCCCGXX."

It was these bells chiming in the soft air that so drew the heart of Michael Pupin when he landed in Baltimore, a youth unknown, fifty years ago. On a Sunday morning his ship dropped anchor here and the boy, delighting in the sweet music recalled the bells of his old home. Years later when he came to Baltimore to be honored by the Hopkins he met Cardinal Gibbons, and once more the bells came to the scientist's mind. He told the Cardinal how they had delighted him and how he had been almost persuaded to remain in Baltimore and to become a Roman Catholic. To this the Cardinal, with his quick Irish wit, retorted:

"What a pity you did not; you might today be an archbishop, or perhaps even a Cardinal."

"Ah" said Pupin, "but in that case I should not be taking this degree."

Those who have followed Pupin's lectures will know how constantly he returns to the theme of the sound of church-bells. As a Serbian shepherd boy he heard their melody throughout the night, marking the hours with their lonely music while he tended his flock. Bells are among his earliest recollections, his strongest impressions. Wonderful it would be to think that the bells of the Cathedral have added their note to the "New Reformation."

In the Latrobe house across Mulberry Street lived John H. B. Latrobe, the young man who read Spenser on the advice of Harper. It was he, too, who furnished the excellent cigars and port when the little committee met to read "The MS. Found in a Bottle," a story by the unknown young fellow named Poe. Indeed the life of Latrobe touched Baltimore at many different points. He was, for example, the designer of the famous Latrobe stoves or Baltimore heaters as they were called. Radiators, of course, have practically driven them from the field, but in the old days every parlour and every dining room had as its central object of attraction a deep-bosomed ruddy stove set, as he describes it, "in the fireplace." It came about in this way. The old Franklin stoves stood out in the room, and Mrs. Latrobe complained that they took up too much space, and could be easily designed to set back somewhat more modestly. Latrobe took the hint, and made a stove which satisfied his wife's specifications. At the same time it suited others, and he declared that he could have made more money in stoves than in law.

But to me one of the most interesting stories about him is connected with his boyhood; it throws such a clear light on the mind of a child. When he was twelve he went to George-town College where one of the coveted privileges was watching Brother Henry prepare the wafers used at Mass. A sort of wafflle iron was required in this work, and thin scraps of bread were often left on the edges of the iron. Those who know boarding schools know that in that narrow realm everything assumes great importance, and it is not strange that the boys who were permitted to watch Brother Henry eagerly ate the scraps of bread as if they were a most delicious dish. Latrobe was just as eager to have a nibble as his schoolmates were, but he would not, because he feared that in some inexplicable way the scrapings would make him a Roman Catholic.

Here at the corner of Charles and Mulberry is "the Cardinal's house" as Baltimoreans still love to call it. In his garden the townspeople still watch for the first signs of spring—the crocuses. You can count on the first green tips appearing at Candlemas. Invariably the Sunpaper announces their arrival, and Baltimoreans smile and say hopefully, "Well, it won't be long now before spring comes." Every afternoon about five the Cardinal used to walk up Charles Street or Saint Paul. I can see him now, tall, spare, with a fine sensitive face. Janvier says, "His strong, yet gentle face lighted with its charming smile when he recognized his many friends." And children were his friends, for often when we were playing "King William was King James's son" he would pass us by, with a smile, and a pat on the head. Nor do I ever see the doorway of this grey old-fashioned house that I do not recall the two Cardinals standing there one hot September morning—Mercier and Gibbons, two great Princes of the Church.

In the same square on Charles Street Severn Teackle Wallis, the brilliant Baltimore lawyer, was born. We have mentioned him in conncetion with Saint Mary's where he laid the foundation of his immense legal knowledge. He was devoted also to the literature and language of Spain. But his life was by no means concerned only with law and letters. In the Civil War he suffered arrest and was imprisoned in Fort McHenry. Always he was associated with reform. It was indeed Wallis who banished the Plug Uglies. Another well-know name on this square was that of Mendes Cohen. Miss Cohen still lives on in the old house, one of the few private residences left in this part of the town. Where Bronson's furniture shop now stands was the Athenaeum Club, formerly the home of the Howards. This was one of the loveliest old houses in the town —painted, as I remember it, a pale warm yellow and adorned with the favorite Greek portico, a perfect model, so I am told, of some temple of Athene's. According to one legend the pillars that supported the pediment were all of one piece, and they were brought to this country intact. Another account states that the four fluted columns were ordered at the Beaver Dam Marble quarries at Cockeysville, and that "in due time they were started from the quarry to add to the beauty of North Charles Street then just beginning to extend." This last seems more probable, but whatever their origin these stately columns have an interesting subsequent history.

In 1910 when the Athenaeum was being destroyed to make way for a modern store, J. Alexis Shriver conceived the idea of transporting the columns to his country-place, Olney. Thus the monoliths were saved the ignominy of being broken for paving stones, and Olney gained a heritage of beauty.

By Courtesy of the City Librarian

THE ATHENAEUM CLUB

NORTHEAST CORNER OF CHARLES AND FRANKLIN

FROM ROCHAMBEAU TO A GREEK

Again to quote Janvier: "Under the Club was the famous barber shop of Emil Caye. . . . When I was a boy, barbers, many of them at least, did a great deal more for suffering humanity than laying on hot cloths for headaches. Some of them were experts in cupping and leeching." This brings to mind a dingy shop on Park Avenue where before the Great War a leecher practised his ancient profession. In the window was a small dish of worms giving evidence that the humble creatures were within call. Gone is the old Athenaeum, and quite, quite gone the cuppers and leechers of another generation. Even the barber poles, once striped symbolically red and white to signify the trade of surgery, have added a blue band in meaningless fashion, and thus have become one hundred percent.

Across from the Athenaeum is the Unitarian Church designed and built by Maximilian Godefroy, a French architect who settled here early in the past century. Godefroy shared the ideals of his day and sought inspiration in classic designs. He succeeded here in making a fine contribution to the architecture of the city. The five doors are copied from the Vatican, and the ghost of the dome of the Pantheon rises anew in Baltimore. But these are guide book details. The façade is always impressive, but never more so than at the close of a winter day when the street is full of ruddy light, and the portico lies in shadow. A wistaria vine grows on the south wall. Once I saw it sheathed in ice, bearing long crystal pendants like sprays of ghostly purple. Glittering in the low red sun it was a miracle of beauty. In 1819 Jared Sparks was called to be pastor. This brilliant man found the society of Baltimoreans most congenial, and it was not long before he had made a marked impression on the intellectual life of the city. He was soon drawn into the circle of the Delphians, and shared the literary feasts of Tusculum. Nor as a pastor did he fall short. His people were warmly attached to him and his family. This church is also associated with William Ellery Channing, a name famous in Unitarian annals, and it was here that some of his most remarkable sermons were preached.

Where the Rochambeau now stands there was once a house solid and square with generous double windows on either side of a Greek portico. It was the sort of house that should have been inhabited by a Greek spirit. Such was the case. Here for fourteen years lived Doctor Osler, that famous physician, and his almost equally famous wife. She had been warned that she was marrying a man who had books all over the floor, but marvelous to relate she did not care where he strewed his books!

Although a Baltimorean only by adoption it would be well to pause a moment to learn something of this man who was to mean through Baltimore so much to the world. Far away in the Canadian woods in 1849 was born the child who was to be such a bright figure in the medical history of this country. The family life in the parsonage hidden in the wilderness was a strict and rigid one. To the end of his days Osler said he could never see a person reading a novel on Sunday without suffering a reflex shock! At school the boy came under the influence of a most remarkable teacher—the Reverend William Johnson, or Father Johnson, as the boys affectionately called him. Johnson was a strong Tractarian—what we should call an Anglo-Catholic, but the term father was an innovation in those days—father, I mean, as applied to Anglican priests. O course there had been for some time Roman and natural fathers. But to return. This teacher took Osler fossil hunting, and then showed him how to mount specimens for slides. Johnson even went to the length of reading to his pupils the new book "The Origin of Species," and discussing it with them. Bring on some more fathers like this! At any rate William Osler determined to make science his life-work.

I have called Osler a Greek spirit, and this is what I mean. There was in the man a balance, a poise truly Hellenic. His marvelous work in science is well known, but here is evidence on the other side of his nature. He writes: "Sitting in Lincoln Cathedral, and gazing at one of the loveliest of human works, the Angel Choir, there arose within me, obliterating for a moment the 'thousand heraldries and twilight saints and dim emblazoning,' a strong sense of reverence for the minds which had executed such things of beauty. What manner of men were they, who could build such transcendent monuments? By what spirit were they moved? Absorbed in thought I did not hear the beginning of the music. Then in response to my reverie rang out the clear high voice of a boy: 'That Thy power, Thy glory, the mightiness of Thy kingdom might be known unto men.' Here was my answer." Skip all of this if you wish, but there is a sharp vignette of Doctor Osler.

Such was the man who lived in the old Curzon Hoffman house. Walk east on Franklin Street where the perilous edge of Preston Gardens begins, and looking off across the city you will see the dome of the Hopkins Hospital. This was the scene of Osler's work. The Hospital opened in 1889, the first English speaking hospital to be organized in units, each under the direction of a head. It was Johns Hopkins who said that there were two things sure to endure: "A university, for there will always be youth; a hospital, for there will always be suffering." Therefore in 1873 he left seven million dollars to be equally divided between the two—the university and the hospital. Someone has neatly remarked that three of Baltimore's hills were dedicated to three aspects of life: medicine, the Hopkins, took one; religion, the Cathedral, chose the second; government, or George Washington, pre-empted the third. We are now on religion's hill gazing across at science, but the gulf between is purely illusory; we are fellow citizens of one town. In a little group of buildings on the edge of the city Hopkins began its great work with a few men, a small group, but mighty. Read the names: Remsen in Chemistry, Martin in Biology, Welch in Pathology. On Osler fell the responsibility of organising the clinic. On the opening morning, May 6, 1889, five patients appeared at the dispensary, and on May 15 the first case was admitted to the single medical ward. Osler in the highest spirits writes to a friend, "'spital booming."

And these young doctors had a merry time. All were bachelors except Hurd, and all lived together in the hospital. One night when Richard Mansfield was playing at Ford's, his role required him to be stricken with apoplexy. Hurrying back to Hopkins it occurred to the young medical theatre-goers that it would be fine to play a good joke on those who had stayed home. Consequently Osler—I think it was our Greek—stuck his head in the door and announced, "Sudden death; immediate autopsy necessary." Up jumped Councilman and Abbott and went at once to the laboratory, and brisky made all the arrangements. Then they waited. Nothing happened. The hospital was as still as the grave. Finally they telephoned to the ward, and learned the hoax. Some of the finest young sprigs of the medical tree actually did come near death that night, but not from apoplexy.

The Oslers drew people to them, and there was a group of young men known as the "Latch Keyers." Each possessed a key, and had access to the house at any time. Furthermore a plain gold ring was given to each latchkeyer "for protection when travelling abroad." Doctor Thayer and some other young men rented Number 3 Franklin Street, and this became in a sense an annex to the Osler House. It certainly had this practical advantage: a telephone was installed there, an abomination that Osler would never permit in his own abode.

On Sunday, May 15, 1905, Doctor Osler left the house for the last time, escaping Mrs. Osler's humorous comment: "Willie's motto may well be 'aequanimitas' because he always flees when things like this are going on." "Things like this" meant moving away forever. On Tuesday the old house was scrubbed from cellar to attic; on Wednesday it was demolished. Someone took away the doorplate behind which the faithful Morris had served for years. This quotation from Doctor Osler's farewell speech in New York before he sailed for England might well be the epitaph of this truly great physician, and truly great human being.

> "I have loved no darkness,
> Sophisticated no truth,
> Nursed no delusion,
> Allowed no fear."

Didn't I tell you the man was a Greek?

OUT CHARLES STREET

CHAPTER XIV

EHIND the Unitarian Church runs a quaint little street named as some say for the great Secretary of the Treasury—Hamilton. The houses are small and English in type—the sort one finds tucked away in odd corners of Eastern cities. John Henry Keene, the lawyer, lived in the square between Cathedral and Charles, but today artists affect Hamilton Street. A few months ago a proposal was made to change the name of the street to some such Babbitry as Prospect Avenue or Maybelle Boulevard. A storm of protest arose, so violent and intense, that the advocates of the heresy withdrew precipitately. Baltimore will not suffer change unless compelled by an act of Providence; to Wit, the Great Fire.

The Thomas Buckler house on the corner of Centre and Charles afterwards known as "Miss Trippe's" is still standing, but it is only a question of time before this corner, too, loses a familiar landmark. Opposite is the Saint James, spick and span in rejuvenated brick. Across the street from the Saint James is now the fine art gallery of the late Mr. William T. Walters.

OUT CHARLES STREET

Here, says Mr. Poulney, was McNally's school for boys. Later Miss Bataille had a boarding house here, and beyond that was the residence of Orville Horwitz.

But before we go any further, turn down Center Street, east, and stop a moment at the New Mercantile Library. On Charles Street just above Saratoga there was for many years an institution greatly loved by the old residents of the town. The institution had its origin at Market and Holliday Streets where in the ripe years of the past century—in 1839—a group of young men of literary taste procured comfortable quarters and opened a reading room. To be sure there was the old Baltimore Library, already long established, but the young merchants and "sprightly clerks" were eager for something more up to date. Baltimore had indeed had a library since 1809. There was Robinson's at the corner of Market and Belvedere Streets. Begun in 1809, it had by 1819 grown rich in the accumulation of seven thousand volumes, "all standard works including the most authentick." The proprietor had established correspondence with London, thereby promptly receiving all the first editions, few of which are ever reprinted in this country. Mr. Robinson also announced "an upwards of twenty English and Scotch periodicals." I wonder if among them was to be found Blackwood's and the Quarterly which at this time were so bitterly attacking Keats? In that very year, indeed, in which Robinson was advocating the latest British authors, did his patrons by any chance come upon a poem called "The Eve of Saint Agnes," or perchance "La Belle Dame sans Merci"? Mr. Keats had recently published them—but not in Blackwood's!

By 1839 Robinson's was outmoded, and the Mercantile began its career. Its founders were eager to increase the culture of the day, and John Quincy Adams was invited in 1840 to speak on Society and Civilization. Imagine a group of young merchants and tired business men hearkening to Adams—or

anyone else—on such a topic. It gives us a shamed feeling
similar to that which overwhelms us when we read that Greek
cobblers enjoyed the tragedies of Aeschylus. Later it became
advisable to move from Baltimore to Charles Street, and John
W. McCoy, the possessor of a fine library and a patron of the
arts, was much interested in the proposal. This is the McCoy
who appreciated the work of the sculptor Rinehart long before
he was popularly acclaimed. In the old Howard Street
epoch of Hopkins's development McCoy Hall was proud to
bear the name of this distinguished man. The old New Mercantile—Baltimore has an odd nomenclature—was a long low
room encircled by a gallery. At the right, at a small desk, sat
the Librarian, Miss Margie Watkins. Shrewd, kindly, sensible,
Miss Watkins knew all who entered her bailiwick, and she
had decided opinions on each. Beside her on the desk sat a
fat bulbous jar filled with slips of paper; what they signified I
never knew and I dared not ask. The room itself was the Victorian age in miniature. Strips of bright carpet were stretched
in convenient spots, and wicker rocking chairs were set accurately and thriftily before each strip. In the centre of the room
there was a circular seat built up around a central column, the
whole structure topped off by a fern. It was as uncomfortable
as it sounds. The walls were lined with books scarlet, blue,
and brown. At the rear of the library there was a tiny little
carpeted staircase leading to the gallery where fame and dust
contended. Those who knew the old Library will never forget it. In summer it was a cavern of coolness and repose. In
the winter when the streets outside glittered like a jewel box,
here was dusk and shadow, the atmosphere for dreams. At
length at five-thirty Miss Watkins, bearing a large sheet,
approached the table devoted to new books, and with a
motherly gesture covered them up for the night.

OUT CHARLES STREET

In 1856 when Mr. Thackeray, the celebrated English humorist, was in town delivering his lectures on the Four Georges, he know this library well; indeed on his departure from England he gave as his address "The Mercantile Library, Baltimore." In later years Hugh Walpole visited the library, and found it a small strait Victorian island not unlike, in truth, the England of his boyhood.

The new New Mercantile on Center Street is a charming room. The walls are covered with a tapestry of books. The fireplace and the rugs and comfortable chairs add much to the home-like quality of the new quarters. Above the bookcases are interesting Baltimoreana—such as old membership cards and framed copies of the Sunpaper. Upstairs among the theological volumes are some of our ancient friends, the old chairs and tables from the Library in its Charles Street days.

Alas, it is stated authoritatively that this, too, must go. The young merchants read elsewhere, and "the sprightly clerks" are no longer interested in Society and Civilization.

The site of Miss Bataille's boarding house is now occupied by the Walters Art Gallery. In 1861 William T. Walters went to Paris where he lived for several years, gathering together the nucleus of his collection. It was the period of Ingres, Millet, Delacroix and Puvis de Chavannes. In sculpture Barye was, at last, earning that recognition that came too late, "when he had lost his teeth." We have spoken of the magnificent collection of bronzes in the gallery, and a visitor can see for himself the fine examples of Barye's work in Mount Vernon Place. On the death of William T. Walters the gallery became the possession of his son Henry. At first this fine private collection was housed in the Walters' mansion on Mount Vernon Place, but some years ago a handsome Renaissance building was erected for the proper arrangement of its treasures. Unfortunately this gallery is not open to the public except in the months of January, February, March, and April, and then only on Wednesdays and Saturdays. What a blessing it would be to the town if the people—the plain people—could have access to these beautiful works of art on Sunday! We certainly have much to learn from the French. In Paris the galleries and museums are filled with working men accompanied by their children studying keenly the great masterpieces of painting and sculpture. And on Sunday too! Oh, those immoral French!

On the first floor there are cases of carved ivories exquisitely wrought; there are enamels; there are Japanese porcelains. But much more interesting than these are the small rooms exemplifying various periods of design. In the French room is spread a rug, in warm pastel colours, bearing the monogram of Marie Antoinette. The Jacobean room is dark with heavily carved mantel and massive chairs. The Gothic room, however, enshrines the loveliest thing in Baltimore. It is a small wood-carving painted in bright living hues. Four ladies young and gracious are leaning together on the window sill of some old mediæval casement. Their heads are poised as delicately, as lightly, as birds. They seem almost to speak in subtle raillery, perhaps, of some knight in the tourney yard below. Each wears the hennin, that tall peaked hat beloved in the days of Villon. A light wind from the Seine ruffles their veils. They smile, and talk in low tones:

"Il ne bon bec que de Paris"

I envy Mr. Walters this lovely bit of old France.

Upstairs are the pictures, admirable early Italians and all sorts German primitives. For my own part I like the pictures that I have seen there since I was a child—old-fashioned work —*The Sheepfold at Night, Gerôme's Christian Martyrs with* the so-real lions, *The Attack at Dawn, The Fête Dieu, The Revocation of the Edict of Nantes.*

234

OUT CHARLES STREET

On the southeast corner of Mount Vernon Place is the Peabody Institute, the center of the musical life of the town. It was designed, as Peabody said, "to diffuse and cultivate a taste for music—the most refining of all the arts—by providing a means of studying its principles and practising its compositions." Famous names have been associated with this institution, none more so than Sidney Lanier's. Born in Georgia and serving in the Confederate army, he came after the War to Baltimore and obtained a position as flutist in the Peabody orchestra. You will recall that it was his flute that so attracted Tabb, also a poet and a Confederate soldier. Mr. Frederick Gottlieb knew Lanier well, and on each birthday celebration at Saint Paul's Rectory he tells a story here and there from the poet's life, or better yet, plays on his flute the melodies once dear to the poet. Mr. Gottlieb was in the Peabody orchestra and had the privilege of knowing Lanier in a very close and sympathetic way.

George Peabody himself is even more interesting than the institution that bears his name, and if you will seat yourself comfortably on the marble bench beneath O'Connor's Lafayette I shall tell you his story. Certainly no one's family name has a more thrilling or dramatic history, and whether it is true or false it is too good to miss. There was in the days of Boadicea—of course you remember her; one of the earliest wild women—a fierce Celt named Boadie. This Boadie after a conflict with the Romans fled to Wales bearing a helmet as a trophy on which was engraved a device of two suns. The intrepid Celt established himself in the mountains, or *pay,* as they were called in the Welsh tongue (and you know how curious the Welsh tongue is, so none dare deny it.) There Boadie prospered, and his sons, a valiant line, took the name of Peabody. In time of peace this family devoted itself to agriculture, and therefore the sheaf of wheat appears in the coat of arms.

From this warlike stock came George Peabody, born in Danvers, Massachusetts, in 1795. The house in which he was born was painted a bright yellow, perhaps in memory of the wheat or the Roman helmet. However that might be, the family was by this time the reverse of wealthy, and George had to leave school at eleven. When but a youth he and his brother opened a little store in Newburyport, but, alas, a fire destroyed it, and then Peabody determined to go South.

In May, 1815, he set out for Georgetown where he hoped to make his fortune, but it was a bad year for fortunes. The British—those "tourists in red"—came along breathing out threats and slaughter against Washington. Now uprose the Blood of Boadie, and, remembering Boadicea, Peabody promptly enlisted. He was sent to Fort Warburton in Maryland and there he met two famous men—Francis Scott Key and Elisha Riggs. Later he met another Baltimorean, then a lad—John P. Kennedy. I do not know whether this meeting took place in Baltimore or not. Kennedy gives a vivid picture of his life at Fort McHenry, and it may be that Peabody met him at that time. Kennedy noted with pride the swanky uniform of the day—"the dark blue and red suit, the leather helmet with the huge black feather." The rations were almost as gorgeous. Imagine a private eating "cold fowl, cold ham, beat biscuit and wine." At any rate, says Kennedy, "nothing in life has ever equalled those nights at the Fort." After the war Riggs and Peabody set up business in Baltimore, and then Peabody went abroad to negotiate a crop of cotton grown for Lancashire. In 1837 he decided to make England his home. But that did not mean that his interest in Baltimore was dead. On the contrary he always recalled the town with sincere affection, and knowing Kennedy's love for the city the banker consulted him about the best possible sort of foundation. In 1868 the foundation was established, and no one can estimate its influence on the life of the community. But not in music alone is this great institution notable. The Library is a veritable storehouse of knowledge, and what is more unusual, it has a corps of librarians unequalled in courtesy, efficiency and general agreeableness.

For over twenty years Harold Randolph was the head of this famous school, and its success and influence today is due in large measure to his direction and wisdom. The Peabody Annex under the guidance of May Garrettson Evans is an interesting development in the teaching of music to children. Nor should one fail to mention the work of Frederick Huber, director of municipal music. Baltimore is the only city in the country which has a separate department of music. The Baltimore Symphony Orchestra under Gustave Strube has done fine work in presenting at moderate prices the works of the great musicians. Back of all the musical life of the town is the Peabody—a fostering mother to a family of sturdy sons and daughters.

* * * *

Seventy-five years ago Charles Street north of Madison presented a wholly rural picture. The ground rose in a red clay bank at the present site of the University Club, and along the top of the bluff ran a narrow straggling path. Just where this ended I do not know, but before long Howard's woods must have swallowed it. All acounts of the period speak of these woods as a sort of glorified Druid Hill Park. I say glorified because there seems to have been utter freedom in this domain. Lovers strolled therein, and made decorous early nineteenth century love under the great forest trees. Duels, too, were fought there by young fire-eaters, and though the custom was highly disapproved it flourished secretly in the dark shadows

237

on a moonlight night. Nor were the youngsters absent. There band of small boys met to play robbers or Indians or other games of that character, and, when they had grown more desperate, stone battles raged frequently. The vast estate, however, was slowly being cut up into streets, and little by little the town was encroaching on what had been primeval woodland.

At present Charles Street is in a transition stage. It is half residence and half trade, but in the nineties it was at the height of its glory. The Baltimore Club then occupied the brown stone building on the west side of the street, and young men gathered at the windows to watch the belles of Baltimore go by in the Sunday after-church parade. Across the street the Misses Cary had their school for young ladies. Here the blinds were discreetly drawn, and the young ladies were properly protected from the rude gaze of the populace—especially the gentlemen across the way.

The sombre brown stone house on the corner of Eager and Charles, now the headquarters of the Arundel Club, in old days belonged to the Bonsals. Further up the street was the home of the Munnikhuysens, and then on the corner where Hynson and Westcott has a fine drugstore was the Perin's home. Across the street is the Belvedere Hotel named, of course, from the old Howard estate. The mansion stood some distance east of this corner, just at the intersection of Calvert and Chase Streets. A gigantic office building now towers on the site of the house where the McLanes and Perots lived. There was a large garden here surrounded by a high forbidding wall but over it grew an aged wistaria vine—a thing of beauty in the spring. Business and trade have swallowed up the old garden, and the mark of the beast is on the whole long thoroughfare as it slopes steeply down to Union Station. In the nineties there was no dust and dirt to mar the spotless steps, and the traffic, except for a leisurely cable car, was negligible. Some of us indeed can recall even the horse cars of long ago. These strange vehicles always had great difficutly in making the Charles Street hill in wintry weather. In those days, in spite of Mr. Nunn, the snows were much heavier and much more frequent than they are now. The floor of the car was covered with straw to keep the passengers feet warm, and the driver, standing on an open platform, was securely wrapped in a heavy blanket from the waist down. At Eager Street the car generally went off the track, and all of the men promptly arose and aided the half frozen driver to restore the car to the proper position on the rails. This was no slight task, but it did warm up the blood, and certainly it added to the excitement of a simple street car ride. Along the route many housekeepers ordered hot coffee for the men during the winter storms, and surely a driver who negotiated this steep hill from Eager to Chase deserved a steaming cup.

On warm and pleasant Sundays in the nineties or on crisp winter days the streets were filled with gentlemen in high hats and ladies in gay apparel. The children walked demurely by their parents saying little, for children were seen and not heard, but they missed nothing of the passing show. They wore their locks in curls shadowed by floppy leghorn hats; their frocks had "berthas." The houses, now so forlorn and uncertain in appearance, were then spotless, brass rails shining, and lace curtains stiffly draped before each window. At Mount Royal Avenue the procession ceased, though some continued their walk as far as North Avenue then called the Boundary.

At the corner of Maryland and Mount Royal Avenues stood the Cyclorama, a round building painted a dismal pea-green. But its mysterious shape indicated something unusual and alluring. Here once was held a "marvelous spectacle—the Battle of Gettysburg painted on a monster canvass. I remember seeing this but all that remains in my mind is the strange twilight, a sort of livid under the sea atmosphere. Later pure food shows were held here and we were introduced to Sunny Jim. Last of all came Bostock's Zoo for a glorious and exciting winter. But, alas, one night the old cyclorama burned—to the great sorrow of all Baltimore children.

In the seventies there was a skating rink where Union Station now stands, and it was the smart thing to belong to this private rink and to walk out through the country on cold winter afternoons. Then after the rural walk you presented your ticket, and off you glided across the pond.

No street in the town has changed as much as the Boundary or North Avenue. In the beginning of this century it was almost entirely a residence street. Where the walls of the new Market House are going up there were three houses known as the "Cottages." Theye were delightful houses with gabled roofs and deep porches approached by wide steps. Each house was set back from the street in a garden shady with great trees, and fragrant with box and crepe myrtle bushes. Now where cars are parked in oily magnificence was a pleasant little square called Taney Place. It was a modest square but green and refreshing with stiff flower beds and neat gravel walks. Across the street on the south side were old red-brick houses, substantial, at least—certainly not shoddy. There were no electric signs, movies, Fords, traffic towers or any marks of a highly advanced civilization. The Fremont Street cars turned just west of the Charles and North traffic tower before they started on their down-town trip. Those were leisurely days when the amiable conductors—I must say, however that our motormen and conductors are invariably amiable—waited for the Goucher "city girls" to board the car at this point. They always waited for us in rainy weather, and—what is more—on

BALTIMORE HARBOUR IN THE NINETIES

one occasion the long-suffering conductor let me pay my fare with three cents and a postage stamp. That *was* service.

There is nothing to be seen between this point and Wyman's Park. The section is filthy and sordid beyond words. A ghastly filling station defiles the corner, but a newly erected bank building somewhat counteracts the monstrosity. At Twenty-third Street the Goucher College buildings begin, and if you are interested walk around on Saint Paul Street for a better view of them. First Methodist Church and Goucher Hall are the work of Stanford White. The hedge now gives some privacy to the pocket handkerchief campus, but it will not be long, probably, before Goucher moves to Govans, and there it will have its true and proper setting. The college founded by John and Mary Goucher has had an enviable record in the academic world, nor is its achievement in any sense diminished under its new leadership. The foundation laid by Doctor Goucher has been sufficiently deep and broad to carry the superstructure of later years. Dean Van Meter told a story of some visitors who came to him in vacation asking to see the college.

"But you can not do that," said the Dean very gravely. The visitors naturally were astonished, and the Dean continued, "The college is away on its vacation—you can see the buildings, but only the students can show you the college—they are the college."

Visit Goucher if possible when the college is present.

As one wanders in this part of the city today one can hardly realize that thirty years ago all north of Huntingdon Avenue or Twenty-fifth Street was country. Charles Street Avenue was a sleepy, dusty road. On the northeast corner of Twenty-fifth and Charles stood a house with a few fruit trees, and all sorts of mysterious sheds and out-buildings. Directly back of this

entrancing garden was another house, a grey, retired place
which still stands as a witness to the past. Beyond, this point
there were fields and wooded lots—maybe a few houses, but
practically none at all. To the east Huntingdon Avenue ran
into the York Road. The Avenue itself was an unpaved dirt
road with grass and dandelions, to say nothing of a good crop
of daisies, growing along the gutters. Nothing, by the way,
has ever been written about the Baltimore gutters, and they
deserve notice. The water flowed along on flat stones, rather
large and well-shaped. From the curb a bank sloped gently
down and this bank was set with neat little rocks in whose
interstices grew rich green moss. Occasionally dandelions took
root on the miniature terrace; sparrow grass grew abundantly.
Along the curb grass flourished. This was an abomination in
the eyes of a Baltimore householder, and a sharp knife was
employed to keep the "front pavement" neat. Huntingdon
Avenue in the nineties had nothing half so sophisticated as
stone gutters, or, if they were in place, the weeds grew so high
that a child at least could not distinguish them. Where the
public school now stands was a great shadowy car barn, and
on the corner of Saint Paul and Huntingdon there was another house set in a generous yard.

Beyond Calvert Street on hot August afternoons one heard
the long-drawn howls of joy from the bleachers. Here in the
old days was the Oriole Baseball Park. The pavement stopped
at the Sadtler's house on the corner of the alley, and Huntingdon Avenue boasted no sidewalk beyond this point. A high
board fence shut out the coveted view of the diamond, but
there were a few convenient knot-holes. These were great days
in the history of baseball. In 1893 Baltimore had a poor team.
It stood last in the twelve-club national League, but Hanlon
was gathering in a fine set of men: Muggsy McGraw, Joe
Kelley, Hughey Jennings, Wilbert Robinson. These men were

HOMEWOOD, HOME OF CHARLES CARROLL OF CARROLLTON

fighters. Jennings was the fellow, by the way, who invented the phrase "Attaboy." With such men as these Baltimore won the pennant. . For three years the Orioles were invincible, and the town went baseball mad. Men went out to the field in droves. They hung on the cable cars like flies. This old field saw some thrilling contests. It has vanished now, and smug houses are built over the old diamond. But Babe Ruth still maintains Baltimore's baseball tradition.

We have chosen Charles Street as an axis, but surely we have swung far afield. Now we must return, but before we walk out Charles Street Avenue, go in memory with me to Sumwalt's pond which lay west of Maryland Avenue in the neighborhood of Twenty-seventh Street. Here was the favorite skating rendezvous in those cold frosty winters of long ago. Where Wyman's Park is now laid out in formal beauty there was a stretch of woods famous for its violets and spring beauties. Down in the sunken garden, approached by neat concrete steps, was a little stream meandering through marshy ground. It was wild unspoiled country, and though the Park is lovely, there was a rich enchantment in those woods. The Mansion belonging to the Wyman family was remote and sheltered behind a thick grove of trees. If one ventured as far as the green lawn surrounding the funny old house, someone chased you away, not with words, but by waving—well, really it looked like a red flannel petticoat, but I could not swear to that. At any rate it was thrilling to venture, more thrilling to flee. For a long time all this was a wild preserve.

Just north of the park shut off by high paling fences was the glorious Carroll Mansion—Homewood. This house built in 1803 as a residence for the son of Charles Carroll of Carrollton, is one of the finest colonial houses in America. Every detail is perfect—the rich colour of the brick-work, the broad low steps, the gracious pediment. It is now the property of

243

the Johns Hopkins University, and it has served as a pattern for the future University buildings. Gilman Hall, named for the first president, Daniel Coit Gilman, carries on the Georgian tradition. But the history of Hopkins has yet to be written in this place. Its roots lie in the town, in the shabby dismantled buildings on Howard and Eutaw Streets. Hopkins prefers men to bricks. Even now she plans plain and simple buildings, and that is in accordance with her past ideals.

University Parkway has a lordly sound. It sweeps in a great diagonal across north Baltimore, and few there are who remember that once it was only a little lane—Merryman's Lane. Here at the junction of Charles Street Avenue and University Parkway was a toll-gate, and a small box of a house where the toll-gate man lived. But there is one landmark left. West of the toll-gate there is an old-fashioned country house, and on the lawn a boat filled with flowers. So it was even in the days when Merryman's lane was sweet with locust trees. I wish I knew the history of that boat.

Sometimes if the wind was from the east we could hear "Saint John's grey bell, that grieving bell." Today the spire is hidden behind the huge bulk of overgrown apartment houses, but in another age it rose above the trees, pointing out the village of Waverly, once called Huntingdon. This quiet appanage has now been merged into the noisy life of the city, but once it was full of lanes, and apple trees, and bird songs. Those who know Miss Reese's poetry will recall a dozen folk who lived there. Surely you have not forgotten Old Saul who lived near the hawthorn tree in Tinges Lane. He came from Kent in the old country—"born English." And then there was Little Henrietta, sister perhaps to Lydia who "is gone this many a year." True enough; and yet one evening in Saint Paul's Rectory she seemed to live again in her cloak, "gilt and faded green." The sexton's wife, you know, had three quince trees, "Cloud-like about her gusty door." Nor for worlds would I forget Charity and Phyllis who plucked the daffodils. And is this the Rector of the parish?

"A tall man stooping not with years but books;
Part Sussex he, so frank deem him hard,
Part Donegal, and so both warm and quaint."

I do not know. Perhaps he has another cure of souls, but he seems somehow to belong to Huntingdon.

GREEN MOUNT

CHAPTER XV

AS one comes down the Old York Road there is small glamour; it is, in fact, a drab neighborhood. One place of legend remains, however, one spot touched by romance: the lawn of Saint Ann's Church. Everyone knows that Saint Ann is the protector of sailors. Brittany is full of churches under her patronage, and pardons are held in her honour, nor is she without suppliants in this country. The old anchor has to do with one of these.

In 1833 when the clipper ships were at their height, a young fellow named William Kennedy commanded a ship called the *Wanderer*. She was a lovely bark, and he a gallant skipper, but the *Wanderer* had a rival in Miss Mary Ann Jenkins. Finally the lady made the captain promise that he would give up the sea and become a landsman, a proposal very uncongenial to Kennedy. But he loved Mary Ann, and with the old anchor hanging at the bow of the *Wanderer* he made a last voyage to Mexico. At length when he had almost reached port, a terrific wind blew from the north, and Captain Kennedy was compelled to anchor in the harbour close to a rocky island, Sacrificios. In the tempest which lasted all day and all night, one anchor was lost, and Kennedy vowed that if the second held he would retire from the sea and build a church in honour of Saint Ann. Some sceptics say that this is an embroidery of the real vow, but there is the church as a witness! Furthermore, when Kennedy returned he married the lovely Miss Jenkins and went to live at his father's country place, Oak Hill, which lay along the York Road, or Greenmount Avenue, above North. On the lawn before the mansion the faithful anchor had an honorable place. In after years remembering his vow, Mr. Kennedy gave the land and the money to build a church on the York Road at Twenty-second Street. The cornerstone had not been in place a year before Mr. Jenkins died, and was buried in the sanctuary of Saint Ann's. There, too, his wife was laid beside him when she came to die. It seems to me a happy and pious coincidence that the patron saint of sailors and Kennedy's wife both bore the same name.

The northeast corner of Greenmount and North Avenues is now occupied by a prosaic shop. It was not so of yore. Here in the bygone days the Circus spread its huge tent. When the big top went up, what bliss untold! Spangles and pink lemonade! Here too used to be held those wonderful spectacles known as *The Fall of Pompeii* and *Lalla Rookh*. There never were such rockets before or since, such soft splutter of green, blue and rosy fire, such adoring "ahs" of delight. In those days the Avenue was little more than a country road leading in to market. Great lumbering wagons piled high with fragrant hay rumbled by on their way to the hay scales. But this is not utterly changed. The circus has long since departed to Bentalou Street, but on the old scales, down by the Belair Market, business is still active.

The low stone wall at North Avenue and Greenmount Avenue marks the north end of the famous Baltimore cemetery, but to enter we shall have to walk south for a square or two. Small shops of butchers, bakers and candle-stick makers line the western side of the street. Along the other side is the rough stone wall of the graveyard. Once the wall had a flat and hospitable top which accommodated the circus crowds of former years.

Across from the main gate of the cemetery there used to be a line of humble brick houses with a row of stiff poplars before the door. The Lord Baltimore Press has swallowed most of these, but the Hansel and Gretel house remains. This is the house with the peaked roof, and the air of a witch. I must admit, however, that the witch is losing her potency; possibly because the high buildings are rapidly crowding her out. Opposite the witch's low-browed dwelling is the gothic gateway of Greenmount, a gateway so proudly described in the *Baltimore Clipper*: "this gothic gateway to the city of the dead is fast approaching completion. If beauty and quiet surround the scene at present who can portray the interest that will be thrown around it a hundred years from now?" There is more in the same vein about the "couch of genius," and the "solitary passenger." *The Baltimore Clipper* might well be the "Token," that book beloved of ladies in the thirties. And how immensely pleased the citizens were with that gothic gateway. Echoes of "The Castle of Otranto" were in the air, and crenellated towers and "Ivanhoe" were still popular. But this entrance is by no means unpleasing. The stone is well-surfaced, and the years have given it a warmth with the passing of time.

It would, nevertheless, be false to imagine that Greenmount had always been a graveyard. Far from it. It was the estate of Robert Oliver, a Baltimorean of wealth and prominence. In Oliver's time the property lay on the edge of the town, beautifully situated in rolling country, comanding a fine view. Josiah Quincy of Massachusetts writes: "Any social meetings more hearty, easy and friendly and in all respects agreeable than those which characterize the Baltimore society of 1826 it has never been my fortune to attend. My stay seemed like a long English Christmas—such as one reads in books. The beauty and grace of the ladies and the charming ease of their manners were very taking to me, reared among the grave proprieties of Boston." How these Bostonians do expand in the Southern atmosphere! Later the New Englander speaks of "dancing and dining at Mr. Oliver's noble residence." Noble it must have been, a great house situated on a commanding knoll with a fine prospect over the rolling, undulating countryside.

But no man has all the gifts of the gods, and Oliver had a headstrong daughter. At this point I should warn you that historians pooh-pooh this legend, but it is so full of dramatic quality that I can not resist it. The daughter was as beautiful as she was spirited, and the lovely headstrong creature fell in love with a young man not acceptable to her father. Robert Oliver forbade him the house to which this thoroughly modern girl replied that she would meet her lover willy-nilly in the groves of the estate. When the father discovered that his daughter was as resolute as he, his rage was unbounded. Now he played his trump card. He declared that if the suitor was seen on the estate he would shoot the lad on sight. And Oliver was a good shot.

But Baltimore boys are not lacking in spirit, and nightly the young fellow met his beloved. One evening the daughter dressed herself in boy's clothes the better to escape detection, and set out for the meeting. What she planned no one knows —an elopement, a final parting, or a merry prank. Robert Oliver was on watch, for he suspected that something was afoot. Presently when the form of a young boy glided along through the trees, the father fired. Alas, it was his daughter who lay at his feet. Where she fell she was buried, and later he, too, was laid to rest beside her. The tall slender shaft on the north slope

249

BALTIMORE

of the green mount marks the spot. Thus into the "noble residence" came pride and sorrow and death.

After Robert Oliver's death an organization of twenty gentlemen was formed to secure the property known as Greenmount. The purpose was to use it as a cemetery. As usual, intense antagonism to the scheme prevailed. All sort of dreadful predictions were made; it would be desecrated by scoundrels; it would be overrun by the vulgar horde; it would be a common tea-garden. But the proponents went ahead with their plans, and let the townspeople howl. To prevent any unseemliness tickets were distributed to lot holders. Of course nothing untoward ever occured, to the intense chagrin of the calamity howlers. In connection with the sale of lots some odd facts are revealed. Forty thousand dollars was to be set aside as a permanent fund for maintenance, and the further proceeds were to be used as follows: two-fifths for the use of the cemetery; one-fifth to temperance; one-fifth to Sunday-schools; on-fifth to the seamen's home and apprentices' library.

The first burial in Greenmount was in December, 1839, when Oliva Cushing Whitridge, "two years, two months and twenty days," was buried here. Teackle Wallis wrote some verses on this occasion, and though tinged with the melancholy of the period, they are not without grace and charm.

"The city of the dead hath thrown wide its gates at last,
And through the cold, grey portal a funeral train hath passed;
One grave—the first—is open, and on its lonely bed.
Some heir of sin and sorrow hath come to lay his head.

Perchance a hero cometh, whose chaplet in its bloom
Hath fallen from his helmet to wither on his tomb;
It may be that hot youth comes, it may be we behold
Here broken at the cistern pale beauty's bowl of gold.

* * * * * *

Green home of future thousands! How blest in sight of heaven
Are these the tender firstlings, that death to thee hath given.
Through prayer and solemn anthem have echoed from thy hill,
This first fresh grave of childhood have made thee holier still."

250

Greenmount was opened in the summer, the Reverend William E. Wyatt of Saint Paul's dedicating the ground, and John P. Kennedy delivering the address.

In Greenmount many famous people lie buried, but perhaps there are none more famous than the Booths. When you enter the main gate, turn sharply to your right, and you will see the tall monument that marks the Booth lot. Here lies Junius Brutus Booth, the father of the great Edwin. But the elder Booth was himself an actor of the finest calibre. A man of ardent and fiery temper, he lived his roles with such completeness that once as Richard Third he chased Richmond across the stage, down the aisle and the whole way around Holliday Street to Gay. I can not vouch for this, but it certainly displays Booth's impetuous nature. Close by, at the back of the lot, is buried John Wilkes Booth. According to several authorities, including Mears the undertaker, John Wilkes' body was brought to Baltimore where it was identified by four persons—Colonel William M. Pegram, Magistrate Hagerty, Basil Moxley and a Dr. Micheau. Hagerty had lived across the street from the Booths when they spent the winters in Exeter Street and Moxley was the doorkeeper at the Holliday Street theater. At the time that John Wilkes was brought to Baltimore for burial in 1869, feeling was running very high and it was only natural that the burial should be quiet and secret. When Mears who had charge of the lot—the marking of the graves and similar matters—asked Edwin Booth what should be done about John Wilkes, the great actor threw up his hands and said: "Let that rest as it is." Here rests that wild, misguided, singularly fascinating youth whose mad deed had such fearful consequences. He was his mother's favorite son, beautiful in face and figure with a wild romantic beauty. Says Clara Morris: "Mr. Booth came, such a picture in his Greek

BALTIMORE

garments as made even the men exclaim at him." He *must* have been extraordinary.

Far away on the north side of the graveyard lies another great artist—Sidney Lanier. Lanier and Tabb, you will remember, were both in the Confederate Army and both suffered imprisonment. It was there that the poet's flute brought such delight to the other captives, and even soothed the rancour of their jailers; and it was this magic flute that gave Lanier an *entrée* to the Peabody. Lonely and unfriendly as he was, Lanier found a full measure of sympathy and understanding in Lawrence Turnbull and his wife. Their house was ever open to him, and it is due to their encouragement that the poet kept on at his work. *The Marshes of Glynn,* one of the greatest of American poems, was written in Baltimore, and likewise *The Ballad of the Master.* At his death Lanier was buried in the Turnbull lot, and later his two friends came to rest beside him. Over his grave is set a rough boulder, a fine, strong rock, bearing a bronze tablet. On it the sun rises over a stretch of water, and the words "I am lit with the sun" are chiseled below. A rose bush, like a little tree, has grown up beside the stone, in summer showering its blossoms across the boulder, in winter making a net-work of wavering shadow. Here by his grave one recalls Lanier's *"Stirrup Cup."* Bitter was his struggle with poverty and sickness, but Lanier faced life bravely, and prepared for the last journey with a high heart. Thus he wrote:

"Death, thou'rt a cordial old and rare,
See how compounded, with what care;
Time got his wrinkles reaping thee,
Sweet herb, from all antiquity.

* * * *

Then, Time, let not a drop be spilt,
Hand me the cup whene'er thou wilt;
'Tis thy rich stirrup cup to me,
I'll drink it down right smilingly."

THE LONG DOCK—SOUTH GAY STREET

GREEN MOUNT

If you are fond of old graves you will find them along the Ensor Street wall in a sheltered sunny place. The quiet dead who lie here are from all parts of the world—Bermuda, Germany, Ireland and far-off Goa in the East Indies. Here they rest in red Maryland earth, and over them are no stones with the grim devices so common in New England. Here are carven willow trees bending in long flowing lines, or perhaps a rose is cut upon the stone; always death is marked by some gentle emblem, not the hideous grinning skulls of Plymouth or South Duxbury. One stone especially took my fancy: "In memory of Sally," it read; then beneath this inscription was carved a graceful rose, its petals a little dimmed by time. Below the flower one read: "Consort of William Yates, who died 1816 in full assurance of a blessed immortality." Her age came last of all, and in the December sunlight I tried to decipher it, but was it 26 or 86? No, not the last; Sally is too gay for eighty-six. In that case the stone should read "In memory of Sarah."

At the northern end of Greenmount there is a lot belonging to the late Andrew Anderson, that arrests attention by its unusual ornamentation. Set at intervals about the enclosure are handsome vases, some of Oriental, some of fine European ware. The subjects on these vases are classical, in most cases drawn from legend or history, and though they have been in place for many years, the colours are still bright and warm. The story is that the first Mrs. Anderson dearly loved these handsome ornaments and that at her death her husband placed them above her grave.

Where the Green Mount which gives the cemetery its name rises to its full height is found the Riggs memorial, a magnificent bronze figure by Hans Schuler, the Baltimore sculptor. The artist is known best, perhaps, by secular bronzes notably the spirited Marathon Runner and the Ariadne in the Walters collection. But in this solemn and beautiful figure in

Greenmount is found a noble expression of the classic conception of death.

Although Hans Schuler, the Baltimore sculptor, is represented in Greenmount by masterly work there is perhaps nothing finer in the cemetery than Rinehart's Sleeping Endymion. The sculptor, born in Carroll county, died in Rome with the strange interval of his life lying between. William Rinehart worked on his father's farm until he heard that a stone cutter needed an assistant. This was the work that he truly loved, and he was by no means loath to give up the plough for the chisel. He labored unremittingly in the stone cutter's yard, accustoming his eye to precision of line and form, and as he worked, the determination grew in him to devote his life to sculpture. Later he came to Baltimore and there in the marble yard of Bevan and Baughman he obtained employment. Nor were they slow to recognize his genius. The young man was given a studio where he was permitted to work out his dreams. But Rinehart knew that he must study abroad. It was not long before he went to Florence, and after a brief interval in Baltimore he returned to Rome where he lived until his death. This simple farm lad became one of the foremost American sculptors. Nor did his influence cease with his death. His small fortune increased by wise investments was used for the establishment of the Rinehart School of Sculpture. This figure of Endymion is one of Rinehart's loveliest works—simple and graceful. But lovelier still is the thought that prompts someone every year to put into the hand of the sleeping boy a flower suited to the season. At All Saints a small chrysanthemum is slipped between the slender fingers; at Christmas a sprig of holly; at Easter a daffodil. More than half a century has passed since Rinehart's death, but Endymion and the flower still keep him in warm and living memory.

The neighborhood to the west of Greenmount has changed greatly in the last few years. A little oblique thoroughfare running southwest from the main entrance of the cemetery is all that is left of the old Belvedere Road. For many years there was a bridge across the Falls where the turbulent stream made a deep bend at Preston Street, and the Belvedere Road was the link joining this old covered bridge with the rich farm country that lay out along the York Road. Down this road came rolling blue and red wagons of substantial girth loaded with grain to be sold in the Baltimore markets. Often the farmer brought his wife and daughters with him, and as they crossed the Belvedere bridge they felt that they were indeed getting their first glimpse of the metropolis. From the hot sunlight they entered the cool tunnel of the bridge where the dazzling light struck upward from the water of the Falls below, and danced upon the rough beams of the roof. Beyond the horses' heads there was a brilliant patch of green where the path came out into full sunlight. Along the bank of the stream grew locust trees, filling the air with their heavy ivory perfume. To the east of the bridge the water was impounded for a hominy mill that stood nearby, and in hot weather small Baltimoreans added a Greek touch to the already pastoral scene. The banks of the stream afforded excellent locker facilities, and a bath in the Falls was the usual procedure on a hot summer day.

On the Belvedere Road lived a young lady so modern in tendency that I must recall her. She was of literary turn, and is described as "a wild and wayward writer somewhat in the George Sand school." Imagine that in peaceful, provincial Baltimore! This lady contributed to the *Baltimore Visitor,* and one day when the editor called, he found her "clad in a loose muslin frock and unbound hair," seated upon a fence rail! George Sand school with a vengeance, and all this in the age of innocence. There is more, but I won't tell it; suffice it to say that this bold young lady "distributed her hair most freely over her shoulders." The minx!

But the George Sands were the exceptions. Most of the people who lived near the Falls were not in the least like the French writer. They, moreover, had comfortable houses, with lawns or gardens sloping down to the stream. On high ground overlooking the Falls was Belvedere, the home of John Eager Howard. This old house stood until 1870 when it was torn down and Calvert Street was cut through. Farther down stream was the home of Josias Pennington, which stood practically in the bed of Chase Street. Farther south still was Appold's tan yards. This warm, sheltered, and redolent place was the favorite spot for boxing matches on Sunday morning —after Sunday-school. Tan bark is a potent scent; even now it stings the nostrils with reminiscence. Mr. Fred Tyson's flour mill was on the square below, and by all these honest little industrial plants ran the Falls, a jolly yellow stream when in a good mood, but a roaring destructive torrent in flood.

JOHN EAGER HOWARD'S NAMESAKE

CHAPTER XVI

ONE of the most interesting streets in Baltimore is changing rapidly—Howard Street. Long ago when the Howard family owned all the vast tract of land bounded roughly by the Falls, Pratt, Eutaw and South Streets, there was no sign of this important north and south thoroughfare. At the end of the Revolution all the land in the neighborhood of Howard Street was undeveloped. At the beginning of the century, as we have seen, western trade brought about a change in land values at this end of the town. Inns were established, roads cut through linking up the town high with the western settlements. But for all this Howard Street for many years remained a sleepy little back street of no particular importance. Today it ends in a tangle of the tracks of the Baltimore and Ohio. Originally it ran down to green fields, and beyond were the waters of the Middle Branch of the Patapsco. Gradually small shops sprang up here and there, serving the needs of sailors and mechanics—a ship chandler or two, a tobacconist's shop with the familiar Indian standing outside the door. Then small houses were built—neat houses with gardens where people could cool off in the hot summer afternoons. All this of course has gone. If you seek for these romantic details you will be disappointed, and forced to console yourself with warehouses and Armour & Company headquarters. It is not, indeed, until one visits the upper reaches of the street that anything of the old-time flavour is found. This, too, is swiftly disappearing. Before we leave the vicinity of Camden Street I want to remind you that it was on this dingy thoroughfare that Mergenthaler perfected his invention of the linotype machine. Otto Mergenthaler was a watchmaker, not a practical printer, and as he made model after model of the machine he called in the men who worked in the composing room of the Sunpaper and asked their suggestions. These they most willingly gave, and at length the new invention was complete. There was the usual hue and cry about men being forced out of work, starving, bread taken from their mouths and so forth. Finally the New York *Tribune* adopted the linotype, and in forty years Mergenthaler's invention has revolutionized type-setting.

The old Wheatfield Inn hung out its sign—a golden sheaf—where now the Howard House offers hospitality, but apart from this, all marks of the ancient country road have vanished. Around the corner stands Ford's theatre, large, rambling, old-fashioned, but maintaining its fine theatrical tradition. Here many of the most famous actors of the American stage have delighted audiences. On these boards James O'Neill the father of the distinguished modern playwright, gave his fine interpretations; here Creston Clark, young and gifted, played his brief part upon the stage; Here, too, came the bewitching Floradora sextette, and Viola Allen. "All, all are gone."

Forty-five years ago a group of Baltimoreans, frequenters of Ford's theatre formed what was known as the Lobby Club. Once a year they occupied the Royal Box at the right of the stage and then dined nobly on terrapin and champagne. Commodore Thornton Rollins is the last surviving member of the Club, but he still celebrates the traditional banquet. Now the champagne is measured by the bottle instead of the case, and the diamond-back which was once three dollars a dozen is now thirty-four to forty!

In another chapter we have spoken of the Baltimore shops and therefore no more will be said about them. They are excellent, and I commend them to you, but I shall proceed to other matters. The corner of Howard and Mulberry seems an unlikely place of worship but it is here over a meat store that Mount Calvary Church had its origin. It was, of course, a mission of Saint Paul's, and in its early days here was its humble start. A few squares farther up the street—at Franklin, to be precise—the Conestoga wagons used to pack the roadway so thoroughly that citizens sought to have a new street cut through to help in the solution of the traffic problems. Just at this point we shall make a detour into Eutaw Street, returning to this corner later on.

On the west side of Eutaw Street about midway between Franklin and Mulberry there is a bare austere building which has played an important part in Methodist history. The property was purchased from John Eager Howard for the sum of five thousand dollars, and the building erected seemed to the people of that day a fine and handsome structure. When one compares it with First Methodist Church one is impressed with the advance in church architecture. But though the old building was destitute of beauty, it was, nevertheless, distinguished in its ministry. The pulpit, long filled by able men, was removed to Mount Vernon Methodist Church, and there the relic of the past is carefully preserved. In this pulpit Bishop Asbury in May, 1808, preached to an immense crowd of people who had pressed in from all sides to hear his discourse. In the vaults below the church Asbury was later buried, and also Emory, for whom Emory Grove is named.

The square above Franklin yields little that delights the eye. The one old landmark left is at the corner of Druid Hill Avenue and Eutaw—the Hopkins laboratories. They were never much to look at, for as we have noted, Hopkins provided that the endowment should not be spent in buildings. But it is well to remember that ugly and commonplace as these structures are they mark a new era in American scholarship. Across the street, where now a gaping hole meets the eye, was once Levering Hall, a favorite rendezvous of old Hopkins men. At all times of the day young collegians (the term was not known) could be seen adorning the wide windows, and glancing out upon the common herd with careful nonchalance. On one April Fool's day they descended from Olympian heights, and cemented quarter to the pavement. Then they awaited developments. Nor were they unrewarded, and merriment prevailed. At last a darkey came along and stooped, but in vain; the coin could not be moved. Loud roars from students. The darkey showed every tooth in a broad grin and departed. In about ten minutes he returned with a chisel, pried loose the quarter and pocketed it.

At Monument and Eutaw was the Orthodox Friends Meeting, a plain building with a tranquil expression. The meeting has moved to the Homewood section, and the old meeting house has passed into the hands of trade. Just above this corner was a lending library kept by two English gentlewomen, the Misses Harman. Long ago they came from the beautiful town of Winchester, and began life in the new world. Their little shop was like a picture out of the past, neat, Victorian. Their books were covered with a brown wrapper, and were read by many distinguished patrons—indeed the Harman library was one of the earliest ventures of its kind. At the corner we pause to look down Madison Street to the spire of the First Presbyterian Church. You will see it often from many angles, but this is one of the most satisfying views. At dusk on winter evenings the starlings wheel around, circling endlessly, shrilling their wild cries before they settle for the night. And now comes a different recollection, for at our right hand where the automobile stores have established themselves was Gordon's a most uproarious inn. Probably though it was not as black as it has been painted. It was a long, low weather-beaten building sadly in need of paint. It, too, has vanished; but it shall draw no tears from me. I like to recall, however, that it stood here; how various is life!

The old brick church standing on a mound is most appropriately named Mount Calvary. It has had a long and arduous career since those first days over the meat store. In the past century when other ways prevailed it stood firmly for the principles of the Oxford Movement, that unfolding of the Catholic heritage of the Anglican Church. The old Rector, Robert Hitchcock Paine, is remembered with grateful love by many Baltimoreans.

Hamilton Terrace, as the east side of Eutaw Street is called, wears yet a quaint old-fashioned air. The houses have changed but little since the days of the Civil War. At what is now numbered 819 Hamilton Terrace Wilson M. Cary had his famous school for young ladies. At 855 at the extreme north end of the square lived the Cary family. About the beautiful Cary girls centres one of the most thrilling stories in Baltimore history, but to tell it I shall have to go back first to a young English teacher.

When the Civil War broke out James Ryder Randall, a Baltimore man, was teaching English literature in a small college in Louisiana. He heard one day that the Massachusetts troops had passed through the town of Baltimore, and that the people, in the intensity of their feeling, had attacked the Yankees. This brought a volley of shots, and the first blood of the war was shed. That night far from Maryland and his own people Randall could not sleep. The incidents of the attack passed vividly through his mind. He says, "About midnight I arose, lit a candle and went to my desk. Some powerful spirit appeared to possess me and involuntarily I proceeded to write a song of Maryland, My Maryland. The whole poem was dashed off rapidly when once begun. It was not composed in cold blood, but under what may be called a conflagration of the senses, if not an inspiration of the intellect." On the following morning Mr. Randall read the song to his class in literature, and at their eager suggestion he sent it to a newspaper known as the *Delta*. Rapidly the poem seized the popular imagination, and the whole South took it up as a rallying cry. But where was the music needed for these stirring words?

There was in Baltimore on Hamilton Terrace a house known as the headquarters of Southern sympathizers. Meetings of all sorts were held here, and frequently patriotic music added zest to occasion. One night in June Miss Jenny Cary had charge of the program and she had racked her brains to find some new way in which to express the ardent feeling of the hour. Nothing, however, seemed to present itself. But Hetty, the beautiful Hetty, had a brilliant idea. Why not set Randall's Maryland, My Maryland to a tune? Splendid! The two girls found the newspaper containing the fine martial poem, and Hetty sat strumming the piano and meditating song.

"Ah" she cried, "I have it! Lauriger Horatius; it couldn't be better." And sure enough, the tune matched perfectly. Imagine the suppressed excitement of that June night. Can't you see the room—a spacious dignified room crowded with young men and girls. It was warm weather and the windows were open. Someone poured out a big pitcher of lemonade;

JOHN EAGER HOWARD'S NAMESAKE

the girls were lovely in their crinolines, and the young men—
well, they are never nicer than when they are going off to war.
In the midst of this, Jenny sat down at the piano and struck
the first thrilling chords; then—

> "The despot's heel is on thy shore,
> Maryland, My Maryland!
> His touch is at thy temple's door.
> Maryland, My Maryland!
> Avenge the patriotic gore
> That flecked the streets of Baltimore
> And be the battle queen of yore,
> Maryland, My Maryland!"

In a second the men and girls had taken up the familiar
words, and with shining eyes and flushed cheeks they sang—

> "Remember Carroll's sacred trust,
> Remember Howard's warlike thrust,
> And all thy slumberers with the just,
> Maryland, My Maryland."

On the pavement below voices picked up the melody, and the
street rang with the stirring strains. For a second time Baltimore had given the country a song of national character.

The old town was an exciting place in those Civil War days.
There were many Union men in the city, but the Southern
sympathizers were more ardent and warm-hearted in their
devotion. Indeed so much was this sympathy displayed that
General Butler, the Federal officer who was in charge of the
town, gave orders that all women and children who wore red
and white—the Confederate colours—should be arrested. An
organization known as The Monument Street Girls particularly delighted in devilling the General, and he, poor humor-
less soul, was at his wit's end. All who sang *Maryland, My
Maryland* were to be arrested and this only added to its popularity. Rebecca Lloyd Nicholson, one of the Monument Street
Girls—she lived by the way next door to the Historical

Library—wanted to have the song published, and took it to
Rozier Dulaney. He refused, however, for Butler's edict was
fresh in his mind. Not daunted by this, Miss Nicholson herself had the song printed. And Butler probably gnashed his
teeth. He could not understand Southern girls; even now
Yankees have their troubles.

But to return to the Carys. Hetty was a famous Confederate
spy, and went back and forth between the lines constantly. On
July 4, 1861, the two sisters ran the blockade from Baltimore
to Orange Court House. They had daring and beauty, but
their most valuable asset was mother wit. That, plus sheer
feminine charm—"it"—carried them through grave dangers
A few days after their safe arrival, the Battle of Manasses took
place, and amid wildest enthusiasm the Cary girls were invited to visit the camp. According to contemporary records
Hetty was a beauty. She had "titian hair, roses and lilies com-
plexion and a magnificent figure." She had, too, a modest
"come hither" as I have indicated, and it is small wonder that
she turned the heads of Southern soldiers. When she appeared
a shout went up—

"Let us hear a woman's voice!"

And Hetty Cary standing at the door of her tent began to
sing *Maryland, My Maryland*. A chronicler reports that there
was not a dry eye in camp or a rim on a soldier's cap.

No were the Yankees impervious. Once she stood at the
open window of her home and waved a Confederate flag over
the heads of the marching Federal troops. This was immediately noted by the colonel who, when asked if she should be
placed under arrest, said, "No, she is beautiful enough to do
as she damn pleases." Gallant fellow!

Butler, however, a little later had Hetty Cary arrested and
thrown into prison. All sorts of absurd measures were taken
against the Confederates. For instance when Captain William

Brown, who had been killed at Gettysburg, was buried in Greenmount all of the males in the party were arrested as they left the cemetery with the exception of the parson. And why? Because the corpse wore a Rebel uniform! Jesse Hunt of the Eutaw Savings Bank was likewise arrested because, forsooth, he spoke to a prisoner, a friend, passing in a wagon. But the funniest of all—R. Q. Taylor was threatened with imprisonment for having a red and white umbrella, the sign of his business, hanging above his shop door. So the opera bouffe went on. But this is not the place for a history of the Civil War. Our business is to return to Franklin and Howard Streets whither we set out.

On the southeast corner of Howard and Franklin George Baxley bought a fine farm and built there a country house much to the displeasure of his wife. She, good lady, protested that this out of the way spot was entirely too isolated and for her part she preferred a more urban location. Could anything more clearly proclaim the growth of the city? And this northward sweep is a continuous process. That loud and garish building called the Stanley marks the site of the old Academy of Music. The famous old house was built in 1875, and many are the memories connected with it. Here Marlowe and Sothern played, drawing great crowds of people to the pit. In vain the young Irish policeman sought to hold back the hordes of students who tried to rush him. At length another officer appeared, a more seasoned veteran, crying out "Hold your ground, Pat, it's always like this when Miss Marlowe comes!" A good-natured laugh surged through the crowd, and they made a wild dash for the stairs. Ah, who can ever forget that rush up the stairs! With what joy one burst into the empty gallery leaping nimbly over the benches to get the best seats. Then out came fudge—we made it in those days—and out came physics or biology that must be scanned before the morrow morn. To my mind no one has expressed one's feeling for the Academy of Music as well as Folger McKinsey, the Bentztown Bard; he has struck in this poem the authentic note. You can see the lights growing dim, and Como with its magic mountain peaks, and that one bark with her rose coloured sail.

THE OLD ACADEMY

I once saw Booth perform in "Hamlet" here,
And Irving give his "Shylock"; Marlowe, too,
Poured the sweet music of her matchless voice
Across this stage of storied atmosphere;
And old comedians taught us to rejoice
In modern quips that made the ancient new.

Good-by, Lake Como; Many a night have I
Looked with content upon that curtained sky
Of peace and beauty, and translated been
To other lands, where on some antic green
The herds before the shepherds' pipes advanced
And in their spell like goats of Bacchus pranced.

Oh, falling walls, it makes us sad to see—
So famed and honored as you came to be—
The workman's mallet strike to tear ye down!
Here Barrett once received the kingly crown
Of Cawdor, and these boards could still rehearse
The ravings of McCullough, murdering verse!

These once so lovely hangings, boxes where
Beauty and fashion sat to watch the play!
Ah, what do time and progress ever care!
But here again like ghosts for many a day
Old-timers will come back to dream the lore
Of that sweet past of lovely Baltimore!

Next door to the Academy was the City College, an ugly building in the worst possible taste, but so closely associated with the men of the town that it is cherished with a warm affection. So strong indeed is this feeling that several old students wrote to the Sunpaper expressing no envy of their new

266

Gothic building. Well, they are right. After all a school or a university is largely association. "Mark Hopkins at one end of the log and you at the other."

Across a rough cobbled alley-way, in the shadow of an aged sycamore tree, was the first home of the Johns Hopkins University. Few of the buildings are left—this ramshackle red —brick structure facing Howard street and the forlorn laboratories in the rear. The Astronomical building on Monument Street still stands, but McCoy Hall which was opposite has long since been destroyed to make way for modern buildings. To tell the story of this unlikely spot is to recount one of the most thrilling pages in American education, for the Hopkins is the only real university that the United States ever had. It began in a small way, and after Gilman's death it began to turn itself into a College as some clever critic has said. Now, however, it has had the courage to return to its deals, and it will not be many years before Hopkins again takes its place as the mother of scholars rather than the cherisher of the coon skin coat. "Truth shall make you free."

This neighborhood, in spite of furniture stores and bowling alleys, is associated with great names and great projects. Those who are familiar with American scholarship can never forget the work of such men as Rowland, Sylvester, Gildersleeve, Remsen, Martin, Morris and Gilman. These seven men made up the first faculty, and the task of selection fell largely upon the young president, Daniel Coit Gilman. The purpose of the University was to "promote scholarship of the first order, to encourage investigators, to develop the principle of research." Gilman kept his eye open for men who gave promise in this direction, and fortunately he saw a young assistant instructor in Van Rensselaer Polytechnic Institute. This man was Rowland. He had already published an article in the Philosophical Magazine, and Gilman, convinced of his ability, took the young man abroad with him that they might become better acquainted. Gilman's diary of this period records: "Rowland of Troy 25 years. $1600 paid now. Work not appreciated. W'd like a chance to work. Sent papers to New Haven, thrice rejected—'too young to publish such.' "

In those days the German universities were the models, and Brice himself said that Gilman would find no men for his purpose at either Oxford or Cambridge. But gradually the men were brought together. At the first faculty meeting which took place in the second story of the Bible House on Charles Street there was no one to remark "this is not our way;" they were all, with the exception of Sylvester, young men—fresh material. We have mentioned Rowland's marvelous gifts as a scholar, but it is pleasant to know that he loved hunting. His favorite maxim was "think of the fox and not of the ditch," and when rebuked for his recklessness he said that he generally could calculate his orbit, and thus his head was not in danger. Nor was Rowland devoted only to hunting; he was fond of sailing. On one occasion he designed a boat and instructed the builders to paint the waterline at a certain level where he had calculated that it would come. The men objected, but Rowland stood firm. When the boat was launched the builders smiled when they saw that the line was far above the water. "Good," said Rowland; "now put in the mast." When they did so the boat sank exactly to the proper level. "Yes," said Rowland, thoughtfull, "that is what I had calculated on."

Sylvester was the absent minded professor, and numerous were the yarns told in illustration of this quality. There is the famous one about making mathematical calculations on the back of a hansom cab; and the equally famous story about walking round and round Washington's Monument and wondering why it took so long to reach the University. But most curious of all was his joy in light. He said it was a powerful tonic and once he bought a pound of candles, and set them all a-burning in his room when he was particularly in need of inspiration. For casual reading he carried the Odyssey! An amusing story is told of Sylvester and Teackle Wallis, the brilliant lawyer. There was a meeting of some sort at the Academy, and Sylvester was asked to respond to a toast, but when he rose to speak, he was obviously unprepared, and mumbled an apology—"Excuse me—I went to the opera last night;" then he sat down. But Wallis, quick as a flash replied—"Ah, I see it is a case of opera non verba." And this rounded off the situation very neatly.

Perhaps I have delayed too long, but these anecdotes make the men real and living people, not simply great names in education.

The University opened in 1876 with a most inadequate equipment. Two dwellings on the west side of Howard Street were bought, and there was also an annex capable of seating two hundred people. In addition to this there was a well-lighted room for a biological laboratory, and a reading room provided with forty thousand volumes. This was the nucleus of the Johns Hopkins. The emphasis was to be placed upon men and scholarship. Sylvester illustrates this well in a comment on teaching. He said: "As the barnyard fowl can not understand the flight of the eagle, so it is the eaglet only who will be nourished by instruction. Among your pupils will be one genius for geometry, and he will derive knowledge and enthusiasm and add more to the reputation of your institution that ten thousand who will complain of the obscurity of Slyvester. For them you will provide another class of teachers." Hopkins was meant to nourish eaglets.

The opening exercises of the University were held in the Peabody and Huxley, the distinguished scientist, was invited to make the address. A hue and cry arose because the champion of evolution was thus honored. A naive comment ought to be considered before we pass on. "It was bad enough to invite Huxley. It were better to have asked God to be present. It would have been absurd to have asked them both, but it is possible yet to redeem the University from the stain of such a beginning."

Thus was the University launched. Later on, McCoy Hall was built and it became the center of the University life. There was housed the fine library, there were the lecture rooms, there in a large central hall were held the public lectures of the University. Around this central room ran a spacious corridor adorned with pictures of Rowland's great discoveries in light. One of Sargent's most memorable canvases had here a place of honor. It is The Four Doctors—Osler, Kelly, Halstead and Welch. The four men are grouped about a table, Halstead standing, his hand upon an open book; Doctor Kelly, well-known in Baltimore civic life as well as in the field of medicine, sits thoughtfully in the shadows; Osler, the Greek, hold a pen in his long sensitive fingers; Welch, firm, assured, executive, looks out frankly at the spectator. It is a marvelous piece of portraiture and one of the University's greatest treasures. Here, too, was another of Sargent's portraits, that of Miss Mary Garrett whose generous gifts enriched the Medical school, and made possible the medical training of women. A bronze bust of Sidney Lanier had also a place of honour. This bust is the work of Ephraim Keyser, the well-konwn Baltimore sculptor and reveals Lanier with great charm. It is a true and noble memorial to a fine poet. This was the man— lecturer in English at the University—of whom it was said, "He never entered a horse car without everyone being conscious of it. Let him come upon the stage and there was a buzz through the audience. Always gallant, always quickening."

270

one day a German pathologist who had never heard of Lanier stopped before Keyser's bust and looked at it. "He was," said his companion, "a poet greatly beloved and greatly mourned by us all." The scholar looked closer.

"H'm," he mourned, "tuberculosis."

A few days later another who had known Lanier slightly looked at the same work and said,

"Yes, Christ-like."

There was a small alley known as Ross Street, I believe, that opened like a tunnel at the east side of McCoy Hall. Here in their moments of ease after intellectual labours the boys matched pennies; it was before the day of craps for the gentry. In the basement Walter, the barber, reigned supreme. Here he lathered the academic face and talked meanwhile on politics national and local. It is said, too, that he gave sage advice on many matters including those of the heart. But these days are no more. The boys have gone; Walter has shut up shop. A bowling alley covers the site of the "Cage" where lacrosse was first nourished in Baltimore. Even the landscape is changing. Over the old Visitation wall Baltimoreans once got their first glimpse of spring—the pear-trees in a foam of blossom. Now great gashes have been made in the wall, and cars are parked in the once lovely garden. Every trace of beauty has been destroyed with elaborate care. Sinclair oils dominate the scene. But no description of Howard street would be complete that did not take account of the Convent that used to be. It has a long and romantic story.

The Order of the Visitation came to America in 1799, but it was already old in Europe. The founder was none other than Jeanne Francois Fremiot de Chantal, the grandmother of Madame de Sevigné. The little Jeanne was a most unusual child and many interesting stories are told of her precocity. One day for example she listened to a long discussion between her father and a Protestant visitor. Unnoted by the two men, the child understood with great quickness the drift of the argument. At length she could bear it no longer and burst out impetuously "Then you don't believe that our Lord is present in the Blessed Sacrament? He said that He was. Do you think Him a liar?" The Protestant laughed and tried to mollify the child with a piece of candy, but the little Jeanne cast the bonbons into the fire and said with true Calvinistic ardour "Thus, monsieur, will heretics burn in hell." The fiery small champion of the Faith was destined to be disciplined by life until her ardour was given the proper direction. When she was marriageable she was wedded to a fire-eating baron who was later killed in the hunting field, and not long after, her oldest son was killed in the English wars—put to death, so the legend goes, by the hand of Oliver Cromwell himself.

The old ardour and passion for God were now to run into new channels. Madame de Chantal determined to devote herself to the religious life. In 1604 she met Saint Francis de Sales and a warm friendship sprang up between them. She poured out to him her grief for her husband and son, and told him of her earnest desire to serve God as a religious. To this he gave not only approval, but suggested that she should form a new order, one devoted to the poor and the sick. Now a struggle with her family ensued, her young son flinging himself upon the threshold and crying dramatically, "I am not strong enough to hold you back, Madame, but if you leave us it must be by stepping over the body of your only son." It seems that the spirit of little Jeanne had descended to the small son. There was fervour enough in that family to found six religious orders.

Well, bear these thoughts in mind when you look at this bleak and featureless Convent. It has a link with seventeenth century France. Who would imagine that on Howard Street one would catch a glimpse of the great Bishop of Geneva. If Saint Chantal seems too austere for your taste keep in mind that she provided trousseaux for her daughters with her own hands—frilly, frivolous French trousseaux. And never forget that she was the grandmother of that wholly bewitching woman, Madame de Sevigne.

The Convent is empty now and is soon to be torn down; the Sisters have moved to their new home in the country, but many Baltimoreans will remember the old place with deep affection. For eighty years the Convent has been a Baltimore landmark. Many generations of school children have recited in those walls, and played up and down the garden paths. It was a quaint place, that garden, a great square bounded by high walls over which loomed the city roofs of the neighboring houses. The grass grew in neat plots with brick walks between, warm mellow brick walks, the kind that once made Baltimore so charming before our progressive days. These paths did not make the garden any the less green; indeed they afforded a pleasant passage between the flower-beds. The whole place breathed the formal air of an old-world garden sweet and remote. Along the Centre Street wall grew a wide border of purple flags. At the western end stood those fruit trees—old gnarled trees that once bore fruit as Sister Raphael said, but now bore only white blossoms. But what blossoms! They made a fitting background for the Virgin's statue. Daffodils were shining everywhere, and along the north wall wistaria hung in heavy lilac sprays.

Don't you remember that Convent in Les Miserables, the Little Picpus? The Visitation has always been the prototype of that Parisian house. I can see Javert skulking in the shadows, and Jean Valjean and the so- silent Cosette dropping down behind the high bleak wall.

273

BALTIMORE

The Visitation will pass as the other landmarks have vanished. It is inevitable. Perhaps best; one must not be a Bourbon. I am glad, however, that I can remember the Sister's gentle voice at the grill, the quiet hospitality, the polished floors, the clean conventual perfume. There is one thing left— the old blind colored man who has sat beside this wall for years untold. Patiently he sits with his Sunpapers on his knees. In the winter his feet are wrapped in bright carpet to keep him snug; in the summer he pulls his hat down over his eyes to protect his head from the sun's burning rays. So changes come; may the old darkey long remain.

On Centre Street, east of Howard, there is a row of tiny houses freshly painted now, and trim, but old in years. No one specially grand or mighty ever lived in them, as far as I know, but they were the homes of comfortable and happy families. Someone who lived there loves to tell of the elegant appearance of Mrs. Charles Joseph Bonaparte when she drove out in her fine Victoria and chestnut horses. But more impressive even than the shining harness and the liveried footman was the "dolly varden" frock and the small foot and dainty hand of the lady herself. You remember that the Bonaparte house was on Park Avenue opposite the Convent. It was a curious house full of strange nooks and crannies with staircases in unexpected places, and crammed full of lovely, priceless things. Here Betsy's younger grandson and his wife lived for many years. Charles Joseph, Bo's younger son, was born almost twenty-one years after his brother, so that he was, in effect, an only child. On holidays he was always taken to his grandfather Patterson's house where the old man delighted in teasing him with being a French boy. To this Charles stoutly replied, "I am not a French boy, grandfather; I am an American boy." And as he grew to manhood a good American he proved himself to be. He and Severn Teackle Wallis

274

worked unceasingly for reform. But in spite of his ardour Bonaparte was not on "the lunatic fringe," as Roosevelt wisely said. He was always practical and canny. The five story red-brick house on the northeast corner of Park Avenue and Centre street was an old Baltimore landmark. On the first floor Mr. Bonaparte had his offices and on the floor above were the Napoleonic relics now owned by the Maryland Historical Society. Here you will find most interesting souvenirs of Baltimore including the famous Gilbert portrait—the three-fold portrait. Gilbert confessed that he had painted glorious Betsy thus because, for the life of him, he could not decide which view of her was loveliest.

The Maryland Historical Society occupies the splendid old house once the home of Enoch Pratt. This fine mansion and a fire-proof addition on the southwest corner of Park Avenue and Monument Street was the gift of Mrs. H. Irvine Keyser in memory of her husband. The treasures within these walls are priceless. By all means visit the picture gallery and ask to see the Bonaparte room.

Next door to the Historical Library was the home of Rebecca Lloyd Nicholson who delighted in singing *Maryland, My Maryland* to the harrassment of Butler. We have mentioned this intrepid young lady before, but as you pass her house you may like to recall her. Across Monument Street, at 214, Doctor Remsen lived. Remsen was to chemistry what Gildersleeve was to Greek and Sylvester to mathematics; they were trainers of teachers and scholars. All over America men taught by Remsen are holding positions of honour and distinction. Nor should the humble college student be forgotten; thousands have diligently conned Remsen's familiar "chemistry book" bound in dingy brown cloth. But the boy Remsen was not intended for a chemist. His father had decided that medicine should be his son's profession, and therefore the boy was placed under the direction of a physician. But it so happened that the physician taught chemistry in a medical college, and one day the doctor gave Remsen a textbook on the subject and bade him read it. The book was unreal and meaningless, for Remsen had at that time no knowledge of the science at all. Finally, he came across the statement that nitric acid acts on copper. Remsen determined to what this meant. He found a penny in his pocket, and the nitric acid was ready to hand on the doctor's shelf.

"I opened the bottle marked nitric acid, poured some of the liquid on the copper cent and prepared to make an observation.

"But what was this wonderful thing I beheld? A greenish-blue liquid foamed and fumed over the cent and over the table. The air in the neighborhood became coloured dark red. A great coloured cloud arose. I tried to get rid of the mess by throwing it out of the window. I learned that nitric acid acts on fingers. The pain led to another unpremeditated experiment. Nitric acid acts on trousers.' "

Remsen, the first professor of chemistry at the Johns Hopkins, became the second president of the University in 1901, a position which he held until 1912, when he resigned. During his administration the School of Technology was established, and plans to move to Homewood were completed.

The house next door to Doctor Remsen's old home—216 West Monument—is one of the most charming houses in Baltimore. It was a keen delight to watch the work of restoration proceeding with intelligence and judgment. Finally when the last apricot curtain was in place I felt a thrill of satisfaction as if the house were mine own—though I have never been across the threshold. It is representative of the best Baltimore traditions. There are other delightful old houses in the square, but business is crowding them out little by little. Long ago the

JOHN EAGER HOWARD'S NAMESAKE

Hopkins Club at the southeast corner of Monument and Howard was destroyed by the wreckers, and a row of futile one-story shops was built on the site.

RED BRICK HOUSES—WHITE FRONT STEPS

CHAPTER XVII

HOWARD Street from Madison to the Richmond Market is an odd mixture of the new and the old. The character of the street is rapidly being destroyed by "up-to-date-fronts" and such atrocities. There are, however, a number of old houses left. For instance 722, just south of Madison Street. Here lived Madame Foudriat and her brother. The house is small, red brick, with the ubiquitous white front steps, an iron handrail and a neat foot-scraper. On the door a tarnished silver plate bears Madame's name. In her time the little house was immaculate. Madame herself slender, grey-haired, was a typical French bourgeoise. Laces were her specialty, and the most delicate and fragile point de venise or chantilly she mended and "blanchisseused" with infinite care.

The eight hundred block, however, has a more antique air. Here for example is Smith's bookstore. It exists for books alone; and they dominate. They line the walls; they trip you up on the floor; they slither about on the counters; they teeter in drunken piles on the step ladders. They make you walk around them as a pet cat does. Smith's is the autocracy of books. But the Smith's themselves control even this apparent autocracy. The two men are walking volumes of information —two editions. Instantly they put their hands on any book for which you may inquire. The store may look like a maze to you; they thread it forthwith. And all these books breathe out an atmosphere. They carry with them not only the story printed on their leaves, but the story of their one-time owners. For every volume on the shelves (and other places) there is another story belonging to the book itself—its personal adventures. The cellar overflows with books, the shop likewise overflows. In the dim light that wavers overhead, you swim in a sea of books; the shadows are murky, but the light strikes out a rich scarlet binding, or a tarnished golden edge. I wish I had a wood-cut of Smith's; it would be a lovely thing. Outside by the door are two tables of very old and very cheap books. For ten cents once I bought *Advice to the Clergy*. It proved to be a practical and useful book. This is merely a sample. All sorts of tastes may be suited here.

Across the street most of the shops have been modernized, and consequently have lost all character. The little sea-food shop still remains. It is, however, painted in a most unappetizing colour. The food may be delicious; I do not know. The Doll's Hospital gives you an idea of what these old houses were like. The floors are uneven; with wide boards, and the ceilings are so low that a tall person can easily touch them with his hand. If this shop were kept by Jenny Wren it would not surprise me in the least. It has a Dickensian manner.

It would not be fair to leave this neighborhood without mentioning Madame Fagret's known to generations of Baltimore women. Madame Fagret, a French woman, attended to ladies' hair in the days when chignons were fashionable. Later the business descended to her son, but on his death Madame

279

Emerson continued the old tradition. The house shines with wax-like order and precision. On the walls of the waiting room—furnished with fine old mahogany chairs, by the way, are pictures of the Tuileries gardens brought over, no doubt, by Madame herself. A large grey and white Persian cat does the honours of the establishment, seating himself when undetected in the best and most comfortable chair. For business purposes a large modern window has been cut in the front of this old house, but within all is old-fashioned, charming, gracious—as Madame would have it. *Voila!*

There are those who love to prowl in antique dealers' haunts. There is a long string of them here. And cheek by jowl one finds a bakery and a general store flaunting a yellow slicker or a pair of "overhauls" as the colored people call them. But before we turn aside to other things, Dunlop's is the place to go for oysters. You may carry them away in neat cartons, or if you prefer make a delicious meal of every variety right there in the shop itself. Nor would it do to neglect to mention Lehmann's Hall, once the rendezvous of fashion, the scene of the Monday Germans. It is still nightly filled with merrymakers, but fashion has departed to the Alcazar.

The hall over the market house was long used as the Fifth Regiment Armory, and that regiment itself deserves some notice. Baltimore's "Dandy Fifth" has had a long and distinguished history. There was a time when every young man in the town belonged to the Fifth. There were drills and parades, when, to the shrilling of the fifes, the grey files went marching by, the Maryland colours flying in the breeze. Those who saw the Fifth's return from Tampa after the Spanish American War will remember that brush with the realities of conflict. Years later there was to follow the service on the Border and then the journey over seas. But this period in no sense belongs to the old Armory. We shall speak of that later.

In this old hall, however, the Confederate bazaars were held in the last years of the nineteenth century. Ah, those were the days! The Stars and Bars floated as of yore—this time quite harmlessly—and every Southern heart, and those not so Southern, thrilled at the rebel yell lustily roared by the old soldiers from the Pikesville home. The Southern poem was on every lip—

> "Furl that banner, it is weary
> Round its staff 'tis drooping dreary,
> Furl it, fold it, let it rest;
> For there's no one left to wave it,
> And there's no one left to lave it
> In the blood that heroes gave it;
> Furl it, fold it, it is best."

But do not imagine for a moment that these bazaars were melancholy occasions. Far from it; the youth and beauty of the land was there. Baltimore, a small and homogeneous town thronged to the Armory, and any melancholy that we felt was purely sentimental. We had not yet "supped full of horrors" in the Great War. In all innocence we sang. "Hurrah for the bonnie blue flag", and went home well content with the stars and stripes.

A short distance from Howard Street the huge span of the new Armory arrests the eye. Using this to orientate ourselves we come out into a jumble of streets just east of Richmond Market. Biddle Street, once the home of gentlefolk, is now given over to the darkeys. A few courageous artists have salvaged a house or two where they have established studios. Otherwise the neighborhood is "gone," as we say. From Biddle a small street named Bolton runs north and ends at the Armory. We shall have to make a detour to reach the front entrance of this very handsome granite structure. Above the yawning door is a splendid bronze commemorating the men of Maryland who fought in the Great War. But, as I stand here, I am not thinking of the Armory or the War. This whole space covered by this huge building was once a quiet country estate belonging first to the Grundys and later to the Spence family, an estate named Bolton. All this was long ago, but the memory of that old house is very fragrant. It stood in the center of the ground with a carriage drive sweeping around before the lovely entrance. In the rear the land sloped down to Preston Street where a high board fence shut out the glances of prying neighbors. Great trees gave shade, and the lawns cut smooth and primly were dappled with shadows, Close to the house was a bush of rowan berries—those scarlet berries that the impish Babbie loved to weave into her hair for the undoing of the Little Minister. Mr. Spence, so the story goes, had the bush brought from Scotland. How true that is I do not know, but one dusky evening in the autumn I crept through the fence to examine the old place. The family had long ago departed, and the house stood tenantless, forlorn. The doorway even then retained its spacious, hospitable air, but the windows were dark and black. The rowans, nevertheless flaunted still their scarlet berries.

The history of Baltimore is closely interwoven with the history of the Fifth Regiment. Consequently, at this point it is only fitting to review its long service to the country and the state. On December 10, 1776, at the Flying Camp of the Continental Army the regiment was organised, and then proceeded to Philadelphia for service. In the long conflict that followed it was known as the Maryland Line, and took part in all of the important battles of the Revolution. When Cornwallis surrendered, the regiment marched home, but they did not disband, for Washington advised the men to keep up their military organizations. Some years after this the law required every man to supply himself with a musket and powder horn. The "Dandy Fifth" was prepared. Now the War of 1812 came on, and the British reported that only Barney's men and the Fifth Maryland Infantry gave them any real trouble. But the Civil War brought the severest strain to the organization. Many of the men went South to fight; others went into the Northern Army. At length peace was restored, and gradually the men came drifting back to town, the old bitterness forgotten. Once more they organised the regiment. In Henry Loney's law office on Lexington Street in 1867 six men met to take the first steps toward reorganization—Stricker Jenkins, Henry Loney, J. D. Lipscomb, S. O. McIlvain, R. H. Conway and L. M. Catlett.

And now a flag was needed. It was recalled that before the war there had been some work done on a handsome silk flag, but the terrible strife had interrupted this labour, and the flag was put away until a happier day. Apparently that day had arrived. The flag was soon completed, and on Washington's Birthday a grand presentation was held in Concordia Hall. The ladies were present, lovely and blushing, and when Teackle Wallis made the presentation speech his peroration was "God bless the ladies of Maryland." These sentiments were cheered to the echo. Every one of the five hundred men in the Regiment heartily endorsed both the flag and the ladies. The new uniforms were grey, because it was in that colour that most of the men had made their names as soldiers. Epaulettes of white and caps with pom poms completed the really stunning ensemble. Such is the record of the Dandy Fifth.

Probably the most thrilling scene that the Armory has witnessed was the nomination of Woodrow Wilson as Democratic candidate in 1912. Champ Clark's men filled the town declaring that nobody should kick their dog around. The Great Commoner clad in a linen suit and a broad brimmed panama was a familiar figure in our streets. The thermometer

283

rose with the excitement. On the John Street cars, as the conductor passed McMechen Street he called out "Wilson next."

"Hell," replied a member of the opposing camp, "you mean Champ Clark." For hours on hours delegations chanted determinedly, "We want Wilson, we want Wilson," and on a scorching afternoon Wilson won the nomination.

The part of Baltimore that lies north of the Armory—like happy nations—has no history, but it is one of the oldest unspoiled residential sections left. The eastern boundary of this neighborhood is Mount Royal Avenue, named from one of those outlying farms in the original grant of the town. The unkempt houses that lie between the Armory and the foot of Mount Royal Avenue hill, are certainly nothing but an eyesore. One hopes that the extension of Howard Street—that consummation devoutly to be wished—will eliminate all this nest of negro houses. A short cut, however, across the grass of the B. and O. Station brings us to Dolphin and Mount Royal. The Lyric is on our right, an ugly building, but for Baltimoreans full of the echoes of operas and symphonies. Now we are ready to climb the steep hill.

At the top there is a monument to Watson of Monterey, the work of the sculptor Edward Berge. Surely this is not his finest work. Berge was happiest in modelling children, as his *Sea-Urchin and Wildflower* so admirably prove. But to return to Watson. When war was declared with Mexico in 1846, Colonel Watson comanded the battalion from Baltimore. In the storming of Monterery Watson became separated from his men while leading the charge and was struck by a musket ball which killed him almost instantly. The name of this gallant soldier came immediately to Randall when he wrote *Maryland, My Maryland*—

> "With Ringgold's spirit for the fray
> With Watson's blood at Monterey."

RED BRICK HOUSES—WHITE FRONT STEPS

In 1903 the Mexican War Veterans unveiled this monument. Around the base of the statue are cannon balls neatly piled one upon the other. Some years ago a few enterprising boys rolled this ammunition down the steep hill, and when morning came the balls were found distributed in various places around the Revolutionary shaft which rises so gracefully at the intersection of Cathedral and Mount Royal. Since then, the balls have been firmly cemented in place.

Immediately across from the monument is the fine Renaissance building of the Maryland Institute. The early history of this art school we have read in another chapter. It has made steady advance ever since the days of its foundation on Harrison's Marsh. The fire of 1904 destroyed the old buildings and all of the records kept throughout the years. But while the city yet burned plans were on foot for a new building. Michael Jenkins gave the site on Mount Royal Avenue, and in 1906 the Institute was complete. The Mechanic Arts are still taught at Market Place, but the Fine and Practical Arts are housed here.

North of the Institute is Corpus Christi Church, a Gothic building that makes an interesting contrast with the architecture of the Institute. The Jenkins family has done much to enrich this square on Mount Royal Avenue.

That section that I have described as north of the Armory is roughly bounded by Dolphin Street, Eutaw Place, North Avenue and Mount Royal; all of this is by no means characteristic of old conservative Baltimore. Some of it is fast slipping down hill, but for all that, here you will find what one calls real Baltimoreans. Here are red brick houses and white front steps; here, even now, on warm nights people "sit out front"; here there is a homogeneity and friendliness not often found in large cities. This part of town has for its axis Bolton Street, and there is no one in this locality who did not know the

Bishop of Bolton Street as he was often called—Doctor William Meade Dame, the beloved rector of Memorial Church. The church itself has had an interesting evolution and it is well worth recalling. Many years ago some ladies at Emmanuel Church started a small mission for men employed by the Northern Central Railroad. This little enterprise—half chapel and half reading room—was on Maryland Avenue opposite the Bolton freight yards. The men crowded in very eagerly and showed such appreciation that within a few years a small chapel was built on Park Avenue between Lanvale and Dolphin. This chapel soon proved inadequate; the neighborhood was growing, and the people demanded a larger church. So the old chapel was abandoned—it later became the Enon Baptist—and a new church was built at Bolton Street and Lafayette Avenue. This church was a memorial to the Reverend Henry Van Dyke Johns under whose guidance the little mission had first been undertaken. From year to year the parish has steadily grown. Doctor Dame was succeeded by his son, popularly called "Page" by all and sundry, and dearly beloved by the community. Memorial has a beautiful art treasure— a painting of the crucifixion copied from Rubens, but so great was the genius of the copyist that the power of Rubens shines forth in every line and contour. The church is open for prayer. Go in.

Linden Avenue once called Garden Street is a commonplace street, perhaps, but it still has some tiny pocket handkerchief front yards left. And General Gary's beautiful garden has not yet been turned into a filling station. While you are in this square you want to remember that here in the twelve hundred block was born, in 1866, Jesse Lazear. He never captured a town or drove the enemy from the fort, but he did a far nobler thing. He gave his life as ransom for many in the field of medicine. I must tell his story, for it is thrilling.

A VISTA OF THE "CHRISTMAS TOWER" OF EMMANUEL CHURCH

Besides, Lazear belongs to this neighborhood. He was born just above Dolphin Street, and he spent his early married life on Lanvale Street between Park Avenue and John Street. Didn't I tell you this was a distinguished locality? But to Lazear's story.

As a boy he spent part of his life here and part near Pittsburg, but when he was ready to enter college he came to Baltimore, of course, he entered the Hopkins. His headquarters at that time were at Windsor, a family country place which later, with the old Mill, gave the name of Windsor Hills to the western suburb. Suffice it to say that Lazear's work in the University and at the College of Physicians and Surgeons was of such a quality that after study abroad, particularly at the Pasteur Institute in Paris, he was appointed bacteriologist on the medical staff of the Hopkins. It was in 1900 that Walter Reed was told to proceed to Cuba to give especial attention to questions relating to the cause and prevention of yellow fever. There he and Lazear met, and these two men and two others made up the Yellow Fever Commission. They had a hard time trying to unearth the bacillus, and met with small success. Finally a doctor who was considered half-mad—Carlos Finlay—said that a mosquito caused the fever, and he gave Lazear some little cigar-like eggs. These Lazear hatched out, and lo, there were some very pretty mosquitos indeed with silver markings on them. But how to test Finlay's idea was a puzzler, for yellow fever can not be given to animals; it must be tested on human beings.

Consequently Reed called his Commission and suggested that the members take the risk first, let themselves be bitten by mosquitos that have fed on yellow fever cases, and thus set an example to American soldiers. The words were no sooner out of his mouth than Lazear volunteered. Carroll, another member of the Commission, did the same, and Reed,

287

called to Washington, left explicit directions to the two men. Lazear took his mosquitos into the wards where the men lay yellow as a kite's foot with the loathsome disease. He bit those men with the striped mosquitos and then took the blood-filled beasts back to their little glass houses in which there were saucers of water and lumps of sugar. When the mosquitos had digested their meal all was in readiness for the test. "Then Lazear collected seven men who were likewise willing to submit themselves to this test. First to himself he applied those poison filled mosquitos, and then to each of the others. And to their deep regret not one of them died. Then Carroll said 'Why not try me?' So he, too, was bitten by the most villainous mosquito in the collection, and he nearly died, but at last came through."

In all, they had bitten eight men, and only two of them had had the yellow fever. Lazear was by no means satisfied with the way things were going. Perhaps those men had been in the danger zone; perhaps Finlay was wrong. So he went about feeding his mosquitos on the patients, and planning always the perfect test. One day as he went about his work a mosquito settled on his hand. "Oh, that's nothing," he said, and let the creature stay. In five days he was ill, and on September 25, 1900, he died. But he had done his work. Walter Reed wrote, "As Dr. Lazear was bitten by a mosquito while present in the ward of a yellow fever hospital one must at least admit the possibility of this insect's contamination by a previous bite of a yellow fever patient. This case of accidental infection can not fail to be of interest."

From that accidental infection experiment after experiment followed until today yellow fever is practically unknown. Lazear's heroism has brought life to thousands, and has delivered the tropics from a terrible scourge. I have not described the Hopkins Medical school as a separate entity. Its great work interpenetrates the whole community and, indeed, the world. If you are interested in medicine go over on Broadway. The dome broods above the town and is a landmark like the Monument. Lazear's name is one among many who have labored there for the good of humanity.

Eutaw Street which parallels Linden Avenue was formerly called Gibson Street from the Gibson estate of Rose Hill which crowned the long steep slope from Biddle to Lanvale. In 1853, however, this property was offered to the city by Henry Tiffany. Gradually houses were built, and a charming old-fashioned parkway was laid out for several squares. Eutaw Place, as the locality is now called, offers refreshment to the hundreds of apartment dwellers who live in the neighborhood. For six or seven squares there are green lawns neatly trimmed, set with stiff delightful flower beds. Indeed the planting in Eutaw Place is one of its chief charms. There is no attempt at modern landscape gardening; here flourish the gaudy cannas, the flat, pale, green rosettes, flowers like subdued cabbages, and the prim Victorian coleus. All these posies are arranged in straight geometric designs much in the style of the 'seventies. To match this is the Centennial fountain, a monstrous ugly thing found north of McMechen Street. Originally fat cupids placed at neat intervals about the bowl blew water through their cast-iron conch shells. Mercifully, their respiratory tracts became impaired, and they are no more. The loveliest of all the squares is the one between Lafayette Avenue and Mosher Street. The little fountain there although of the same dreadful period has nevertheless a lyric charm. The water sings a gay tune. The swallows bathe on the wide, shallow bowl and here pigeons preen their opal throats and flick the water with their quaker wings. Those stone monuments—*Winter* and *Spring*—that you have noticed on the lawn before the Phoenix Club are said to have come from Belvedere, but I can not vouch for it. They have a stiff and melancholy look. *Winter* wraps his mantle sadly, and even *Spring* casts her flowers with an elegiac manner.

There are few trees more beautiful than horse-chestnuts, and Eutaw Place has a splendid row of them. In the winter their rough black boughs stand out sharply against the sky; in the spring the white blossoms gleam like tapers.

> But now in late October
> With frosty nights and cold,
> There is more poignant beauty
> In their dim tarnished gold.

Where Rose Hill spread its broad acres, the Hebrew Temple now crowns the hill. It is a beautiful building, its fine dome a distinguishing mark against the skyline as one walks south from North Avenue. Seen in an October dusk between sunset and the rise of the moon the dome looms above the trees, unreal and dreamlike—an image of the East.

Where the Marlborough lifts its huge bulk there was once an old house and another one of those Baltimore gardens so numerous in this part of the town. The garden was rapidly going to seed when I knew it, but the rose bushes bloomed riotously, and a crepe myrtle flamed like a banner in the spring. Down on Linden Avenue many houses have small garden plots set out with flowers and shrubbery. City people grow to depend on these seasonal barometers. For instance, in this neighborhood the first sign of spring is the budding of the pussy-willow bushes in a pocket handkerchief garden or a neighboring back yard. Another house pridefully tends its white lilac bush. The Hospital for the Women of Maryland was once like a country house with a goodly yard around it. The lawn was by no means spruce; dandelions grew at will, and all along the paling fence on John Street there was a tall hedge of Rose of Sharon bushes. Time and necessity destroyed the garden, but it is worth remembering. Where a hideous row of sordid little houses has sprung up on McMechen Street between John Street and Mount Royal Avenue there was once a tangled old remnant of an apple orchard called Addisons. Here the boys and girls played "catchers" and "I-spy" and all sorts of early-century games before the movies had been heard of as a popular diversion. Park Place has yet a formal beauty, and may it long continue!

Just north of Wilson Street on the Place is Friends Meeting House and School. This Meeting is a descendant of the old Friends Meeting on Lombard and Howard Streets where the Washington, Baltimore and Annapolis Station is now situated. The ancient Meeting House has long vanished, but while Charles Yardley Turner's picture remains we can never forget the atmosphere of that old place of worship. *Moved by the Spirit* shows an interior plain and austere but redeemed from any suggestion of coldness by the warm golden light that floods in through the windows. The men and women clad in sober garments sit quietly, each face marked by that repose which so strongly characterizes the members of the Society of Friends. It has been said that these faces are portraits but the artist denied this. However that may be, these worshippers are veritable flesh and blood; whether Turner willed it or not he painted actual men and women. The speaker is the painter's grandmother. Moved by the Spirit she gives her simple testimony, and before her, on the benches, the Friends listen intently, earnestly.

Associated with the Friends School is the name of a man very well-beloved—Cousin Eli Lamb. This man who did much for early education in the town had conducted a school of his own at the Lombard Street Meeting for many years. After a time he moved to McCullough and Preston Streets where he opened a new school. But Cousin Eli had one weakness—that of generosity, and because of this he often found himself in practical difficulties. The new Meeting House had been built on Park Avenue since 1888, and a small school had for several years been conducted in the rooms above the Meeting, but Jonathan K. Taylor was anxious to form a school under the direction of the Monthly Meeting. Consequently a proposal was made to Cousin Eli that he should bring his school up to the new Park Avenue site and join with the small nucleus already established. This Lamb decided to do, and the Friends School was opened with about two hundred pupils. Cousin Eli had charge of the Intermediate school, and the present headmaster, William S. Pike, was his assistant. Cousin Eli was a most lovable man, a man of wide acquaintance with all sorts and conditions of men. If one walked down the street with him, it was impossible to go more than a few steps without observing how numerous were his friends. Everyone knew him; everyone loved him. He was particularly a friend of Cardinal Gibbons and the two men, each great in his sphere, often met together to talk over matters of education or to discuss in simple friendliness some matter of common interest.

Edward C. Wilson who served the school as headmaster for a quarter of a century is another name beloved by many Baltimore boys and girls. A new field of service awaits this old school in its new setting at Homewood. A generation that knows not Cousin Eli has come to the front, but his ideals go marching on.

When Baltimore town was first laid out in 1729, the old Mount Royal farm was an irregular tract of land lying roughly north and west of the present Mount Royal entrance to Druid Hill Park. On this estate was built a manor house which is still standing and is now happily the property of the Friends Meeting. The old house long the home of the Bond family stands high above the present-day street level, but that height was once the original elevation of the land. It was hilly rolling country that sloped up from the Boundary. But long before even the Boundary—North Avenue—was dreamed of, these high forested acres rose in gentle swells from the low-lying section around Dolphin Street. A straggling footpath scarcely more than a country lane ran in approximately the direction of Mount Royal Avenue, skirting the Bond manor. Beyond this farm lay the Brooks place. When, therefore, the streets above North Avenue were opened up the manor house was left in a position of seclusion. The garden became the sanctuary for birds of all kinds. The great silver poplar tree on the west side of the house was astir with wings in the nesting season. Now that the old house is more populous, the birds flock to the neighboring gardens. One winter when snow was on the ground I saw two cardinals in a nearby yard. And my bird-loving friends assured me that grackles, sparrows and even blue birds were no infrequent visitors.

Around the corner from these ornithological delights live Doctor and Mrs. Morley. It sounds absurd to describe them as the parents of Christopher, but such is the case. Of the Morleys I should like to say much, but *they* would not like it at all. I must add, however, that they are as warm, as delightful and Morleyish as Christopher's best essays.

THE WEST END

CHAPTER XVIII

BALTIMORE is fond of using names to designate certain localities in a rather vague manner—"the Point," "the Space," "the West End." To a townsman born and bred these terms are well understood and each has its own significance and flavour. To the outsider the West End sounds nebulous. And indeed when confronted with the task of describing it geographically some difficulty arises. At the risk therefore of correction I shall give that name to the portion of the city lying west of Fremont Street and south of Lafayette. This is a sizable wedge. The eastern boundary, Fremont Street, branches off from Pennsylvania Avenue at Bloom Street, and cuts diagonally down to Hamburg Street. Allen K. Bond says "A lover of old streets can not fail to be struck by the curious diagonal course of Fremont Avenue. It is a very ancient thoroughfare and was undoubtedly a short cut from the old Wagon Road of Mr. Digges to the Great Eastern Road where it left the city." In the early years of the nineteenth century this western section was country pure and simple. Then gradually streets were cut through, and after the Civil War this neighborhood was filled with people who had come up from Southern Maryland and Virginia, seeking in most cases to mend their broken fortunes. Many little Squares still preserve the small-town atmosphere—Lafayette, Union, Harlem, Franklin, and, tiniest of all, Perkins. The country pressed hard upon the city in those days, and boys brought up in the West End can recall the free and joyous adventures of life in that unsophisticated region. Beyond the city lay great estates; to the south, Mount Clare the home of Charles Carroll, Barrister; to the west the vast holdings of Richard Caton who married Charles Carroll of Carrollton's daughter; and to the north the lovely rolling country of Gwynns Falls.

Until last summer there was between Baltimore and Hollins streets a very ancient landmark of the West End—Alexandroffsky. A stern forbidding wall at least twelve feet high enclosed a whole city block. On Hollins Street the brick wall was broken by a strong iron gate set solidly in the brickwork. In spite of rust, it still wore a severe and vigorous air. A little farther down the street one came to the lodge gate, and through the entrance one caught a glimpse of a pink rose bush sprawling on the grass, and the corner of a fortress-like house, dark chocolate colour, with high towers—a most un-Baltimoreanish house.

Such was the mansion built by Thomas Winans who went to Russia to build railroads for the Czar. Ross Winans had been established in Baltimore for some years where he was hard at work upon steam engines. Indeed the railroad world owes this man a great debt for his genius. His son Thomas was apprenticed to the same trade, and when Alexander of Russia sent to America for engineers Ross Winans built a locomotive and sent his son Thomas to the Imperial Court to demonstrate its operation. With Winans went George Whistler, an engineer. The Czar was delighted with the two Americans and gave them a shop called Alexandroffsky, not far from the capital. For some years they lived in Russia and when Winans returned he was a very wealthy man. As the chronicler says, "He went abroad a mechanic and returned a millionaire."

With these millions Thomas Winans built a house set in the midst of a large garden, and in memory of his Russian days he called the place Alexandroffsky. At first the spacious grounds were adorned simply with trees and shrubs, but Winans was a man of taste, and it seemed to him that the lawns would be lovelier if there were statues here and there. Consequently Baltimore awoke one morning to find Greek gods and goddesses set about under the fine old trees. Nor were these celestial beings clothed; not at all. The mid-Victorians' sensibilities were shocked, yes, shocked at the bare limbs of Venus and the manly loins of Appollo. The town in fact seethed with moral indignation. That's what came of foreign parts. Scandalous the way those Europeans went about! Then was Winans moved to wrath. He immediately ordered a twelve foot wall to be erected around the garden, shutting off forever the sight of those poor heathen divinities. As is ever the case when mysteries are made of privacy Alexandroffsky was reputed by the common herd to be a sinister place, an abode of luxury, Byzantine in its splendour. Those who enjoyed its hospitality knew it to be a solid Victorian house, richly furnished in the massive style of the day. It was, moreover, crammed with rare objects of art. In truth romance and art both flourished here; George Whistler's son married Ross Winan's only daughter, and George Whistler's younger son was James McNeill Whistler. Whistler afterwards became the great artist, and in Alexandroffsky among other treasures of his brush was that wonderful Wapping. In this canvas there is the quick vibrant life of the waterside. It is the very spirit of the Thames. In the foreground three people are seated, two men and a woman, their figures sharply outlined against the criss-cross of rigging and spar. We might have had this picture—I recall John Oldmixon Lambdin—"J. O. L." as he was better known—that brilliant critic on the *Sun* speaking of this matter some time before his death. Now unhappily it has been sold and the thread of its connection with the town is broken.

At the death of Mrs. Hutton, Winans' daughter, the old place was sold. The walls were rudely thrown down and the mystery of many years was laid bare to the public. But there was no mystery. What the curiosity seekers found was an old-fashioned house somewhat forlorn and comfortless. The grass had grown very long, and the flowers and bushes were within a few weeks prodigal and unrestrained. But what a park this might have made for the people in a crowded ugly section of the town. This old house might have been preserved and its tradition cherished. For surely the building of railroads in Russia is a practical enterprise in which even an American might feel a just pride. But no; the land has been cut up into building lots. There must be filling stations.

One word, however, about the iniquitous statutes. Today two of them adorn the steps of a storage house on Charles and Twenty-sixth Street, and nobody stops to register horror at their Greek simplicity. Perhaps we have improved. But I coveted Alexandroffsky as a public park.

If, however, progress has destroyed the Winans estate, there is still much to be enjoyed in the Hollins Street Market. In foreign towns one finds intense pleasure in the primitive open-air markets, but I doubt if many Baltimoreans have ever seen this unusual sight. As you walk along Hollins Street from Poppleton, you mingle with a throng of people intent on buying. The crude wooden stalls are set up twice a week from eight o'clock until two and around these swirls a multitude of marketers. On hot days the stalls are covered with a spread of canvas, or perhaps an old quilt; another has unfurled a red and blue umbrella. If stalls are not sufficient the salesman arranges his wares upon the street itself—but hygienically protecting them from the dirt with old Sunpapers. Many of these buyers and sellers are English-speaking, but a jargon of tongues assails the ear in Pentecostal manner. Germans are buying shrewdly; Jews are feeling the goods with an enquiring thumb and finger; the Irish laugh gayly but keep their eye on the change. It is a merry whirligig. Here there is a different technique from that employed in the Richmond or the Lexington Markets. In Hollins Street the man who sells cherries frankly says that "they are sweet as a kiss" and winks at the nearest pretty girl; nor need she be so very pretty. The flower vender waters his posies and cries out monotonously "Ain't they fine? Ain't they sweet?" The Italian hopes that he will die and perish utterly if there is a sour strawberry in the whole box. But best of all was the china department. Spread out upon the bricks themselves was a fine collection of pots and pans and kettles. Brittany sells quainter china, but here and there the method of selling was the same. A few snowy caps, and I should have thought myself in Dinan. Nor are clothes lacking. Scarfs of every hue hung side by side with cheap lace collars. On the edge of the pavement a patient mother fitted shoes on her stubborn and refractory child. Until you have seen Hollins you do not know Baltimore markets. All of them are charming. I wish I had time to describe each one.

Beyond the red brick market house Hollins Street is very different in appearance. An air of starchy respectability is apparent at once. The street is quiet and provincial, the houses small and neat with an occasional trim garden. An image shop displays tawdry statues much bespattered with scarlet and blue—luridly religious. Indeed this note is not lacking in Mr. Mencken's neighborhood, for in a private house I saw this sign displayed in the "parlour window"—"Prepare to meet thy God." Rather sudden, that!

At last I came to Mr. Mencken's house. No wonder he commutes to New York. Solid and red and white it faces Union Square—one of those green patches that do so much to relieve the tedium of brick in the West End. Over the door is a gay striped orange awning and a silver plate engraved in slender script says 'August Mencken.' The iron hand-rail distinguishes this house from others in the block, and oddly enough the design used is that of a lyre. I hardly think that a suitable emblem for one who smites the strings with such berserkian gusto. This comfortable house looks out upon green grass and trees all day long. The sun pours upon it from dawn to late afternoon. Could one get this in New York? In the centre of the Square is a pleasant fountain, and nearby one of those structures that used to be found in City Spring—a sort of Belvedere with a prim Greek cupola. Neat flower beds planted in the manner of the seventies with coleus and petunias give colour to the spotless lawns. Old men dozed in the sunny corners; a horse occasionally clop clopped by on the north side of the Square. Mr. Mencken has chosen an abode of peace.

As one walks along Lombard Street and looks south he sees a stretch of red wall and buildings towering over it. This is the Mount Clare shop, the cradle one might say of the steam engine. The yards themselves are not of interest to the casual visitor, nor do I suppose that one would be admitted, but the history of the shops is well worth calling to mind while we are in the neighborhood of old Alexandroffsky.

BALTIMORE

On July 4, 1828, all the roads to Baltimore were thronged with people. Gentlemen went by in gigs with fine horses in the shafts. Large nondescript family carryalls also journeyed townward, crowded with the whole family—the ladies heavily veiled to protect them from the sun and rude men. Small boys in pea-jackets and frilled shirts rode fat ponies, having much ado to keep up with the family coach. Cato, the family dog, sprinted along nimbly, his pink tongue lolling, but nevertheless determined to maintain the reputation of a good coach-dog. But what was the event? The Iron Horse was about to be born and all the real horses were on the way to see the spectacle. Fortunately, the Fourth was cool, for dense crowds packed Baltimore street, fifty thousand townsmen out to see the great parade as it moved westward from Bond Street. All the guilds were there, stone-cutters, masons, carpenters—every man jack of them and all Baltimore and the County as well had assembled to greet them. In the midst was borne the Union, a model of a clipper ship rigged at Fells Point, the pride and joy of every seagoing man, and all the land lubbers too, for that matter. Charles Carroll of Carrollton rode in his barouche—the dear old gentleman now very aged and white-haired. When a spot two and a quarter miles from town south of the Frederick turnpike was reached, the long procession halted, for here was to be laid the cornerstone of the Baltimore and Ohio Railroad. Under a canopy Charles Carroll of Carrollton took his place, while the young and common folk stood smiling in the sun, but they did not care. This was truly a great occasion. Then two mercuries stood forth and begged that the printers be furnished with a copy of the speeches so aptly made and that copies be distributed among the citizens. Then up stepped the blacksmiths and stone-cutters and presented a spade and pick and hammer to the revered Signer. Next the stone itself which was to mark the beginning of the railway was set in place. Wine and oil were poured out in classic fashion and heaven's blessing was invoked. Then after more speechifying and ceremony the procession went to town. The county people returned to their estates. Fathers adjured their sons to mark that day, for they had seen the beginning of mighty works. They had truly. Two years later from Pratt and Poppleton Streets one could ride out to the Carrollton Viaduct and back for nine cents. Think of it; the car ran upon the rails, and a horse pulled it! What a thing progress is! The beaux and belles with appropriate giggles and manly reinforcements mounted these cars and got the most tremendous kick.

This was just the beginning. The horse car was not the solution of transportation, and many minds were set to work out this problem. Peter Cooper of New York was interested in the Baltimore and Ohio, and he designed the *Tom Thumb* the first American built locomotive to show what the Iron Horse could do. The first trip was made to the Relay. This was such a success that the daring experiment of venturing to Ellicott City in this *Tom Thumb* was next proposed. Though feeling some misgivings, twenty-three men accepted Cooper's invitation, and they set forth. The train went at the terrifying speed of a mile in five minutes. The town was reached in safety. Said Peter Cooper in the *New York World*: "This was the first passenger engine built in America, and the first passenger train that was ever drawn by an engine on this continent."

The coaches used on the first railroads were naturally copied from the stage coaches which had immediately preceded them. The engineer sat on the outside, and the passengers within faced each other. In England the old terms driver and guard were retained, but in America new words took their places. In Baltimore the coach maker was a man named Richard Imlay

BALTIMORE

who had a shop at Monument and North Street. He took
intense pride in his work and bestowed upon every detail the
most loving care. Nor were the coaches dull in colour. Not at
all; they were gaily painted, and named the Dromedary, or
the Sea Serpent, or more decorously the York, and the Atlantic.
After Imlay had put the finishing touches upon these little
coaches they were exhibited in Monument Square and everyone stood around marvelling at the advance of science.

It is a far cry from these diminutive coaches to the powerful
engines of today, but the Fair of the Iron Horse, the Baltimore and Ohio Centenary, gave a vivid picture of this development. Nothing could speak more eloquently than the program itself which, in part, I have included here. Those who
visited the Fair will recall it as one of the memorable celebrations in the history of a railroad, and indeed of a nation.

THE FAIR

OF THE

IRON HORSE

BALTIMORE AND OHIO

CENTENARY EXPOSITION

AND PAGEANT

1827 - 1927

IN THE DAYS BEFORE THE RAILROAD

American Indians with pack horses and *travois* pass in review.
They are symbolic of early travel, crude and slow. These Indians
are members of the Blood and Piegan tribes of the Blackfeet Nation, and come from Glacier Park, by courtesy of the Great Northern Railway.

2   *Pere Marquette.* The famous missionary and explorer accom-
    panied by Joliet and two aides, sights and blesses the Mississippi.

THE WEST END

3 *Early River Transport.* Showing the crude *bateau* by which the first settlers traveled the great interior rivers, carrying their household goods preparatory to setting up their homes and clearing the wilderness.

The scene turns to the highway. Roads have been cut through the forests; over them come the steadily increasing army of pioneers; first on horseback and then transporting their goods, far beyond the reach of water transportation, by the first rough forms of road wagon. The post chaise shows itself, and so does the post rider.

4 *Canal Days.* Better by far than the rough and frequently impassable highway was the man-built water highway that developed in Eastern America. The float shows one of the early craft that plied these artificial waterways, and carried still more settlers into the West.

More and more the highway is used for transport. There come the tobacco rollers, a unique form of hauling freight one hundred years ago. There ensues the Conestoga Wagon, once a distinctive feature of the turnpike roads. A curious vehicle at this time is the so-called George Washington coach in which one sees Henry Clay riding over the National Road. It is followed by the historic coach *Kearsarge;* in turn by another of the same sort. The *Kearsarge* has been loaned by Mr. Henry Ford; the other coach by Mr. Fred Stone.

THE BIRTH OF THE RAILROAD

These modes of transport offered no solution of the problem of the development of the nation. Faster, more dependable transportation; transportation upon a far larger scale was necessary. The railroad brought it. The problem in Baltimore had been made acute by the fact that the then new Erie Canal was taking trade away from the city. Because of this a meeting of the prominent citizens was called at the home of George Brown.

5 *The Birth of the Baltimore and Ohio.* There is shown one of these meetings—held in February, 1827—at which the bold project of a railroad was discussed and brought into actual being. In addition to Mr. Brown, Philip E. Thomas, who was to become the first president of the new railroad, and other prominent Baltimoreans of that day are shown gathered at the table.

The broad roadway is now the principal street of Baltimore City. On it is now reproduced the historic parade of July 4, 1828, held in celebration of the laying of the First Stone of the Baltimore and Ohio Railroad. For this the trades of the town furnished many

303

floats. From the carefully preserved documents of the day, four are reproduced. The First Stone rides upon a huge car, preceded by the Band (the Mount Clare Band of today), playing the *Carrollton March*, written for the parade of ninety-nine years ago. The black-smiths are represented by the Sons of Vulcan; the carpenters by a Doric Temple and the shipbuilders by a vessel, the *Union*. Charles Carroll of Carrollton, the only surviving signer of the Declaration of Independence, rides in a barouche.

6 *Surveying for the Railroad.* Gradually the new railroad project takes definite form. Army engineers are shown surveying its route. In the early thirties, the Military Academy at West Point was the only school of engineering in the land. Its graduates therefore often were called upon to serve industrial enterprise. Tribute to these army builders of the Baltimore and Ohio is paid in this float, depicting Captains McNeil and Whistler and Lieutenant Thayer, making its first reconnaissance.

The Horse Car. The new railroad was first built with no certainty as to its motive power. The men of Baltimore decided that the horse—reliable and dependable, not the uncertain steam locomotive of which they had heard vague reports from England—should be the motive power for their railroad. The Horse Car shown is a replica of the one which in May, 1830, began its daily trips between Mount Clare, Baltimore, and Ellicott's Mills, fourteen miles apart.

7 *The Treadmill Car.* Many ingenius devices were introduced to make horsepower applicable to railroad cars. One of these on the Baltimore and Ohio was the Treadmill Car by which an ancient mechanical device was applied to rail transport. The Treadmill Car ran into a cow, was ditched, and thereafter abandoned.

8 *The Sail Car.* More ingenius was the Sail Car, which Evan Thomas, a brother of Philip E. Thomas, devised and placed upon the road. A replica of this was sent to the Czar, who considered its introduction upon the Russian railroads.

THE COMING OF THE STEAM LOCOMOTIVE

The horse car was not the solution of the motive power problem. Peter Cooper, of New York, financially interested in the Baltimore and Ohio, designed the Tom Thumb, the first American-built locomotive to show what the Iron Horse might do for them.

By Courtesy of F. X. Milholland. Baltimore & Ohio R. R.

THE "ATLANTIC" LOCOMOTIVE

THE WEST END

9 *Tom Thumb*—1829-1830. A replica of the Peter Cooper engine. It weighed only two tons but it served to demonstrate to the men of Baltimore that the steam locomotive was practical. Peter Cooper is seen driving his engine.

10 *York*—1831. So convincing was the lesson the *Tom Thumb* taught, that the directors of the Baltimore and Ohio offered a prize of $4,000 for the most effective steam locomotive. The *York* came as the answer. It was built by Phineas Davis, at York, Pa.; weighed three and one-half tons and was capable of carrying a load of fifteen tons at a rate of fifteen miles an hour.

11 *Atlantic*—1832. No replica this but the actual locomotive, which continued in service until 1893. It, in turn, is much heavier than the *York*, weighing six and one-half tons. It hauls two Imlay coaches, exact reproductions of passenger cars built for the Baltimore and Ohio in 1831 by a famous Baltimore coach builder.

12 *Thomas Jefferson*—1835. This stout little engine (the original) was the first locomotive to operate in the State of Virginia, being employed on the Winchester and Potomac Railroad in 1836.

13 *William Galloway*—1837. This locomotive is a replica of the *Lafayette,* built by Richard Norris, of Philadelphia, and was the first engine with a horizontal boiler to be used on the Baltimore and Ohio. It hauls two flour cars, typical of its day.

14 *Memnon No. 57*—1848. Another original locomotive built by the Newcastle Manufacturing Company, at Newcastle, Del., and being for her day very fast was used in passenger service.

15-16 *The Birth of the Telegraph.* These two floats depict the first commercial use of the telegraph on May 24, 1844, when the world-famous message, "What Hath God Wrought," was flashed along the lines of the Baltimore and Ohio from the national capital at Washington to the railroad station at Baltimore. Professor S. F. B. Morse, the inventor, seated at the desk.

Again the scene shifts to the highway and one sees another form of communication in the United States. This is the Pony Express and the early western stage coach (contributed to the pageant by the American Railway Express Company), which once gave glamor to the famous name of Wells Fargo and Company.

17 *William Mason*—1856. The original locomotive was built by the William Mason Company at Taunton, Mass. Mason's beautiful engines were the forerunners of the standard American type locomotives of today.

305

BALTIMORE

18 *Mr. Lincoln Goes to Washington.* A critical journey was that of Abraham Lincoln over the Baltimore and Ohio in February, 1861, to his first inauguration. He arrived at Washington in the early morning and is shown here with his guards, Allan Pinkerton and Colonel Ward H. Lamon.

19 *Thatcher Perkins No. 117—1863.* Designed along the lines of the Mason locomotives but far greater in strength were the ten-wheel engines built by Thatcher Perkins at Mount Clare in Civil War days. The *Perkins* is painted in its original colors and hauls a passenger train typical of its day.

20 *Destruction of the Baltimore and Ohio Tracks.* In modern warfare severe measures ofttimes are necessary. Baltimore and Ohio lines traversed the scene of much Civil War fighting. Frequently its tracks were torn up and destroyed, first by one army and then by the other. The money loss was very great.

21 *Ross Winans No. 217—1869.* The camelback locomotive invented by Ross Winans was for many years the most distinctive feature of freight transport of the Baltimore and Ohio. One is shown here, hauling a typical freight train of sixty years ago.

22 *J. C. Davis, No. 600—1875.* This locomotive when exhibited at the Philadelphia Centennial Exposition of 1876 was said to be the heaviest passenger engine in existence. It weighs forty-five tons. Engines today may weigh three hundred tons and upward.

23 *A. J. Cromwell No. 545—1888.* A very successful consolidation locomotive designed by A. J. Cromwell, a former Master of Machinery of the Baltimore and Ohio.

24 *The Coming of the Electric Locomotive—1895.* This float shows the first electric locomotive to operate on a steam railroad. It was run in the Baltimore and Ohio Belt Line tunnel, under Baltimore, and was originally operated by overhead trolley. The third-rail system is now used in the tunnel, which thereby is kept free from smoke.

25 *No. 1310—1896.* The inauguration of the famous Royal Blue Line between Washington and New York called for locomotives capable of tremendously high speed. No. 1310 was built for this service. Its 78-inch drivers rendered it extremely suitable for the difficult work it was called upon to do.

306

26 *Muhlfeld No.* 2400—1904. This, the first Mallet ever built in the United States, was designed for the Baltimore and Ohio by John E. Muhlfeld, then the roads General Superintendent of Motive Power, and more recently the designer of the *John B. Jervis* of the Delaware and Hudson Railroad, which is also shown in this pageant.

With the Baltimore and Ohio is linked up the thought of the telegraph, for along the lines of the B. & O. the first message from Washington was flashed to the railroad station in Baltimore. But we must go back a little in the story.

In 1837 Samuel F. B. Morse asked Congress to help him perfect an invention on which he had been at work for many years. It was an electromagnetic telegraph which would enable persons to communicate with each other over great distances; indeed it would link up cities as far distant as Washington and New York. To this plea Congress turned a deaf ear. In fact they were somewhat amused at this absurd proposal, nor were those lacking who thought the whole idea had a slightly impious sound. Search the Scriptures as you will; there is no mention of a telegraph in Holy Writ. Poor Morse! Much learning had made him mad. However, in 1842, John P. Kennedy, Chairman of the House Committee to which the bill had been referred, became much interested in the plan, and strongly urged Congress to appropriate thirty thousand dollars to test the applicability of the new invention. Morse's delight knew no bounds and with eagerness he set to work to demonstrate this marvelous new principle. All that he needed was money and a hearing. Accordingly he gathered together three men, Leonard D. Gale, James C. Fisher, and Alfred Vail, who at the magnificent salary of fifteen hundred dollars a year set themselves to solve the problems of the electric telegraph. Later on Fisher died and Ezra Cornell, the founder of the Cornell University, was appointed at one thousand a year!

BALTIMORE

The first plan was to lay the wires under ground along the sleepers of the Washington branch of the Baltimore and Ohio Railroad. Between Baltimore and the Relay lead pipe with four insulated copper wires inclosed was buried twelve inches below the surface. But alas, when the test was made the insulation proved faulty, and the underground method was abandoned. Poor Morse, trembling in despair at the expenditure of fifteen thousand dollars and at the public contempt heaped upon him, was almost frantic. Everyone said "What did I tell you? Wasting the people's money."

But as the winter came on Morse and the faithful three began to figure out a new line of attack. It was decided to string the wires on poles, and Ezra Cornell got the job of pole-setting There was no precedent for such a method, and the work was crudely done. To establish a current a wire connecting with the pole of the battery was soldered to a copper sheet five feet by two and a half set in the dock at Pratt and Light Street in Baltimore. In Washington the wire was buried under the pavement in the dusty cellar of the Capitol.

After many months of labour the Sunpaper announced: "Professor Morse's electromagnetic telegraph in course of construction between Baltimore and Washington is now in full operation a distance of twenty-two miles. When cars from this city on their way to Washington on Wednesday were within twenty miles of the latter city, information of the Whig's nomination for President and Vice-President was communicated through means of the telegraph." This was exciting enough, but, finally, on May 24 the line was complete and all arrangements were made for the transmission of the first formal message. Magnets and recording instruments were attached to the ends of the wires at the depot of the Baltimore and Ohio in Pratt Street, and similar preparations were made in the Supreme Court in Washington. Miss Ellsworth, daughter of the Commissioner of Patents, had been the first to tell Morse the joyful news that Congress had given him the coveted appropriation. Consequently he promised her that she should send the first message when his dream should become reality. When everything was in order Morse gave her the signal, and the message "What Hath God Wrought" came clearly as the first dispatch to Baltimore. Morse had won and all the Jeremiahs were put to confusion.

From that day messages sped over the wires between the two cities. The first Presidential message was transmitted exclusively for the *Sun,* that great newspaper which has done so much to make Baltimore. In the forties Pratt Street was a lively place. It has fallen now to base commercial uses, but then it wore the high air of politics. Before the War with Mexico men packed the street from curb to curb avid for news from New Orleans. Both the eastern and western mail arrived amidst intense excitement. So violent indeed did the Baltimoreans become that Morse was obliged to issue a statement.

"For the purpose of preventing any misunderstanding or jealousy in the transmision of news by telegraph I wish you to make it known that at six p. m. each day or as soon as the Southern mail arrives the government telegraph will send to Baltimore any public intelligence that arrives by that time. Each person at Baltimore wishing the same shall be allowed to come into the office and by paying the charges, two words for one cent, can take a copy. But when news is being received, you are to shut the door. Let the people in but no one out until all is completed. If news arrives here before the mail, it must of course have precedence. S. F. B. Morse."

Whether this calmed their ardour I do not know. When the war actually began the *Sun* ran a pony express from the landing in of the Southern Mail boat to the telegraph office in Seventh Street, Washington. Dispatches were prepared as the boat steamed slowly up the Potomac then at the wharf the pony rider snatched them up and flung off to the office. Thus light for all was shed abroad. Good old Sunpaper!

The people in general were thrilled with the new invention and constant crowds gathered in the streets to observe, if possible, this new marvel. Between nine and twelve and four and five the offices were thrown open. Then the public came surging in. Henry J. Rogers who was in charge was then a busy man, and Morse sometimes had to take a hand—in writing—and lay down a few regulations. Games were soon played over the wires, and draughts particularly, a spirited contest being waged between Alfred Vail and John Wills. Wills won. Then Washington challenged Baltimore to chess again, and again Baltimore won. Nor was the city backward in the more modern sports; the first murder transmitted over the wires was news of a Baltimore murder—McCurry vs. Roux; McCurry winning. You can't down the Irish!

FROM FEDERAL HILL

CHAPTER XIX

ECHNICALLY South Baltimore begins at Baltimore Street and embraces all the land lying south of that east-and-west thoroughfare. In reality you do not get the flavor of the neighborhood until you are south of Pratt Street; indeed, one might say at Barre. There one has a feeling that the inner harbour lies north; there is a new orientation. But this is purely fanciful, for on Conway Street stands one of the oldest landmarks in this neighborhood, the Otterbein Church, built in 1785. This old structure was built of bricks—brought from England (yes, we know well how this brick question has been disputed) but there the church stands today solid and four square with a steeple like Wren's, only more substantial, more Teutonic. The windows are very lovely, of plain glass with delicate tracery. Above, in the belfry, are the ancient bells brought over from Bremen many years ago. The Rev. William Otterbein, the founder of the United Brethren Church, came to Baltimore in 1773, but did not settle here permanently until 1774, and then until 1813 he carried on a fine work ministering to the German people of Baltimore. A little further to the east,

BALTIMORE

at the northwest corner of Charles and Camden, was situated
another of those springs that supplied Baltimore with water
in the early days. This was a specially convenient one for all
sea-faring men, and often small boats would be sent ashore
to fetch back a supply of fresh water for some vessel outward
bound. Most of the antique air of the neighborhood has long
since vanished, but the names of the streets still bear a record
of the past. Conway and Barre successfully opposed the Stamp
Act in the Parliament, and these old streets commemorate their
courage. Sharpe Street was named for Governor Sharpe—that
able colonial governor, whose fine estate, White Hall, was
one of the notable mansions in the province. Camden, of
course, commemorates the battle in the Revolutionary War.
Montgomery, a little farther south, was named after a hero of
the Seven Years' War, and, needless to say, Key Highway bears
the name of the illustrious Francis Scott Key. Hanover and
York recall the days before the War of Independence, and
Armistead records the commander of the Fort in the War of
1812.

Walk south now to Montgomery Street, and you will see
rising before you, blocking the eastern horizon, Federal Hill.
A steep flight of steps leads up to it, but if you are wise you
will take the left hand road at the first landing; this will save
you a great expenditure of breath, and at the same time it will
present a shifting view of the harbour. Frankly, although
from a commercial and sociological point this neighborhood
is much improved, from the standpoint of picturesque beauty
there has been a sad loss. The old clutter of houses and
wharves, the tilted roofs, and disreputable sheds have vanished
forever. All is neat, clean and prophylactic. But do not lose
heart. Federal Hill still has charm. No commanding hill
lifted above a great harbour can be without significance. I
look back upon the old days of clutter and wild beauty with

312

THE OTTERBEIN CHURCH—THE MOTHER CHURCH OF THE UNITED BRETHREN
DENOMINATION. BUILT 1785 BY PHILLIP WILLIAM OTTERBEIN, SHARP AND
CONWAY STREETS, BALTIMORE, MD.

regret, but there is still quiet and a sense of withdrawal on Federal Hill.

Now, doubtless, you have reached the top, a place of level lawns and old trees. On the benches one could dream away many hours if one had them, for here the light and colour of the harbour changes every moment, and there is always something fresh, something varied, and mutable. The Inner Harbour lies at our feet. Above the ugly roofs of the docks rises the skyline of new Baltimore. The office buildings tower aggressively against the blue; there the elegant dome of the City Hall suggests old and classic things; the pyramidal mass of the Penitentiary menaces. What would John Smith have thought could he have seen this sight? Imagine him there where Light and Pratt Streets join, seated upon a sandy beach surrounded by his sturdy Elizabethans, eating roasted maize. Jones Falls then ran down from the Green Spring Valley in a clear limpid stream. The marsh later known as Harrison's was a lowlying stretch of ground where reed birds built their nests. Perhaps this hill was a high green knoll rising percipitately from the water's edge. We can see the Captain looking out across the harbor as he munched his Indian corn, and thinking rather idly that yon green hill would make a goodly fort. No doubt, or rather possibly.

At the top of the hill there is an utterly hideous monument erected to General Armistead, who as the inscription reads was

"The gallant defender
of Fort McHenry
Near this city
During its bombardment by
The British Fleet
13 *and* 14 *of Sepember* 1814."

This tight precise block of stone is unworthy of the brave and dauntless men who withstood the fire of that hostile fleet.

313

BALTIMORE

But fortunately one does not have to look at the monument. The changeful interplay of light and shadow, the movement of the boats and the sounds strangely muted give plenty of occupation. Here is a quiet rarely found in a city. The putter of engines, the raucous scream of steel on steel, the hoot of a whistle—all these come dreamily. At our feet the excursion boats lie quietly at the docks awaiting the oncoming throngs. The sweltering summer days see these spick and span white boats crowded with mothers and children to say nothing of youths and maidens, all setting out merrily to Tolchester or Port Deposit or Annapolis. The *Louise* was the most famous of these old boats. Faithfully she plowed up and down the river and back and forth across the Bay to the favorite picnic ground of Baltimoreans. The last I heard of this old favorite she was in the pleasant port of New Orleans. Smaller than the *Louise,* and therefore more intimate, is the *Emma Giles.* She is a lovely little vessel, all resplendent with mirrors in black walnut frames picked out with gold, and with an "elegant saloon" furnished with red plush settees and chairs. Over the main stair-case hangs a portrait of Emma Giles herself, the little girl for whom the boat is named. She is a pretty child with rosy cheeks and appropriate curls. Often I have gazed at her picture and thought how wonderful to have a boat named for oneself—a whole boat! Oh, those marvelous sails when one was ten! There are few sounds in life as thrilling as the splash of the great ropes in the water when the darkeys on the dock cried "Let 'er go!" Then the wind freshened, and the Emma Giles turned and headed for the Bay. Fort Mc Henry slipped by, a green romantic spot; soon Seven Foot Knoll, appeared, a curious name when one is young, for there was no knoll—nothing indeed but a lighthouse and the sound of a bell. Mysterious and dimly seen on the horizon was Fort Carroll built by Robert E. Lee. This lonely deserted island

314

was always a place of enchantment, and to this day it lies there desolate and forlorn the grass growing upon the ramparts, and perhaps a lone fisherman to give a hail and farewell. Ships carry one's thoughts very far, but the voyage on the *Emma Giles* is only in memory. There are more things to be discovered in this neighborhood. The Bay boats must wait.

Indeed I have discovered nearby the ideal Baltimore house. It stands on the steep edge of Warren Street, almost toppling down into the harbour. All its eastern windows are open to the sun. It is a perfect location; peace itself. To keep the natives from tumbling off the hill a stout row of stumps runs along the edge inviting the foolhardy, but warning the wise. I followed the line of these stumps and descended a flight of wooden steps; and found myself in a narrow court more like a country lane than a city street. It was a poor place, but by no means forlorn. Bits of garden were tucked in here and there, and as it was wash-day the lines were strung with red, orange, and green. If there is anything more decorative than a line of rainbow rompers I would like you to name it. This whole neighborhood is a network of little courts and alleys. They must be sought for, but they can be found. Grindalls Court for instance is a tiny place with not more than five or six houses on each side; Compton has its mansions set in sawtooth fashion, like a chevron molding. The roadway was muddy—very—but the houses themselves are small and quaint and gaily coloured. One was pale green; One sported a bright yellow transome and window sills. This neighborhood tucked away under Federal Hill is anything but drab.

In the Civil War Federal Hill was strongly fortified. Here Benjamin Butler was in command, and a sad time he had of it with beautiful Confederate blockade runners, and the "Monument Street girls," to say nothing of "Secesh" babies appearing in public with red sashes around their rebel waists. Mysterious tunnels have been discovered under the Hill and all sorts of theories have been advanced in explanation. These labyrinths are quite extensive, many of them running for at least two blocks directly to Federal Hill. They have been blamed upon both beer and Butler. It is true that in the past—the remote past—many breweries were established in this neighborhood, but it is not at al llikely that such lengthy chambers would have been needed in the cooling of beer. On the other hand Butler never mentions any tunnels, but refers solely to a cave found on one occasion. This, by the way, gave Butler and his men a terrible fright, for it was thought to be stored with explosives. The mystery, therefore, is not yet solved, which leaves something to future historians.

At the corner of Light and Montgomery there is a small shop with a peaked roof, and in the yard some rough blocks of stone where two men were busily at work. This drew me at once and as I came near I saw on the left of the doorway a long panel of stone set with a small spirited bronze horse. There I read this inscription

"The City put the
(horse)
In the cellar
But the business on
a mountain
But I am still making
tombstones
on the old corner
And selling them for
Less money than you
Can buy them elsewhere."

Not in every day's walk does such an adventure befall. Who was the horse? Why did the city act in such an inexplicable

By Courtesy of the City Librarian

CIVIL WAR SCENE ON FEDERAL HILL

manner? Nor did Mr. Wingrove, the owner of the business, seem averse to telling me.

"Now," said he, "young lady, I'll explain; you come with me." Meekly I went. He showed me an old stable where the fine horse—the "grand stud horse"—once lived. Now the stable was at least six feet above the level of the pavement.

"That," said Wingrove, "is where my horse lived. That was my stable. But along come those smart fellows from the City Hall making improvements—oh this has all been wrote up all over the country—and they cuts down the street to make this here Key Highway to improve things. Huh! And there is my horse, my fine stud horse in the stable high and dry. What am I to do?"

"What?" said I, for ignorance is always best when a man is mounted on his hobby and a fine stud hobby at that.

"Come here," he said patronizingly, "look through this chink. Well," says he, surveying me as if he were Dr. Norwood of Saint Bartholomew's or Dean Inge, "What does I do, young lady? I lets down a plank from the stable to the next room, see? Then I gets the horse out! Then I made this monument just to let folks know what they done with their improvements, and I puts it up in memory of my horse which was as fine a horse as you can find in Maryland and that's saying something."

It is. Billy Barton may have a finer monument, but Bruce will be no prouder of his horse than Wingrove is of his.

Interesting as Federal Hill undoubtedly is, the chief landmark of south Baltimore is Fort McHenry. During the Revolutionary War the citizens had begun fortifications, but when peace came they were abandoned. Later, however, it seemed wise to commence the work again, and in 1794 the fortress built at the mouth of the harbour passed under the control of the Federal Government. This small compact fort was named after James McHenry of Maryland, who was Secretary to General Washington during the Revolution, and Secretary of War from 1796 to 1800. In 1805 the fortress was completed, nor was it long before its worth was sorely tested.

Great Britain determined to put an end to the pretensions of America on the high sea, and having disposed of her foes in Europe, she now turned her attention to her former colonies. Baltimore, the "nest of privateers," was especially in need of a severe lesson. A well-known British statesman declared that Baltimore was "the great depository of the hostile spirit of the United States against England." Said a London paper: "The American navy must be annihilated; their arsenals and dock-yards must be consumed; the truculent inhabitants of Baltimore must be tamed with those weapons that shook the wooden turrets of Copenhagen." In fact, Baltimore and Washington were the two towns appointed to suffer. This reputation for valour delighted the high-spirited citizens of the town and they made ready for defense. The inhabitants of the city were summoned to deposit at the courthouse, the market house at Fells Point, or the riding school "all wheel-barrows, pickaxes, spades, and shovels that they can procure." All classes of men in well-organised groups were enjoined to participate in this important work of defense. To the stirring sound of 'Money Musk' or 'Yankee Doodle' the men and boys marched each day to the appointed place in the line of entrenchments. The water approach was by no means neglected. A four-gun battery was constructed at the Lazaretto, and between this point and Fort McHenry across the harbour a number of ships were sunk, thus effectually blocking the entrance to the inner basin.

On September 6 the British embarked, weighed anchor, "and stood with a fair wind for the Chesapeake." A day or two of suspense followed during which the intractable Balti-

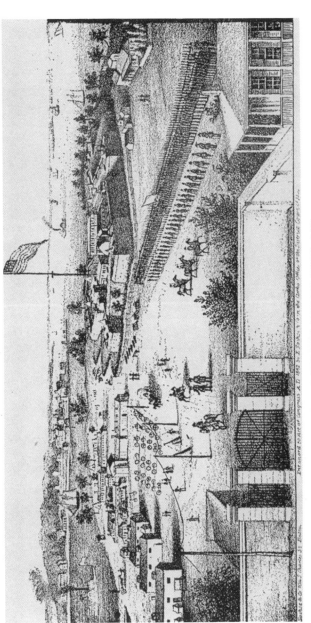

FORT McHENRY, BALTIMORE, MD.
IN 1862

By Courtesy of the City Librarian

moreans worked like beavers on their fortifications. Finally, on September 11 about seventy enemy vessels anchored off North Point. Now the city became an armed camp. Under the brilliant light of the moon the citizens led by General Stricker marched out to "feel the enemy." At the Fort Lieutenant-Colonel George Armistead was in command of about one thousand men. Among them as a volunteer private was young John P. Kennedy, just out of college and entranced with his giddy uniform and that helmet with the huge black feather. Kennedy often said that nothing in his after life ever was half so thrilling as those nights at the Fort.

The Battle of North Point we have described earlier. Now we have only to defeat the British on the sea and all will be well.

Poor Ross had been killed at Gorsuch farm, you remember, and the battle had not been a marked British success. The army, soaked by the rain, halted a while and waited for the fleet to lend its assistance. A few hours bombardment would reduce poor little McHenry to ashes. It was about two o'clock on the morning of September 13 that the enemy opened fire. All day long and into the night the harbour shook with the roar of bombs. To this the Fort made no resistance, for the enemy was out of range, and they took good care to keep at a respectful distance. This twenty-four hour bombardment was met with a passive resistance trying to nerve and valor. Occasionally the enemy would venture nearer, and then the sullen guns spit out such a venom that the British retired hastily. Until midnight there was little change in the method of attack, but about one o'clock boats were seen approaching, manned with twelve hundred picked warriors. They carried with them scaling ladders, and all was in readiness for a rear attack on Fort McHenry. But their plans failed. At a signal Fort Covington and Fort McHenry opened a terrific fire. The whole

BALTIMORE

Harbour glowed like a furnace, and the little town trembled under the heavy gunfire.

Out in the river that night on board ship was a young lawyer named Francis Scott Key, who was seeking the release of a friend taken captive by the British. Key had been courteously received, but told that he must remain with the British fleet until after the attack on Baltimore. When the vessels moved up the river the boat, in which Key was detained, anchored in a position that gave a clear view of the Fort. There above the garrison floated the flag made by Mary Pickergill and her small daughter. Breathlessly Key watched that flag, for to him it meant the delivery or capture of Baltimore. Throughout the night when rockets reddened the sky he saw it still floating on the hot September breeze. In the morning it still fluttered in command of the old Fort. On the back of an envelope he scribbled the words that came crowding into his mind, and then stuffed the poem into his pocket. The flag was still there; the city was untaken; the British fleet departed. Key and his friend reached town in safety. They went at once to the Fountain Inn, no doubt, for breakfast, and there Key showed his poem to his uncle, after making some additions and changes in the original draft. Captain Nicholson was delighted with it, and had it sent straightway to a printer. As to the place where *The Star-Spangled Banner* was first sung authorities differ. Some say it was introduced at the Holliday Street Theatre; others credit the debut to a restaurant next to the theatre. It is immaterial. So intense was the relief after the battle that the townspeople took readily to the strong emotion of Key's song. *The Star-Spangled Banner* set to the well-known tune Anacreon in Heaven exactly expressed their feelings, and from the first the poem found a welcome in the hearts of the American people.

320

But tense as the emotional strain was there were some amusing incidents connected with the bombardment. When the cannonading was at its height a rooster deceived by the bright ruddy glow thought that the morning had come, and lustily crowed as he mounted the parapet. Worn as the men were they had to laugh at the ridiculous fowl. The laugh did them so much good that one of the men swore that if he lived until the next day he would buy that rooster the finest pound-cake in Baltimore. When the day dawned the weary defender was alive, and true to his promise he procured the richest, noblest pound-cake that the town afforded. Then in snug content the enlivening fowl and a group of tired soldiers had a merry feast.

During the Civil War the Fort was used as a prison and many were the Baltimoreans sent thither. In those days men were arrested on the least provocation. Among these were Ross Winans, and Colonel Kane, Teackle Wallis, George William Brown, the Mayor, Henry M. Warfield, and J. Hanson Thomas. All these prisoners were committed to Fort McHenry. Nor were these the only ones. In those day, however, imprisonment in the Fort was a badge of honor; certainly it was the sign of brave and fearless men. The Fort had fallen on evil days, and it had become not a means of defense but an instrument of oppression. The commanding officer (from Hackmatack no doubt) boasted that he could easily shell Washington's Monument, if he had a mind, but evidently he "did not choose." Finally all the Yankees went to their appointed place, and the old Fort was left in peace and tranquility.

In the opening years of this century it was a lovely, quiet spot. The long roadway leading from the gate was lined with maple trees. On the left were the barracks and the parade ground, on the right a line of officers' cottages, neat and trim.

Beyond was the old star fort and the flag pole with the "flag still there." There were guns placed here and there, not much use possibly as defense, but making admirable retreats for any two who sought a quiet place for conversation. Along the sea wall there was utter solitude except for an occasional gull. The view of the Harbour and River was particularly fine. Fort McHenry in truth was a little idyl.

Just before the Great War the Fort was turned into a park, for its career as a defender of the city was undoubtedly over. The Star-Spangled Banner Centennial naturally centered at McHenry, but by that time the War had come and again the Fort was demanded by the Government. Hospitals were erected, and famous doctors came and went, doing marvelous work in plastic surgery. But the war left it a wreck; those who love the old place hate to see it in its present defilement. The good news, however, has come from Washington that once more the Fort will become a park, and here certainly should be a true shrine of American history.

All of South Baltimore smacks of the sea. Indeed one never gets very far from salt water anywhere in the town. Across the Middle Branch of the Patapsco is Hanover Street Bridge spanning what is known as Spring Gardens. Here at the foot of Light Street were two Rowing Clubs the Ariel and L'Hirondelle. In the early years of the century these clubs were sworn enemies, and they met in deadly conflict in races and regattas. The Ariel still remains, "the only rowing club on this side of the river," as an attendant proudly told me. It was a lovely sight on summer afternoons to see the slender racing shells speeding through the water like swift arrows. Up the river at Westport was Flood's, a park reputed for its "Wickedness." One warm summer night the flaming youth of the first decade of the twentieth century sought out this sinister amusement park hoping to see some wickedness in action. Softly they slid along in their canoe, approaching the horrific spot with thrills of unholy anticipation. For a long time they sat out quietly under the summer stars waiting for deviltry to materialize. But alas, all was very dull. In a grove of fine trees lighted by the gasoline torches of the period sat a number of heavy stodgy men, women and children. Decorously they were grouped about long tables, and before them were large schooners of beer. (This of course was wicked but we did not know it then.) Somewhere a girl whined out a sentimental song about home and mother. It was as pious as a convention of elders. Disheartened, the flaming youth stole away.

Not far from the shores of the Patapsco there is a pretty little settlement with the old name of British Consul. The story of this small suburb is so unusual that I must tell it. By stretching a point British Consul may rightly be considered South Baltimore for it lies partly within the city line established in 1918. Moreover, a good yarn is always acceptable.

A man named William Dawson, said to have been the first British Consul in Baltimore, once owned an estate on the old Annapolis Road. A tradition asserts that William Johnson had a brother, a British soldier, who had been banished to Maryland for some act committed in England. The Dawson family was rich and powerful, and they had a curious sentence passed upon this scion of the house: he was to leave England with the promise and understanding that forever after, once a year on a given day, the exile was to be lashed for half an hour.

The unfortunate man settled with his brother in Maryland —at the estate of the British Consul—and yearly submitted to this strange punishment. On the estate there was an immense oak tree, and here the exile bared his back, and strapped to the oak, received the cruel strokes. For a time a man named Hawkes was paid five dollars to inflict the stripes upon poor

Dawson, but the nobility of the exile, and his manly bearing excited the pity of Hawkes. Gradually he softened the blows, but though Dawson shrieked in agony he urged Hawkes to lay on the lashes with redoubled zeal.

No one has ever discovered the nature of the crime. All that could be learned from Dawson was that he had sinned in defense of his own honour. There the mystery rests.

THE GREEN CHAIN OF PARKS

CHAPTER XX

T HE parks of Baltimore are justly famous for their beauty, but they have another claim to interest: in a least three cases they are not only parks but great estates handed down from earlier days as a legacy to the present generation. Of these by far the most interesting as a survivor of the colonial period is Carroll Park, named from the distinguished family so long associated with the history of the state.

Shortly after the War of the Spanish Succession—in the year 1715, to be exact—Doctor Charles Carroll, grandson of Daniel Carroll, who, as we have seen, presented twenty sons fully accoutred for the service of Charles I, came to America and settled in Annapolis. He practised medicine for many years but finally devoted himself to business thus amassing a large fortune, which he invested in land in and around Baltimore. Among these properties was a fine estate rising in a long smooth sweep up from the Patapsco river, until it reached a proud eminence. Close by at present runs the Washington Boulevard, but in those days there was nothing but a narrow

325

Indian trail running south, a foundation for the post road of another era. The river, however, was an admirable highway, and here Carroll built several ships which he used in his extensive business. Indeed he writes to his son Charles "I have found it very convenient at Patapsco (Mount Clare), a planta-tion running down to the river, well wooded with timber. I have sawyers, laborers, smiths, and iron workers, and have in mind to try at building more ships to be launched from thence."

The son to whom this letter was addressed was then study-ing law in the Middle Temple, but not since he was sixteen had he been at home, for at that early age he was sent to Eton. In 1746 he returned to Maryland and in spite of his English upbringing he was devoted to the interests of the Colony and soon became one of her warmest advocates. The society of Annapolis at that period was brilliant and dissipated. Gentle-men fought and drank with equal gusto. About this time regular matched races between pedigreed horses were intro-duced, and the Maryland Jockey Club was formed. Cards occupied the quieter moments of the day, and the play house was ever popular. Into this gay life came Charles Carroll, Barrister. The title added to his name was given because, as he wrote to his friends in London: "There are so many of my name in this town that particular direction is necessary to prevent mistakes. Please therefore direct me to either Counsel-lor or Barrister at Law.

On the death of Dr. Charles Carroll his only surviving son Charles lived in Annapolis, but he found himself drawn more and more to Patapsco. The name of Mount Clare was later given to the stately house built on the hill, a name probably chosen by Doctor Carroll, whose mother was named Clare. However that may be, the old house was still associated with the river which flowed on quietly at the foot of the green lawn. From the mansion to the Patapsco which then flowed nearer the house there is still an underground passage bricked up now for the sake of safety. Long ago when Braddock was defeated and Indians came pressing down upon the city this subterranean passage was used by the citizens as a secret exit. Tradition says this, but positive proof is wanting. One would like to know, however, what purpose was served by a small secret chamber near the house which opened into this mysterious tunnel. Within and without Mount Clare has been beautifully preserved. One cannot commend too much the wisdom and foresight of the Park Board in securing this fine example of colonial architecture, and surely the Colonial Dames have done well in furnishing the mansion not only with "articles collected here and there presumably of the period, but the veritable furnishings and worldly gear, silver, etc., remain in the place for which they were purchased from London."

As to the grounds around the house they are kept with the usual care and attention bestowed by the Park Board. All the necessary modern roads and paths have been laid out in such a way that the spirit of the old place has been enhanced rather than destroyed. The terraces on the east slope are especially worthy of note. The tall slender trees bordering the narrow walk make one think of the terraces of Italian gardens. John Adams described them thus: "There is a beautiful garden and then a fall, another flat garden, and then a fall, and so on down to the river." Today the river lies farther to the east but the beauty of Mout Clare is unspoiled.

Across the city from Mount Clare lies Patterson Park, a very attractive green square of large dimensions set in the heart of east Baltimore. In the early days this outlying section of the town was known as Hampstead Hill. It was high rolling ground commanding a view of all that flat and undistinguished country that spread out along the northern shore of the Patapsco. This part of the town is now called Canton— for the first voyage made from China to Baltimore. The ship, the Pallas, came in bringing a rich cargo, and the captain, John O'Donnell, has given his name to one of the principal streets in the industrial suburb. In the year 1814, however, the outlook from Hampstead Hill was very different. Far to the east lay North Point, and the citizens of Baltimore knew that the British would advance in this direction. That is why they worked so feverishly on that broiling September Sunday. All along Hampstead Hill they toiled at the fortifications that were destined to save the city. Today the green lawns and terraces certainly do not suggest anything warlike, but Rogers' Bastion can yet be seen. It is not far from the main entrance, and to mark it suitably the children of Baltimore have given a memorial by Miller to commemorate the valour of the Old Defenders. The Park itself was the gift of William Patterson, that sturdy citizen, the father of the redoubtable Betsy. Patterson presented it to the city in 1827, but it was not made a public park until 1853.

Both Carroll and Patterson Parks have fine modern recreational facilities. There are well-equipped playgrounds, and extensive playing fields. Carroll has a large wading pool, but in Patterson the Park Board has installed one of the largest and best swimming pools in the country. All of Baltimore's pools are well-patronized. In this connection it is interesting to note that the Walters have given us not only Barye bronzes, but also a system of public baths. It is greatly to be regretted, however, that our waterfront facilities have not been utilized in recreation as they should. A movement in this direction has recently been made in the acquisition of Fort Armistead for camping purposes.

THE GREEN CHAIN OF PARKS

North of Patterson as the crow flies is another great park, Clifton the home of philanthropist Johns Hopkins. The chief charm here lies in the beauty of the grounds. The house is frankly ugly, handsome, no doubt, in its time, but now marked with the bad taste of the period that produced it. The eighteenth century did these things well, the nineteenth, badly. But the lawns, the gardens, the magnificent trees—all these things are well worth seeing. The playing fields and swimming pool are remote from this part of Clifton, and here near the old house and to the north of it are quiet peaceful tracts where one may dream undisturbed.

There is but one monument in the Park—Edward Berges *On the Trail*—a fine bronze Indian who beneath his lifted hand gazes out across the country, alert, intent. This sculptor, dying so young, has left noble work behind him. This is a particularly fine example. In quite another mood is his charming *Sea Urchin* in Washington Place, and his elfish *Wildflower* so successfully placed near the pools in Homeland.

It is said that in Hopkins' life-time there was practically nothing to break the view from Patterson Park to the country seat Clifton. Not so many years ago the neighborhood to the north and west of Clifton was purely country; but now a flock of suburbs has sprung up, and brick houses and concrete sidewalks are the rule of the day. On the Harford road near Clifton is the home of Baltimore's most distinguished poet, Lizette Woodworth Reese. Miss Reese was born in Baltimore in 1856, and all of her life has been spent in this locality. Waverley and Windermere are her familiar abodes. We saw this when we "came down the Old York Road." For years she was a teacher in the Western High School when it stood on the corner of McCulloh and Lafayette. A bronze tablet the gift of the students and alumnae was set up there inscribed with her famous sonnet Tears; and this notable work has been

placed in the new School as one of its most treasured possessions. Baltimore as any public spirited citizen will readily
bear witness is fortunate in many things; but one of its happiest
distinctions is that it is the home of this true poet — not
one of these flash-in-a-pan kinds, but the real, the authentic,
poet. She would be at home with Herbert, and talk robustly
with Herrick. Carew, Lovelace, and Suckling would attend
her most gallantly. Long ago in the dim nineties Miss Reese
was writing steadily, writing grave and lovely verse. Time
passed and the novelties began to appear—vers librists, imag-
ists, symbolists, and other strange Canaanitish gods. But true
to the best traditions of English poetry this Baltimore woman
refused to bow the knee to Baal. She still practised the ancient
art of rhyme and rhythm, and more wonderful still—her poetry was intelligible. All this, of course, was very old-fashioned.
She is like the lavender that she loves so well, small and grey
and both sweet and spicy. With all haste I add spicy, for if
one were to emphasize sweet there would be a vigorous retort in Elizabethan English. For vigorous this poet is, like the
hardy boxwood of her poems. And she has, too, a dash of
mint—how like a julep that sounds, but Miss Reese is too
much in the Cavalier tradition to object to that fine flavour.

Beyond the Park and to the west is Montebello, the home
of General Samuel Smith, commander of the defenders of
Baltimore in the war of 1812, and later Secretary of the Navy
and Mayor of the city. The latest addition to Baltimore's beautiful chain of parks, is a wild stretch of country lying along
the winding course of Herring Run. Thirty-third Street takes
one across town to Wyman's Park, another link in the green
chain encircling the city, and from there it is but a short distance to Druid Hill.

The Mount Royal Avenue entrance is now undergoing some
reconstruction and it is at present anything but imposing.

THE GREEN CHAIN OF PARKS

Those who remember old Baltimore before the days of the motor car will recall the handsome iron gates, the neat gravel road, and the leisurely policeman who had a little sentry box on the right hand side of the entrance. In those days, too, and until recently there was a green slope with a winding path just beyond this sentry box, and at the top of the arduous ascent was a circular stretch of water, enclosed with a spiked iron fence. This was the old reservoir, and from this high level very lovely views of the town were obtained. "Walking around the reservoir" was a well-known occupation on a warm summer evening; it was the favorite spot of discreet lovers.

All this section of the park has suffered a change, but no doubt the new approach will be dignified and beautiful when it is completed. At present Mount Royal entrance has an unshaved look.

Indeed no entrance is worthy of the beauty of Druid Hill Park itself. Eutaw Place is now lined with huge apartments or showy houses. The charm of the Brooks estate has long vanished. Indeed, from Ducatel Street onward there was once a continuous garden. On the square embracing Linden, Eutaw, Whitelock, and Ducatel the Gails once had a fine house surrounded by green lawns. If my memory serves, there was a little lake in the southern part of it. At any rate I know that there were birches growing in a slender group, and around the house there were old trees and the grass was trimmed and rolled until it looked like a billiard table. A few feet above Whitelock street on Eutaw there was an old fence shutting in the meadows of the Brook's country place. A broad gravel path led up to the house which was almost hidden behind the foliage of magnificent trees. The white pillars tall and stately gleamed in the sunlight, but the house had that air of aristocratic withdrawal characteristic of southern architecture. Towards the Park, however, the lawns came to an abrupt end, and where now prim modern houses stand was more meadow land and pasture for the Brooks cows. Even yet some of the oaks are left, but the heavenly smell of honeysuckle on hot spring evenings has long since departed.

At the Madison Avenue entrance we have a very dull gateway designed by no less a person than Latrobe, but for all that it is not beautiful nor adequate. Not far from this entrance was situated Fort Number Five as it was called, a city defence erected in the Civil War as a protection from those rascally Confederates. A fine row of horse-chestnut trees runs straight up from the gate to a statue of George Washington. This statue, the work of Bartholomew, an early American sculptor, used to occupy a niche in a building on Baltimore Street. At the death of Noah Walker, the owner of the shop, the statue was given to the Park, and it is rather well-placed in this leafy background. Off through the trees you can see the William Wallace memorial. This is a fine impressive work representing the Scotch patriot on the heights of Stirling watching the battle on the plains below. Mr. Spence, whose fine old home, Bolton, we have already seen, gave this worthy monument to the city.

Until 1860 when Druid Hill became a public park it was the estate of Lloyd Rogers. The original patent had been taken out in 1688, but in 1709 the property passed into the hands of the Rogers family. Long ago Nicholas Rogers, an aide to De Kalb, had the estate laid out like an English landscape park. He took especial interest in the planting of the trees which he had grouped deliberateley for their effect, and from the sturdy oaks the estate received its name. There are parks in other cities far larger than Druid Hill and far more ornate, but in few of them is the effect of natural beauty so perfectly preserved. It is still a country gentleman's estate. The Mansion stands on a rise of ground which commands a view of the lake. Here the lawns softly curving fall away into long undulating stretches of green sward. In the spring dog-wood trees glimmer through the dark foliage, or judas trees burst out into ruddy bloom. The Mansion itself is certainly not a thing of beauty. It is flat and undistinguished. Think what Mount Clare would look like in such a location, or imagine the antique charm of the Carroll mansion, Homewood, built on this green knoll. Away on the west side of the Park you will find the family burying ground, a melancholy place with fir trees set thickly about it. If you enjoy such things climb over the iron fence and explore among the old stones. It is a neglected spot, and the boast of heraldry has led but to the grave. Here lies the brave soldier who fought with De Kalb. I had to brush away the snow to read the inscription. Many of the old grave stones have fallen. The wind in the trees comes with a melancholy sigh, and it would not surprise me at dusk to meet a ghost slipping in among the slender trunks of the gloomy evergreens.

Druid Hill Park, if you would know it well, must be travelled on foot. To skim by in a car gives you no sense of intimacy. There is a place in the park where the skunk cabbage first appears; there is the haunt of the blue birds; there is a spot where Quaker ladies grow. And long ago there were deer fleeting up the steep hills, or peeping at you from the green coverts. Sometimes you startled them as you tramped the steep leaf-strewn hillsides and they fled before you as if some ancient tapestry had come to life. An arrow from Robin Hood's bow might twang past your ear at any moment.

But lovelier even than the deer is the shepherd with his sheep. The old shepherd with his dog was a familiar sight. Now a younger man takes his place, but the sheep still stray across the green lawns as in times past. We come upon them at evening over the brow of a hill and our thoughts go back to Shakespeare's rustic fellows, or Hardy's Gabriel Oak.

The shepherd brings close to us that simple pastoral world. Indeed, there is no picture of all this changing Baltimore scene that I would rather keep with me than this; out of the shepherd's occupation towns and cities grew, and among all the changes and chances of this mortal life it is well to have with us this abiding symbol of ancient power.

BIBLIOGRAPHY

CHRONICLES OF BALTIMORE
—*J. T. Scharf*
HISTORY OF MARYLAND
—*J. T. Scharf*
HISTORY OF BALTIMORE AND
BALTIMORE COUNTY
—*J. T. Scharf*
THE CLIPPER SHIP ERA
—*Clarke*
LIFE OF DANIEL COIT GILMAN
—*Franklin*
THE LAUNCHING OF A
UNIVERSITY —*Gilman*
STAR SPANGLED BANNER
CENTENNIAL
COMPILATION —*Coyle*
The Sun
The Baltimore Clipper
MARIE ANTOINETTE
—*Belloc*
SKETCHES OF TUDOR HALL
—*Mahoney*
WOMEN OF THE SOUTH IN
WARTIME
Andrews
THE MONUMENTAL CITY
—*Howard*
MARYLAND AND BALTIMORE
—*Griffith*
PICTURES OF BALTIMORE
—*Lucas*
JOHN H. B. LATROBE AND
HIS TIMES
—*Semmes*
LIFE OF CARDINAL GIBBONS
—*Will*
STREET INDEX
—*McCreary*
LIFE OF J. P. KENNEDY
—*Tuckerman*

RED BOOK
—*Delphians* 1818-1819
LIFE OF OSLER
—*Cushing*
GUIDE TO BALTIMORE
—*Bond*
BALTIMORE PAST AND PRESENT
—*Mayer*
EDWIN BOOTH—RECOLLECTIONS
BY HIS DAUGHTER
—*Edwina Booth Grossman*
BALTIMORE, ITS HISTORY AND
ITS PEOPEL
—*Hall*
MOUNT CLARE
—*Siousat*
AT HOME AND ABROAD
—*J. P. Kennedy*
LIFE AND LETTERS OF
MADAME BONAPARTE
—*Didier*
CHARLES JOSEPH BONAPARTE
—*Bishop*
ISRAFEL
—*Allen*
CATHEDRAL RECORD
—*Reardon*
GEORGE PEABODY
—*Payne*
A METHODIST SAINT
—*Asbury*
CENTENARY ALBUM
SHADOWS ON THE WALL
—*Hewitt*
LIBRARY OF SOUTHERN
LITERATURE
POETS AND VERSE WRITERS
—*Perine*

335

INDEX